The Psycholinguistic Nature
of the Reading Process

The Psycholinguistic Nature
of the Reading Process

with a new foreword

Kenneth S. Goodman, EDITOR
Wayne State University

Wayne State University Press, DETROIT
1973

Published simultaneously in Canada by Ambassador Books, Limited
Rexdale, Ontario, Canada

Library of Congress Catalog Card Number: 67–26383

*Grateful acknowledgment is made to the Wayne State
University Alumni Fund for financial
assistance in publishing this book.*

International Standard Book Number 0–8143–1338–8
Second Printing, February 1973

Contents

Tables

Figures

Foreword

This volume contains the papers presented at a symposium held at Wayne State May 3, 4, and 5, 1965.

As I planned this symposium I felt that the time had passed for getting linguists, psychologists, and educationists together to talk about how linguistics *ought* to apply to teaching reading or how linguistic and psychological concepts *might* be interrelated. It was now time to bring people together who were already involved in theoretical and empirical investigations of reading as a psycholinguistic process. I knew that such work was under way though little of it had been published.

Accordingly, I began to gather the names of likely participants. John B. Carroll of Harvard, Doris Gunderson of the U.S. Office of Education, and Harry Levin of Project Literacy, Cornell, were all very helpful. Some potential participants suggested others. The result was the distinguished and productive group whose work you will read.

No attempt was made to limit presentations to completed research since an important goal of the symposium was to bring together people who were actively involved in investigations.

The preliminary announcement carried this statement:

> Papers presented by participants will deal with completed research, on-going research, or theoretical schemata from which researchable hypotheses can be drawn. The symposium will be concerned with assumptions, research techniques and designs, statistical procedures, and outcomes. Related research and development on reading curriculums and materials will also be considered.

The papers in this volume should be read with this pre-stated scope in mind. A new interdisciplinary approach to reading is involved. New frontiers are being crossed, new research methods are being evolved, new insights are being obtained, and a new vantage point for viewing reading as interaction between language and thought is emerging. The hope is that the on-going work and the developing concepts reported here will stimulate more work to challenge and extend these developments. It is hoped that the work reported here will be a step toward a new synthesis in the field of reading.

The symposium was made possible by the Alumni Association of Wayne State University which, through the Wayne State Fund, each year presents two research recognition awards to make such symposiums possible. This kind of concern for the advancement of knowledge is uniquely fitting. I greatly appreciate the personal honor of being in charge of the symposium.

My gratitude for their assistance with the symposium and the preparation of this volume goes to : My associates, Hans Olsen, Elmer Schacht, Clement Kaye, James Kerber, and Donald Protheroe for much general assistance; Louis VanderLinde, Jean Hamilton, Samuel Stone, Sam Weintraub, Irving Sigel, and E. Brooks Smith, who served capably as session chairmen and discussion leaders; and to the last named special thanks for his continuous aid and encouragement; Mrs. Zelda Rose, my secretary; Mrs. Yetta M. Goodman, my wife, and associate; and Debra, Karen and Wendy Goodman for putting up with my constant use of them as guinea pigs and sources of anecdotes.

K. S. GOODMAN 1967

Foreword to the Second Printing

In May of 1965, when the conference was held at which the papers contained in this volume were presented, it was possible to bring together in one room most of the people who were doing research or theoretical work on applications of linguistics and psycholinguistics to reading.

The preliminary announcement of the symposium carried this statement:

> Papers presented by participants will deal with completed research, on-going research, or theoretical schemata from which researchable hypotheses can be drawn. The symposium will be concerned with assumptions, research techniques and designs, statistical procedures, and outcomes. Related research and development on reading curriculums and materials will also be considered.

The title of the symposium which became the title of this book was a wishful assertion: *The Psycholinguistic Nature of the Reading Process*. I hoped to provoke the interdisciplinary group of psychologists, linguists and educationists who gathered to look at the reading process as an interaction between thought and language. I hoped for a new interdisciplinary approach to reading which would cross new frontiers, evolve new research methods, and provide a new vantage point for viewing reading.

Seven years later it is possible to look back over the dynamic development in reading research, theory, and instruction and the key roles in that development which many of the participants have played. The early preoccupation in applying linguistics to reading with phoneme-grapheme correspondence has broadened to a total examination of reading as a psycholinguistic process. Many psychologists and linguists have been actively engaged in reading research. Many educationists and teacher educators have built strong backgrounds in psycholinguistics. Virtually every new published program for reading instruction has drawn on linguistic and psycholinguistic insights.

This volume, then, should be considered a beginning, a base on which the contributors and others have continued to build. The new synthesis in the field of reading which this volume moves toward has not yet been achieved. But the directions are clear. The problems to be overcome in achieving that synthesis are becoming clearer and the list of answered questions has not shortened but has improved greatly in quality.

I wish to thank, in addition to the Alumni Association of Wayne State University whose grant made the symposium possible, the contributors to the volume and those others who have carried the purpose of the book forward by picking up the ideas and questions raised here. And I wish to welcome those who, reading this work, now join the quest for a new synthesis in reading.

K. S. Goodman
Detroit
September 1972

The Psycholinguistic Nature of the Reading Process

Kenneth S. Goodman
Wayne State University

This opening paper is a statement of a theoretical position on the part of the editor in his capacity as symposium host. It should not be construed as a keynote nor should the other papers be viewed as responses in any sense to this first presentation. It will be obvious that there is by no means any consensus among the symposium participants on what the psycholinguistic nature of the reading process is, though perhaps by the close of the symposium all had come to the point of at least agreeing on the areas in which they disagreed.

Editor

The Psycholinguistic Nature of the Reading Process

Reading is the receptive phase of written communication. In written language a message has been encoded by the writer in graphic symbols spatially distributed on the page. The reader does not merely pass his eyes over written language and receive and record a stream of visual perceptual images. He must actively bring to bear his knowledge of language, his past experience, his conceptual attainments on the processing of language information encoded in the form of graphic symbols in order to decode the written language. Reading must therefore be regarded as an interaction between the reader and written language, through which the reader attempts to reconstruct a message from the writer.

In this symposium we are not looking at reading from a special point of view. We are looking at it as a total process. This psycholinguistic process is exceedingly complex. To understand it we must consider the language and the systems of language that make possible communication. We must consider the relationship of oral and written language. We must consider the special characteristics of written language and special uses of written language. We must consider the characteristics and abilities of the reader which are prerequisite to effective reading. We must particularly study how the reader develops the ability to process graphic information to achieve the rapid comprehension that he must develop. In this paper the focus will be on the reading process of readers with normal perceptive ability.

To a great extent research on reading and on teaching reading in the past several decades has been dominated either by a preoccupation with letter-sound relationships, (phonics) or words and the techniques of recognizing and naming them.

Linguistics and related fields have produced new knowledge about language. But to apply these new insights we must let go of our preoccupation with letters and words and see language as a unity. New information about language forces us to look at reading in a new way that produces creative results.

Even some linguists have erred in the direction of a narrow view that focused only on the relationship of letters and sounds. They have assumed that if a reader can equate graphemes and phonemes he is decoding written language. (1, 2). This view is equivalent to saying that oral language decoding is nothing more than listening to an even flow of discrete sound symbols. What they overlook is that phonemes have no real existence except in the flow of language; that decoding cannot really take place except from language, real and complete.

In the pre-literate language experience of children, input has been in the form of aural* language. They have learned to decode meaning from this aural input using the phonemic and grammatical structures of the language. Reading introduces what is basically a secondary representation of oral language. The system is partially based on representing sounds by letters, though it would be more accurate to say that oral sequences and patterns are represented by graphic sequences and patterns. Though the system is a secondary system, it is complete enough for a skilled reader to become so proficient that he can decode meaning from graphic input directly without recourse to oral re-creation.

In the early stages of reading the process may involve a stretching out so that graphic input is *re*-coded (not decoded) into aural input which is eventually decoded for meaning. One might compare this to the receipt of a coded message by radio. Dots and dashes may be recoded by the receiving operator into graphic symbols. But when this recoding is complete he is left not with the meaning but with a still coded message.

The recoding can take the form of assigning phonemic val-

* For the sake of accuracy we draw a distinction between oral output and aural input. The latter is never quite the same as the former. What the speaker's mouth utters is not exactly what the listener hears.

ues to letters. It can take the form of assigning patterns of phonemes to patterns of letters. It can take the form of putting oral names on written word shapes.

A diagram of this stretched-out process looks like this:

Proficiency Level 1

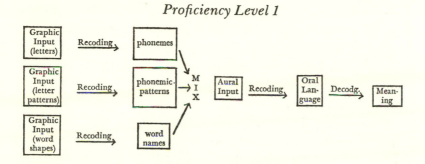

Unless the beginning reader has been taught one recoding strategy exclusive of all others his recoding will probably include all three of these forms in a kind of mix. If, however, he is taught a straight phonics approach, his recoding will tend to be of the "*pig* is puh - i - guh" variety. An exclusive word recognition strategy will tend to result in calling the names (with list intonation) of all known words.

In all cases the reader must go beyond this initial recoding which results in aural input that is not language. He must recode again, supplying additional aural input to create a reasonable approximation of oral language. The aural input that the reader supplies comes not out of air but out of his knowledge of the language. He develops the ability to make his recoding sound like language as he knows it. This he can then decode as he would aural language input in listening. But successful decoding depends on how close his reconstituted oral language approximates real language.

At a certain level of proficiency these recoding processes are probably telescoped so that a diagram of the process would look like this:

The aural input is supplied by the reader simultaneously with his recoding of the graphic input. To achieve this level of

Proficiency Level 2

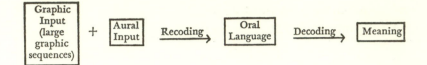

proficiency the reader must perceive letters and words always as parts of larger language units. He must be able to equate these large graphic units with oral phrases, sentences, and sentence sequences.

Words, and sometimes parts of words, have lexical or referential meaning. There is a sufficient association of this fragment of meaning with word shapes or names even in young readers, so that meaning enters somewhat into the recoding process on the morphemic and word levels. A young reader may perceive the word shape <river>, associate it with a splinter of meaning, and call its name <lake>. Thus, not only the word name but the associations it evokes are involved in recoding of word shapes. But decoding must involve some level of comprehension of the entire meaning of large language units. Nothing less than decoding of large language units is reading. Even in the lowest proficiency level the child must be able to get meaning.

In the early reading stages, oral and silent reading are probably quite comparable as processes. The recoded graphic input must be supplemented, principally with the intonational aspects of speech. Sequences of phonemes or morphemes must be perceived as fitting together into sequences of phrases and syntactical patterns. Relative stresses must be assumed, junctures inserted, pitch modulated, so that when the recoding is complete it must sound like familiar language.

But eventually the process is telescoped further. At this point recoding and decoding becomes simultaneous so that, except in passages where the phrasing is complex or ambiguous, the reader is virtually decoding meaning directly from graphic input.

Proficiency Level 3

The speed of processing graphic information at this stage is not limited to the speed at which oral language may be produced by speakers.[5] The silent reader perceives whole graphic phrases in an instant, processes the information and moves on. He is not even limited, as some have assumed, to the small area of type which he can perceive completely and accurately, since he can decode from partially complete and partially accurate perceptions. Thus, he can use the peripheral areas of his visual field and even compensate for incomplete type or illegible handwriting. In fact, reading is a rapid series of guesses, tentative information processing. The less available information the reader uses the more rapid and efficient is his reading.

It seems likely that proficient silent readers edit out a good deal of redundant language information. It may also be that silent reading bears a closer relationship to inner speech than to oral language.

When a reader has reached this stage of proficiency, oral reading has become quite a different process. If a child who spends ten, twenty, perhaps thirty or more hours a week in silent reading is asked to read orally, the process would look like this:

Oral Reading (Proficiency Level 3)

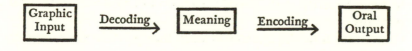

The process of decoding directly from graphic input has become so habitual that the reader must first decode and then encode meaning as oral output. As might be expected, this will result in considerable change from the original graphic input to oral output.

A higher level of proficiency, or perhaps a special skill, is required to produce completely accurate oral reading. The reader must be able to change his normal pace and his mode of information processing to encode orally at the same time he is decoding. Many adults who are proficient readers never acquire this special oral reading skill.

Insufficient evidence is available to indicate here that all children or any individual child *must* pass through each proficiency level. But those I have studied *do* seem to pass through these levels.

It is vital that the distinction between recoding graphic input as aural input and decoding graphic or aural input be understood. Many teachers remark that reading beginners can't really make progress in learning to read until they grasp the concept that what they are reading is supposed to make sense, that is, that it can be decoded. Preoccupation with teaching children to recode may actually short circuit the reading process and divert children from comprehension. It is even possible that children will reach a high level of proficiency in recoding, actually taking graphic input and recasting it as very natural sounding speech, with little or no awareness of the need for decoding for meaning. There are such readers even in secondary schools. Their oral reading sounds as if they understand, but they are in fact only highly efficient recoders. All good adult readers, of course, can recode, as oral language, passages from specialized books they don't understand. One could, for example, read a legal document to an attorney without understanding any of it but do a good enough job of recording so that the attorney could decode from oral output and state what it means.

Consider now the systems of cues that provide the language

information readers utilize in deriving meaning from written language.[6] The systems of cues in the written language itself can be divided into two groups: 1) Cue systems within words; 2) Cue systems in the flow of language. To these we should add a set of cue systems within the reader which he supplies as he reads. Another set of cues are those external to language and the reader. These may be pictures, charts, or direct prompting.

Words are more obvious graphic entities than recognizable units in oral language. The written word is neatly and clearly marked off from other words by white space. While even the beginning reader does recognize some recurrent marked off units in oral language, the one-to-one relationship between written word and spoken word is not self-evident. The child may be taught an oral name for a graphic word entity but he does not necessarily recognize this oral word name as an element in his speech, particularly if he says the word name with list stress and with an uncommon pronunciation. Similarly, the young native speaker of English is continually making fine discriminations between phonemes in the flow of language. But if he is taught to respond to letters with sounds he will not necessarily be able to cement these separate, and perhaps unnatural sounding, sounds into language.

The cue systems *within* words primarily are used by the reader for recoding. Excessive stress, in reading instruction and materials, on phonics or word attack skills will tend to make recoding an end in itself, and may actually distract the child from the real end: decoding written language for meaning. Reading can then become a game of name the word and say the sound.

The cue systems within words which a reader uses in recoding are the letter-sound relationships, the spelling pattern-phonemic pattern relationships, and word shape-word name relationships which were pointed out in the model earlier. The reader learns to respond to these cues either by being taught responses or by self-induction. The advantage of self-induction is that the learner becomes aware of limitations on his responses, whereas direct instruction often avoids examples where the relationship does not hold, leading to overgeneralization. Approaches to reading instruction such as Bloomfield's[1] which attempt to control the process of self-induction by providing materials where each graphic symbol has a constant phonemic value, may lead to quick acquisition of the phoneme-grapheme relationships but they also lead to quick overgeneralization.

To the cues within words should be added gimmicks such as finding little words in big words. These are also devices for recoding written input as aural input. One young reader found in the word <Jimmy>, two little words, <Jim> and <my>. "Jim, my" he said several times. But he was unable to go the next step of recoding his two little word names as a single word name he recognized. Another child was more successful. He pondered over <something>. "Some, thing" he said. "Oh, it's *sump'n*."*

As the reader responds to cue systems that exist in the flow of language, he is able to utilize the same decoding procedures in ultimately decoding from written input, which he has learned to use in decoding aural input. He finds that graphic sequences correspond to the patterns of oral utterances. He finds common grammatical patterns that make it possible to introduce the appropriate phrasing. As he fits his recoded aural input into a familiar pattern, he uses his well-learned knowledge of the structure of the language to test its fit. Any native speaker of English can ask himself 1) "Does it sound right?" (that is, does it sound like an acceptable English utterance) and 2) "Does it make sense?" (that is, can I decode a meaningful message from it).

In reading language that is complete, the child finds function words that serve as markers and structural signals. He identifies noun markers, verb markers, question markers, phrase markers, conjunctions. He uses these, as Alice did when she found the "Jabberwocky," to establish the patterns and struc-

* The latter incident occurs in the NEA documentary film, *Children Without.*

ture of the language he reads. He also finds inflectional endings that he has learned to use in his oral language at an early age and he uses these in the decoding process. These also help define the pattern and the relationship of elements to each other and to the whole. The young reader has well learned, *within his own dialect,* the rules for agreement of inflectional endings.[4] *The boys eat* sounds right to him. So does *the boy eats,* but *the boys eats* doesn't sound right. Fortunately language is redundant. It provides multiple clues to the same bits of information. If a reader misses a cue he can still get the message. If his responses to language cues in reading seem inconsistent he can check back and find his error. Redundancy helps in other practical ways too. Not all possible sequences of language elements can occur in a language. Some sequences do not occur at all; some are rare; some are common; some are very frequent. In any given language context the possible language elements which can fit are very much limited, compared to the universe of elements. The reader can screen possibilities and anticipate elements in language sequences, whether they are phonemes, morphemes, words, or phrases. No doubt redundancy is an important factor in the ability to read incomplete or mutilated text.

Punctuation in written language can at least partially cue the reader to supply appropriate intonation as he re-creates oral language or decodes his re-created aural input. But the reader must supply something more than the punctuation signals. He must sense the ebb and flow of what he reads to make it sound to himself like real language.

The following passage will illustrate how the reader uses the cue systems within words, as well as his knowledge of English sentence pattern, inflection, function words, and intonation, in reading.

A marlup was poving his kump. Parmily a narg horped some whev in his kump. "Why did vump horp whev in my frinkle kump?," the marlup jufd the narg. "Er'm muvvily trungy," the narg grupped. "Er heshed vump norpled whev in your kump. Do vump pove your kump frinkle?"

Literate speakers of English would generally agree on the pronunciation of most of the nonsense words in this passage though they had never seen them before. They have become skilled enough in recoding graphic input as aural input or oral output that they can recode even nonsense, provided that it looks like English and provided that their recoding must result in oral language which obeys the morphophonemic rules of English, that is, it doesn't contain any non-English sound sequences. Of course, there is some ambiguity. Is p-o-v-e /pohv/ to rhyme with stove, or /puwv/ as in prove, or /pǝv/ as in love?

Most good readers could also supply appropriate intonation in their reading of this passage, though some of the subtleties might be overlooked and the reading would probably not achieve its full-natural or dramatic potential. The intonation would result from the reader's interpretation of the structure of the passage. *A marlup was poving his kump* is easily recognized and read as a sentence of the familiar subject-verb-object or noun-verb-noun variety. The pattern is set off by the markers: A——was——ing his——. *A* and *his* mark the nouns, while *was* serves as a marker of the verb *pove,* which also has the expected *ing* inflectional ending. All these signals the mind interprets in the process of reading. From them a kind of structural meaning is also derived, so that some partial decoding can take place; the passage seems to make sense because the structural cues, those in the flow of language, are consistent with each other and with our deeply internalized sense of the structure of the language.

But the decoding must stop short of meaning. The recoding techniques and strategies we have learned or been taught can make it possible for us to create an aural language equivalent of this written passage which has the sound of English. Our deeply internalized knowledge of the structure of our language makes it possible for us to supply a structural meaning. But for complete decoding we must have some experience with the referential meaning of the language elements we have recoded. Just exactly what is *kump?* And in what sense can it be *frinkle?* What happens to *kump* when it's *poved?* We must call forth from our storehouse of experiences those which relate to the situation described in the passage, so that the totality of the message may be understood. A conceptual framework is necessary to deal with the concepts involved, not in the language, but in the message it transmits.

A reader could answer accurately a series of questions about this passage without any substantial comprehension. For example, these:

Answer in complete sentences:
1. What did the narg horp in the marlup's kump?
2. What did the marlup juf the narg?
3. Was the narg trungy?
4. How does the marlup pove his kump?

Do these questions resemble the kind found in school texts as a test of comprehension? If they do, then what is being tested is not the ability to decode the passage, but the ability to manipulate the language.

The cue systems that the reader supplies from within himself are: 1) The recoding strategies he knows. 2) His past language experience, knowledge of the structure, intonation, and vocabulary of the language (if it is his language but a different dialect he is reading, decoding may be impeded). 3) His general experiential background. 4) His general conceptual background.

Some cues are external to the reading process, but they may be used by the reader. Pictures are cues which may be decoded as a substitute or supplement to language. Prompting is actually recoding done by someone other than the reader. Skill charts may supply a recoding strategy not yet mastered. These external cues get between the reader and written language. In a sense they interfere with the vital recoding processes.

Summary: Outlined here is what I believe to be the essence of the psycholinguistic process in reading. It is my belief that no theory of reading, reading learning, or reading instruction can be complete or successful which excludes any aspect of this psycholinguistic process. Research on reading can contribute to the understanding of one phase or aspect but ultimately research must be related to the whole psycholinguistic process. Reading is not reading unless there is some degree of comprehension and therefore at all stages of instruction there must be concern for ultimate decoding of written language.

Reading Temporally and Spatially Transformed Text

Paul A. Kolers

It has been evident to perceptual psychologists for some time that the perceptual process in reading is much more complex than identifying, in succession, the letters or word shapes in the line on the printed page. Having satisfied himself that the rate at which skilled adults read exceeds the speed at which they can process visual input on a letter-by-letter basis, Dr. Kolers designed an ingenious set of experiments using transformed text to gain insights into the perceptual aspects of reading and into the way readers organize their perceptions. His findings suggest the need for a reconsideration of many beliefs and practices in reading instruction based on simplistic misconceptions of visual perception in reading.

EDITOR

Reading Temporally and
Spatially Transformed Text*

The work I write about has its origin in psychophysical experiments I made a few years ago on the detectability of sequentially-presented visual targets (Kolers, 1957, 1962; Kolers and Rosner, 1960). In those experiments we studied the influence that each of two brief visual presentations has upon the appearance or detectability of the other when each of them presented alone has a high probability of being seen. The finding was that the first of two presentations affected the appearance of the second, but that the second exerted a stronger masking effect upon the first. That is to say, under conditions in which the first of two visual targets would have been clearly visible if presented alone, following it at appropriate temporal separations with another caused it to be invisible, an effect sometimes called "backward masking." Studying this phenomenon in some detail, we found that we could identify a "formation time," the interval the visual system required to process an input into a clear perception. This formation time had a value of about 0.3 seconds as a maximum, and was shorter as the intensity, contrast, or size of the stimuli was increased.

* Some of the experimental work was performed at Harvard University, supported by PHS Training Grant 2G-1011 Special from the Division of General Medical Sciences to Harvard University, Center for Cognitive Studies. This work was also supported in part by the Joint Services Electronics Program (Contract DA36-039-AMC-03200 (E)); and in part by the National Science Foundation (Grant GK-835), the National Institutes of Health (Grant 2 P01 MH-04737-06), and the National Aeronautics and Space Administration (Grant NsG-496). This work was done in part at the Computation Center at the Massachusetts Institute of Technology. The faithful assistance of Miss Jan Bettman at Harvard, and Mesdames Ann Boyer and Kathryn Rosenthal at M.I.T. in preparing texts and collecting the data is gratefully acknowledged.

If we assume that printed English has about 5 letters or 5 phonemes per word, and that the skilled adult reads 600 words per minute, he must be scanning 50 letters or phonemes per second, or 0.02 seconds each on the average. (Actually, some experiments of Sperling and Neisser suggest that adults may scan some materials at the rate of 0.01 seconds per item [Sperling, 1963; Neisser, 1964], but those subjects are not reading.) Since these rates exceed the sequential capacities of the system for the formation of visual targets, it must be clear that the skilled reader cannot process into a full perceptual representation every letter or every phoneme of the material he is reading. At 100 or 200 words per minute, or less, he may be; but at 600 words or more per minute, he cannot be. Wonder about what the skilled reader might be doing at the higher rates was one of the stimuli for my experiments.

We have concentrated on two kinds of experiments that distort the material normal, literate college students are required to read. The distortions are either temporal or spatial. For the former, words are photographed one letter at a time on successive frames of motion picture film. When the developed film is projected, the letters appear one after the other on approximately the same part of the viewing screen, their rate and duration controlled by means of a variable speed projector. In some experiments the subjects are required to name the letters, in others, to name the word the letters spell (Kolers and Katzman, *XL*, 1966). I want to summarize a few results.

First, we found that correct detection of letters or words increased in a regular way as the duration for which the letters were presented increased. This should surprise no one. What was interesting, however, was that correct detections were about $p = 0.9$ when the sequence of presentations was about 3 per second, the value previously found to be important for defining an upper bound on visual processing time.

Second, when the duration for which the letters were presented was short, less than 0.150 seconds, the subjects did better at identifying the words than they did at identifying the constituent letters, but the opposite was true at longer letter durations. That is, the subjects did not need to be able to make out all the letters in a sequence in order to identify the word presented with moderately good probability, when the durations were short; but, as it were, they "lost" the word perceptually when the letters were each presented for longer durations. Another way to state this: one can identify a word without being able to identify all of its letters; and conversely, one can identify all of the letters in a word and still not be able to name the word spelled. Spelling a word correctly is no guarantee that one has the word, nor is having a word a guarantee that one can spell it. Truer of *onomatopoeia* and *syzygy,* words we never used, this is true also of *carrot* and *dollar,* words we did use.

The third finding of some interest here is that at rates of presentation of about 10 letters per second or faster (that is, at letter durations of 0.100 seconds or less), the subjects were quite often able to identify all of the letters of a six-letter sequence, but reported them in incorrect order. Given a sequence which we may represent as *abcdef,* the subjects would report, for example, *bacdfe.* This anagrammatizing of letter order, at rates in the region of 10 per second or more, identifies a kind of ordering operator, a property of the visual system concerned not with identifying a target per se, but in representing its sequential properties correctly.

The second kind of distortion we have used varies the geometric properties of the textual material. There are a very large number of ways textual material can be distorted geometrically: direction of scan can be left or right, up or down; orientation of the letters can be tilted, reflected, inverted, or reversed; and so on. The experiments I will describe are based on a selection of seven transformations from this large population. They are illustrated by number in Table 1 where, unlike the material in the experiments, a single phrase is shown in several ways. All of our material was taken from a single source, George Miller's *Psychology, The Science of Mental Life.* The subjects were students at Harvard, paid for their efforts to read aloud as rapidly as they could the text presented to them.

1.   suoᴉʇɐlǝɹ ɥʇᴉʍ pǝllᴉɟ sᴉ ssǝusnoᴉɔsuoƆ

2.   ꙅnoᴉƚɒlɘɿ dƚiw bɘllᴉƚ ꙅi ꙅꙅɘnꙅ␣oᴉↄꙅⴈoↄ

3.   snoitaler htiw dellif si ssensuoicsnoƆ

4.   Ɔoᴎɒᴐᴉoυɒᴎꙅꙅꙅ iꙅ ƚᴉllɘb wᴉƚᴚ ɿɘlɒƚᴉoᴎꙅ

5.   ᴄoᴎꙅᴄʇoᴎꙅυꙅꙅꙅ ʇꙅ ʇʇʇʇɘϱ ʍʇɟᴚ ɹɘʇꙅɟʇoᴎꙅ

6.   ☙☚ʘ☙❦☙ʘ☜ ☚❧☚❦ ☙ʘ☜☚☜❦ ☙☜ ☙☙ʘ☚☙ʘʘ☚ʘ☙☚ʘ☚

7.   ☙☚ʘ☜❦☚☜❦☙☚ ☚☚❦☚ ☚ʘ❦❦❦☚❦ ☙❦ ☙☙ʘ☚☙☙ʘʘ☚ʘ☙☚ʘƆ

Table I. *Examples of geometrically transformed text. Nos. 1, 2, 3, 6, and 7 are read from right to left; Nos. 4 and 5 from left to right.*

In our first investigation with these materials, each of eight subjects read aloud consecutively five pages of one of four transformations, a different one on each of four successive days. On a given page of twenty-six typewritten lines, alternate lines were normal and in one of the four transformations shown as numbers 1–4 in Table 1. The order of presentation of the pages to the subjects was a replicated 4×4 Latin square. The time required to read the materials aloud was measured with a stop-watch. The averaged reading time for each half-page of transformed text and the remaining half-page of normal text is shown for the eight subjects in Figure 1a. An order of difficulty clearly appears there, in which mirror reflection is the most difficult transformation to read (No. 2 of Table 1) and rotation in the plane (No. 1) is the easiest, the other two falling between.

In a second study, five subjects were tested on each of five successive days, reading on each day five pages made up wholly of a single transformation, Nos. 1–5 of Table 1. This test differs

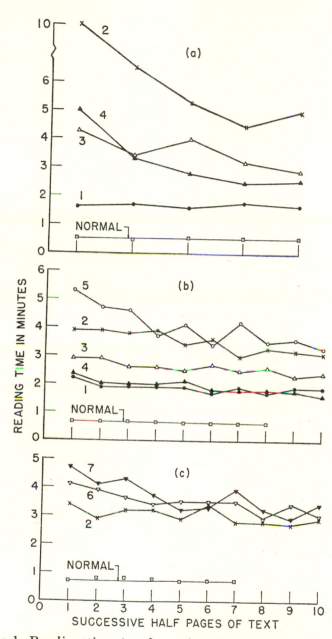

Figure 1. *Reading time for the various kinds of text. A, results for eight subjects who read pages made up of lines alternately in normal text and in the like-numbered transformations of Table 1. B, results for five subjects reading pages made up entirely of a single transformation, numbers 1–5 of Table 1. C, six subjects reading pages of nos. 2, 6, and 7.*

from the preceding in that a different type-font was used (IBM *Elite* in the first study, *Courier* in the second), the entire page contained the transformation, and a fifth condition, No. 5 of Table 1, was added. At the beginning and end of the first day's testing, at the beginning of the third day's, and at the end of the fifth, each subject read a single page of normal text aloud to provide an index of his basal reading level. Figure 1b plots the averaged time scores for these data. They show an order of difficulty similar to that of Figure 1a for the four transformations studied twice, despite the change of font, while the absolute values are different. The Latin square design followed in presenting the material tends to flatten the curves, as discussed below.

In a third study, six subjects read aloud the two transformations shown as Nos. 6 and 7 of Table 1, as well as No. 2, five pages on each of three successive days. Again a basal reading level was inferred from performance on normal text. The averaged data are shown in Figure 1c. Comparing Figures 1b and 1c shows that the subjects in the latter case, for whom all the transformed text was in mirror reflection, read No. 2 somewhat faster than their counterparts in Figure 1a.

The reproduction of the order of difficulty suggests that strong regularities exist for processing the transformations; nevertheless, the range of individual scores is large. All subjects read normal text aloud within $1.5 \pm .50$ min. page; but mirror reflection (No. 2) required from 7.2 to 21.8 min./page to be read when it was presented alone (Figure 1b), and from 6.4 to 26.2 min./page when it was alternated with normal text (Figure 1a). (The graphs are based on reading time for half-pages.) Others, for example No. 5, required from 9.0 to 36 min./page, and even the least difficult transformation, No. 1, required from 2.0 to 9.2 min./page. More interesting than the extended ranges are the correlations between subjects and transformations, the rank order of tests with respect to their difficulty. The ranking of tests, measured with Kendall's coefficient of concordance W, an average rank correlation coefficient, is

0.79 for the four transformations of Figure 1a and 0.66 for the five transformations of Figure 1b. Both of these are statistically significant ($p < 0.01$). That is to say, the subjects agree rather well on the order of difficulty of the tests.

The nature of the skill required to decode these texts is not yet identified. It is easy to point out that classical variables such as direction of scanning movement or similar actional components to the reading task can, in these tests, be associated with unlike scores—witness the comparison of No. 2 and No. 1, which require similar scanning movements, or Nos. 4 and 5. Specific actional components seem to be of limited significance in describing performance on these tasks, without being altogether irrelevant.

To pursue this matter, in a fourth study we examined the amount of transfer of skill that occurred between eyes. Five right-eyed, right-handed subjects read five pages per day of transformation No. 2 on each of four successive days, using the right eye only, the other being covered. On the fifth day each read one page in this manner, and then changed occluders to read the remaining four pages with the left eye, the right eye now covered. Of the five subjects, two were graduate students concentrating in Middle Eastern studies with reportedly a good reading knowledge of at least one Semitic language, and the other three lacked this skill. Average performance of the three subjects unfamiliar with languages normally read right to left is shown in the topmost curve of Figure 2; performance of the two students of Semitic culture is shown below it. There was no overlap of scores between the two groups of subjects at any point. Transfer of skill between eyes is virtually perfect, even though the direction of transfer, in this case, is from the more to the less-favored organ.

The greater part of skill on all of these reading tasks seems to depend not upon the specific "correlation" of action and visual input found important in some cases of adaptation to transformed environments (Kohler, 1964; Smith and Smith, 1962; Held and Freedman, 1963), for here the subject's left eye

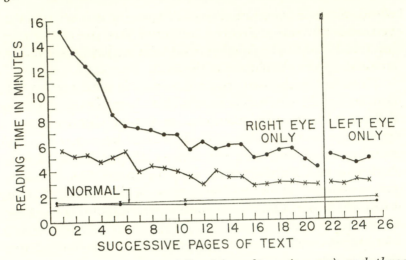

Figure 2. *Two students of Semitic culture (crosses) and three without that knowledge (filled circles) read 25 pages of Transformation 2, the first 21 pages with the right eye only, the remaining 4 with the left eye only. Their reading rates for normal text read monoptically is also shown.*

had no opportunity to form such a correlation, but upon an increase in ability to process serially information derived from unfamiliar actions. By inference, the superior performance of the two Semitists came from practice in reading normal Hebrew or Arabic from right to left, not from skill in reading English in mirror image. A similar generalized facilitation in performance can be demonstrated with the data of Figure 1b. As they stand, those describe performance on each transformation separately, but the transformations were read by different subjects on different days according to the Latin square design. The effect of generalized practice can be examined by summing across transformations within test days. Doing this yields the average time taken for the first page on the first day as 8.7 minutes, for the first page on the second day as 8.1 minutes, and so on until for the first page on the fifth day it is 4.5 minutes. This "generalized practice"—in which practice on any transformation facilitates performance on any other—and the effects of specific practice shown in Figure 2 demonstrate that two kinds of "learning" occur: habituation to the task of reading transformed text generally, and habituation to the specific transformations, which are differentially difficult.

That the learning does not come easily is shown by the fact that no subject ever read a transformed page as rapidly as he did normal text, and by the frequent and spontaneous remarks by the subjects that their comprehension of what they had read in transformed text was poor, improving with an increase in reading speed. Further, there is a "program"-like nature to these reading skills. In all but the first of these studies it often happened that a subject, presented with a page of normal text to read after several pages of transformed text, would stare at it blankly for several seconds, unable to read or even recognize it; but once recognized, it was read off without impairment.

Within the pages of transformed text, subjects unable to read a word were encouraged to spell it out; whereupon, it often happened, they would identify the constituent letters correctly but still be unable to say the ordinarily familiar six- or seven-letter word they had spelled. As we have shown earlier, we show again that recognizing a word as such involves something other than mere recognition of its constituent letters. Recognition of the word always occurred after sufficient respellings or resoundings, and was often accompanied by surprise or chagrin.

Direction of scan and other actional components to these tasks have already been shown to be insufficient to account by themselves for the results. Nor can experience with the various transformations by itself explain the data. For while everyone literate has probably read rotated material at one time or another (No. 1), we have also many times seen mirror reflections of text (No. 2); yet reflection is a more difficult tranformation to master than rotation, and it is also more difficult than the transformations shown as Nos. 3 and 4, which have very low probabilities of occurrence in the normal environment. These considerations seem to suggest the hypothesis that separate mechanisms operate to process the various transformations.

Finally, it is interesting to note that the pre-classic Greeks used a form of writing that the reader read alternately from left to right and right to left, reading continuously, that is, instead of returning to the left margin to begin each line anew (Woodhead, 1959). Called boustrophedon, the text for the right to left scan was most often written in rotated form, as in No. 1. This still seems to be the easiest transformation to read.

As you know, we have required our subjects to read aloud. Reading aloud involves some very different processes from reading silently: the easiest demonstration of this is that almost no one can read aloud intelligibly at the rate of 300 words per minute, while silent rates go much higher. But we were forced into this method on two counts. Had we merely let our subjects read transformed text silently, we would have had no way of monitoring their performance—whether they were really decoding the transformations or merely sliding by them—no way, that is, short of using comprehension tests. But we found that there is no really trustworthy test of comprehension. There is, in fact, no signficant analysis I know of concerned with what comprehension itself is. Some tests of comprehension ask questions of fact or the meanings of unfamiliar words definable by their contexts. These are tests of short-term memory and induction. Others ask for brief descriptions of the content, précis. Such tests measure intelligence and prior knowledge as much as comprehension. Other tests require the subject to complete sentences, to answer multiple-choice questions, and the like, supplying the subject with the very information whose existence in his head is our matter of interest. In fact I have myself taken a number of objective comprehension tests to find out what they are like, and usually scored between 50 and 70 per cent correct on them—without having read the passages on which they were based! Clearly, tests which supply so much of the information that they supposedly are testing for have a limited value, if any, as genuine tests of comprehension.

In other experiments, we have been exploring our subjects' ability to recode other kinds of geometric transformations from the large sample available, varying the linguistic and contextual properties of the texts. Our results to date suggest the following: 1) The ability to decode specific kinds of geometric transformations seems to reflect the action of what we might call "spatial operators"—decoding processes relatively specific to the various transformations. The data already shown reveal that, as nearly as we can define the terms, logically and mathematically equivalent transformations are not regarded as equivalent by the visual system, for equivalent amounts of practice with the various transformations do not produce equivalent levels of skill. Furthermore, the rate of acquisition of skill differs among the transformations, some being learned more rapidly than others, with no clear-cut correlation between level of difficulty and speed of acquisition. 2) In addition, we find that the context of the materials is not particularly important as a variable. We have altered context in two ways: first, bilingual subjects learn to read a transformation in one language and are tested in another; second, subjects are trained with one kind of material, a psychology text, and tested with another, a description of the architectural properties of concrete. In both cases the transfer of training is high. Thus the skills are not specific to type fonts, contexts, or even languages.

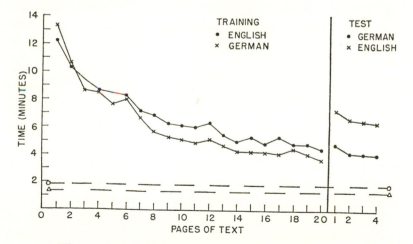

Figure 3. *English and German Training Text.*

We have had a dual motive in using geometrically transformed text. We have wanted to study something about the acquisition of skill with such materials which, because of their unfamiliarity, magnify the reading process somewhat; and we have been interested also in the topic of adaptation to geometric distortion. Our aim, as we continue experiments of this kind, is to find out how the skilled reader extracts information from the little black marks on a page, and to learn more about the nature of the interplay between skilled movement and information processing. What we have found so far does not even establish the limits of the field of study.

Some Thoughts on
Perceptual Units in Language Processing

Margaret Hubbard Jones

A word; what is a word? Philosophers, grammarians, language teachers have taken the answer to be fundamental and obvious. Here, Dr. Jones summarizes her conclusions that the word and the sentence are not really the units through which the spoken language is perceived. This strikes at the very core of modern reading instruction that has literally been built around the word. Controlled vocabulary, sight-vocabulary, word-attack skills, word flash-cards have been major emphases. Perhaps Dr. Jones points the way to a bridge which can be built from the spoken language to the written language.

EDITOR

Some Thoughts on
Perceptual Units in Language Processing

When we seek to relate psycholinguistics to reading, we need not limit ourselves to the area of learning, but should seek to apply relevant psychological principles from other areas. I have in mind particularly perception. Although an occasional piece of research has been done on perceptual factors in reading, there has been little systematic exploration of this essential topic. It seems to me that we need such systematic exploration with an eye both to general principles of perceptual development (cf. Ervin, Walker, and Osgood (13)) and to a comparison of auditory and visual perception.

If we know anything about perceptual development it is that children need more cues than adults, and that they have difficulty in proportion to the amount of information, in the technical sense, in the stimulus. We also know that storage for any great amount of information requires a code, and that certain kinds of codes are easier than others. Language is basically a coding system, operating on visual or auditory perceptions (in the literate adult), and it is only because there is a system for coding input that we can process it rapidly. It seems essential, then, to explore the perceptions, and the codings of them that are language, if we wish to understand the process of learning to read.

The visual perceptions involved in reading come to us already "chunked" into units of several sorts, called words and sentences, and sometimes clauses. But many linguists will admit they cannot define a word or a sentence, and certainly they cannot agree on the definitions. Martinet (39) specifically states, "There is no way of defining the term 'word' in such a way as to make the definition tally with the naïve uses of it" (p. 90). Greenberg (23) also says that there is no satisfactory definition for a word, and Kramers (33) discusses five kinds. As to the instability of a word, one only need remember that two words, used often together, eventually are hyphenated, and finally are admitted to the dictionary as one word. A sentence is a larger unit; it can stand alone; it is a complete statement. But even here the notion is not as clear as might be desired (cf. Kramers (33)). If one examines aural language with an effort to avoid the prejudices of written language, it may be that something of psychological interest may result. The question is what are the natural perceptual units of spoken language. If the aural, or even oral, units are very different from the units used in written language, then the psychological principles involved in transfer of training come into play, and the difficulty of transfer will be increased in proportion to the magnitude of the differences in the two sensory inputs (Bugelski and Cadwallder (5)). Learning to read is certainly *not* "merely" a transfer of auditory signals to visual (cf. Fries (15)) and even that is not a simple problem psychologically. Because visual language is organized in certain ways, due to a series of historical accidents, is no reason to assume that it is the best way. Actually the two-dimensional visual shapes which are our alphabet could be significantly improved in discriminability and ease of learning for six-year-olds. But there are more basic questions still unanswered, namely: 1) What are the units in which the auditory language is processed, and 2) how may a bridge to the units of visual language best be constructed. If the first of these questions can be answered, then the second becomes much easier.

That questions about auditory perception are pertinent to the reading task is attested not only by common sense, but also by several investigations which disclose an auditory component in reading even for mature readers (12, 19, 29, 32, 37, 40, 49, 54). It is likewise true that frequency of occurrence of words in spoken language affects the visual perception of words (7, 8, 9, 17, 58, 59), and natural intonation in reading appears to be somewhat related to its excellence (22).

There arises, of course, the question of the real information-

processing units of skilled reading. It is known that good readers do not process letter by letter, nor even word by word.
Rather, they make relatively few saccadic eye movements per
line, and in training for improvement in reading, it is likely to
be emphasized that the visual perceptual span must be increased. The implication seems to be that a good reader takes
in a larger, but constant physical distance (6), whereas he is
probably using larger meaningful units. This hypothesis could
be further pursued with profit. One could also test the useful-
ness of special visual cues to natural grouping in visual material. Such cues might well aid the unskilled reader in bridging
the gap between his skillful handling of auditory input and his
halting processing of visual input. In such cases, it is fairly
obvious that the visual coding is not being done efficiently. If
one can teach the individual to code properly, he will read
well, and can, without extra training, dispense with any extra
cues which were introduced, since highly practiced perceptions
require only minimal cues.

The crux of the entire problem appears to rest upon knowledge of the natural units of language processing, and in particular the processing of auditory language. There are a number
of attempts to discover the natural language units, based upon
a great diversity of techniques. I shall attempt to group these
loosely, but the classifications are not mutually exclusive. The
factors which have been hypothesized to indicate or to produce
speech units are: 1) intonation contours and/or stress (often
not clearly differentiated), 2) pauses (also linked to intonation
contours), 3) separability of parts, 4) frequency of occurrence
(redundancy), 5) coding efficiency, 6) ease of learning or retention, 7) factor analysis. Some are favored by linguists, some by
psychologists, and one is unique and, apparently, adventitious.

Intonation and stress, which are not separable, are favorite
devices of some linguists. Also included are pauses of certain
kinds, because of the way intonation units are defined. Since
only phoneticians have the skills necessary to study intonation
and related concepts, it is not surprising that they should be in

the majority in this category. I shall cite only a few representative examples of this way of defining units. Halliday (26) posits four phonological units for English, the largest of which (the tone group) is the unit of intonation; the next largest (the foot) is the unit of rhythm, and the two smallest the syllable and the phoneme. Although no simple relationship is found between phonological units and grammatical ones, and although we know very little about the information carried by English intonation, the two grammatical units most frequently coextensive with the tone group are the clause and the "group" (phrase). Martinet (39), as noted above, does not believe the lexical word has any linguistic meaning. He seems to think that "monemes" (similar to morphemes) combine syntactically to form larger units (sentences), and that there are tonal and accentual features of speech which indicate smaller units, whereas intonation, the melodic curve, indicates the larger unit. If one insists on having a unit of intermediate size, he proposes the independent phrase, such as "down the road." He also points out an interesting perceptual principle: when he says that redundancy may be resorted to for the purpose of indicating function, he is invoking for audition the psychological principles of similarity and/or proximity of elements, which are strong determiners, of perceptual units in vision. "He goes" vs. "They go" contains redundant information about singular and plural, but the similarity in number helps form an auditory unit. Ebeling (11) says that sentence intonation "marks a group of words (or one word) as a linguistic unit, a sentence," and that intonation patterns characterize types of sentences. He, too, does not think the word can be easily defined. Stene (55) believes that English has evolved phonologically in such a way that "the sense group" (the phrase or sentence) is a close-knit unit, without a need for pauses and glottal stops. This sense-unit is the unit of speech, whereas the lexical word is important for "language." He thinks phrases in modern English are very like words in Old English in terms of stress patterns. Fries (16) states that intonation patterns are part of the signaling system of English structure and are important indicators of sentence units, but not often decisive for other groups, and not always for sentences. In a later book (15) he seems to think that mature reading requires the supplying, by the reader, of the missing information about complete units which is supplied by intonation in speech. Pike (51) thinks that intonation contours mark sentences, but are intimately related to both pauses and to rhythm, although the three cannot substitute for one another. Intonation contours also appear to define phrases. Stress defines the semantically important word, whereas function words related to it are unstressed. Hultzén (30) believes that the function of the normal intonation pattern is simply to call attention, by its variation, to the imminence of a transition of low probability. These are linguists, but at least one psychologist, Miller (42), thinks that pauses serve a psychological function in providing time for decisions. He also finds that when difficult sentences are finally mastered, the intonation changes and becomes proper sentence intonation. And Goodman (22) found that children who read aloud with "natural" intonation tended to retain more information from a story, which would seem to indicate that intonation segments language into easily stored units.

Pauses are found to be important in several experimental studies. Mosher *et al.* (44) found pauses (either habitual or one-half second pauses between phrases) essential to accurate recording of several sorts of messages. Goldman-Eisler (20, 21) has studied pauses in speech in several situations. She finds two kinds of pauses, some defining syntactic or phrase units, but others, called hesitation pauses, which often fall well within the boundaries of syntactic or phrase units and are significantly longer. She finds that the latter anticipate a sudden increase in information, and, in fact, are necessary for it. (Cf. Lounsbury's discussion of hesitation phenomena as reflections of low probability transitions at the semantic level (36).) This within-sentence hesitancy is significantly less in description than in summaries of the same topic, and with repetition of the summaries there is a decrease in hesitancy. "Hesitation is thus an indicator of the subjective activity of producing information rather than of the statistical entity of predictability of linguistic expression." (20, p. 172) One is reminded here of the findings of Siipola *et al.* (53) where pressure (a set for speed) produces word association responses of a stereotyped sort, but freedom from pressure (time for decision) permits of idiosyncratic responses, which can also be described as creative or in Goldman-Eisler's terms of low transitional probabilities.

Hargreaves (27) found different modal units in different situations and what appeared to be a periodic effect. Speech, he thinks, tends to come in multiples of 600 ms., which corresponds to the utterance time for a single word. The one-half second modal unit is accounted for by a single word utterance, the one-second modal unit by two word responses. But the rate is faster (in English) in longer continuous bursts of speech. Osgood (48) favors the word (not the morpheme) as the unit of perception. Maclay and Osgood (38) corroborate Goldman-Eisler's findings that hesitation pauses are longer than juncture pauses. They analyzed the distribution of hesitation pauses in a moderately large corpus of conference speech. They reported that the distributions by Fries' categories for various types of pauses were significantly different, but the assumptions required by χ^2 do not appear to have been met. There may be biases in the several distributions. In their data, retracing for correction of a lexical item tends to include an antecedent function word, suggesting the boundary of an encoding unit. "Repeats" tend to be a single word, or at most two, but rarely a smaller unit. They believe there are two levels of encoding, lexical and grammatical, and that the units are either words or tightly knit phrase units. Pauses in emitted speech evidence encoding, but not necessarily decoding, units.

There is a series of experiments which are based upon the notion that a unit resists fractionation. Various techniques are devised to interrupt or fractionate it. Ladefoged and Broadbent (34) introduced clicks into a story and had the listeners indicate where they occurred. They were usually heard as occurring on the preceding word. For digits, the bias was not as great, but the click was heard earlier than it actually occurred, close to the pause between the stressed digits. When a speech sound was used as the interrupter, there is some evidence that it was correctly placed when it occurred on a stressed word in a clause or on a pause after "that," but the sample of sentences was not large enough for definitive results. The five sentences produced different sorts of errors. It is a promising technique which needs a good deal of exploiting. Fodor and Bever (14) have indeed attempted to use it in defining the constituent. They designed sentences with a single boundary where a large number of constituents terminated. There was a statistically significant tendency to locate the clicks at the major break, but 34 per cent of the responses either went too far or in the opposite direction. The obvious hypothesis—that the pauses often associated with major breaks account for the results—was disposed of by showing that there was no relationship between the decrease in energy of the sound signal at the major break and the percentage of responses confirming the hypothesis. However, most sentences did show such a decrease in energy, and since there are probably several auditory cues to perceptual units available to adults, the pause is not ruled out as one of these. Furthermore, it should be pointed out that although a pause may no longer be essential for adult perception, since the grammatical units are by then so overlearned as to be automatically units, they may nevertheless be essential to language learning. Children, as we know from genetic perceptual experiments in other areas, require more cues than adults. Likewise, when perception becomes difficult, as with a noisy channel, adults require more cues—and do better with pauses. There are some difficulties with the experiment which should be corrected before this technique is pursued. It is simpler, and safer, to lead both speech and clicks to both ears (cf. 10). Because of learning during the course of the experiment, a steady state should be reached before data are used, as in good reaction-time studies. Also "set" is a problem; probably various, very definite instructions should be tried out, since, with vague instructions, such as used here, subjects use "self-instruction," which is very variable, and a change in set is known to have a significant effect on reaction time. This technique is really a complex reaction-time experiment in modern dress.

Suci (56) is undertaking pilot experiments to investigate three non-linguistic criteria for units: 1) resistance to fractionation, 2) pauses at decision points (Goldman-Eisler's low transition probabilities), and 3) recodability (see below). He finds narrative material most useful with both children and adults, but has no data as yet. Bruce (4) asked children to fractionate words by saying what is left after removal of a certain phoneme, and found that children below M.A. 7 could not do the task. The assumption is that the word is a unit for small children, since they cannot dismember it. Huttenlocher (31), however, asked children to reverse pairs of words or to indicate where the items separated. The results indicate that four- and five-year-olds often do not perceive a single word as a unit, so that Bruce's units may be phoneme clusters of high frequency of occurrence. Both experiments may be running afoul of the short immediate memory span of youngsters as well as their incomplete comprehension of the concepts involved. It may also be that the instructions were simply not understood as intended. The Warrens (57) have shown that young children (but not old ones) do give non-English phoneme combinations, so they are not as rigidly bound by word frequency as one might guess from Bruce's results. Baldwin and Baum (2) tested the interruptability of sentences with three+- and four+-year-olds, by asking S's to repeat after E, but to stop when a light went off, and then complete the sentence when it went on again. Words of two syllables tended to be completed regardless of where the stop signal came, but one syllable words were even less frangible than two. If the signal came before the test word, some S's stopped before the word, but once the word was begun, most children completed it, and there was no relation between the facility with which words were split and the volume drop between syllables. There was also a tendency to complete phrases. Significant differences in reaction time were found between interruption at the beginning and in the middle of both words and phrases. They conclude that words function as units for the older S's and for some of the younger ones, that some phrases are also units, and that there are also even larger units for younger S's. Since work with young children and choice reaction time both are fraught with difficulties, and since the materials used here were not ideal nor varied enough, more should be done with this particular technique.

Frequency is allotted an important role in the formation of groups. A large amount of work has shown that frequency of occurrence of words is an important determiner of their perception and retention (50, 52). Less work has been done with frequency as a principle in the formation of larger groups. Yngve (61) hypothesized that a sentence can be considered as a structure of frequent morphemes with various open positions into which the infrequent morphemes and new words fit. The frequent morphemes and their combinations are role markers for infrequent ones and are important for stating syntactic patterns. He attempted to discover these patterns by gap analysis, a count of the number of words intervening between two occurrences of a word, or between two words, and summing of such counts. He has analyzed so far only a small corpus and that for only six words, but the distributions are anything but random. "The," for example, most often occurs in a structure containing two or three words (a phrase), but "and" most often repeats after fifteen gaps, so is usually associated with larger syntactic units (independent clauses); "of"—"the" has its only significant peak at zero gap, indicating that it is often part of a close-knit group. This technique is promising, for frequency, masquerading as familiarity, is an important principle in perception, and has been shown to be effective even in the perception of "nonsense" shapes with repetition frequency which falls far short of that occurring in natural language (1).

Miller, Heise, and Lichten (43) found amount of information to be the most important variable in correctly perceiving messages in noise; grammatical context effectively decreases the S/N threshold in a manner similar to restriction to a 256 word vocabulary. Decreasing the amount of information is equivalent to increasing the probability of an event and is locked to frequency of occurrence in experience. Goldman-Eisler (20, 21) also hypothesized high transition probabilities as determining structured groups. One of our own attempts to define units is likewise based upon frequency of occurrence plus pause (see below).

Ease of learning or retention in the definition of a unit, apart from frequency, has also been used. Glanzer (18) found that function words are hard to learn as separate units, but are easily learned if put into a group, even if the other clusters of phonemes are nonsensical. Content words are easier to learn alone. He suggests that an utterance is made up of a series of units, some of which are single (content) words, others sets of words which have function words embedded in them. It may be that the critical element here also is frequency, but it should be considered in relation to the principle in the next section, coding efficiency. Braine (3) found that children could learn the form classes of nonsense words by generalization from spatial position (or temporal, or both, depending upon whether visual or auditory cues were predominant). They could do the same with "phrases"—absolute position was easier than relative. He thinks that intonation defines the borders of units for very young children (see above).

Codability was mentioned as a criterion by Suci (56). Miller (41) has also placed great emphasis on this principle. Considering the choice reaction time, he believes that people ordinarily process speech units at only about one per second and that the phrase (of two or three words) is probably the natural decision unit. He finds intelligibility improved by grammatical context, but the same words without syntactic constraint can be understood if sufficient time is given (two seconds per word). It is interesting that Wickelgren (60) finds grouping in 3's most effective in auditory short-term memory. Mosher *et al.* (45) found that listeners could identify couplets (two commonly associated free forms) better if presented in the expected order. Goldman-Eisler (20) is also concerned with encoding units. Although efficiency of encoding is of basic importance in processing and retaining information, it does not solve the problem of how the perceptual units are originally built. Greenberg (24) suggests that the "nucleus" (intermediate between morpheme and word) should be investigated as a possible fundamental encoding or decoding unit. Osgood (47, 48) quite unlike Miller (41, 42) thinks the decoding unit will prove to be small—perhaps Greenberg's "nucleus."

The final category is surprising not only to me, but to its authors, Nihira, Guilford, Hoepfner, and Merrifield (46). A test, called Sentensense, dealing with the internal consistency of ideas or events expressed in a sentence, was designed to test the intellectual factor: Evaluation-Semantic-Systems. It turned out to be loaded not on *systems* but on *units,* together with other tests of semantic units. The test consisted of twenty items (to be done in four minutes) like: "Johnny, who is seven, went with his mother to Europe ten years ago." The explanation for the failure of these two-idea sentences to require the subject to deal with systems is based upon the shortness of the sentences, the high verbal ability of the S's in the study, and therefore the possibility of treating the entire sentence as a semantic unit in the processing of information. This brings up an important point, as well as introducing a technique which could be further exploited in the discovery of units, since "units" is a basic category in Guilford's model of the intellect (25). The point, which has almost reached threshold several times in this discussion, is that units may be different at different stages in language learning. In fact, Nihira, Guilford, *et al.* suggest that more complex sentences might shift the test to the Evaluation-Semantic-Systems category. The converse may also be true: that the present test used with verbally less proficient S's might also shift to the systems category. This approach certainly deserves thorough exploration.

In sum, it appears from the diverse approaches, that perceptual units are formed by rather well-known perceptual principles, principally those of proximity, similarity, familiarity, and continuity, with frequency in a position of prime importance, intonation, pause, and stress contributing heavily at some stages, and agreement somewhat less compelling. The highly familiar groups cohere as units for the encoding process in short-term memory. Verbally facile individuals will be able to deal with larger units. Units, then, may be words, phrases, clauses, simple or complex sentences depending upon the individual and the context. The larger the unit, the more efficient the coding of information, and the better the reader.

Our own investigation of units is in the pilot stage, and is entirely statistical so far. It is based upon speech production rather than reception, but this speech is well comprehended by the peers, and presumably represents, at the earlier levels, what the child has learned from his auditory perception of the speech of others. Four approaches have been looked at: 1) identification of the places at which "noise words" tend to occur in informal speech; 2) a tabulation of patterns of major stress; 3) a rough tabulation of the language frequency of words following pauses in the sound stream; and 4) a count of the various phonemic units bounded by pauses in the sound stream. All these were based upon samples of natural speech of interacting peer groups of three each in first, third, and fifth graders, and adults.

The pilot investigation of "noise" words (er, um, uh, etc.) is based on a very small corpus (one 30-minute tape at each level), so it is only suggestive. For one complete tape at each level (but varying from 3600 to 8400 syllables), "noise" words occur most often for all levels at the beginning of a sentence and with some frequency for all levels after a predicate verb. "Noise" words never occur after the first half of a compound noun, a predicate nominative, a predicate adjective, or an auxiliary. The other spots draw a scattering of frequencies, varying considerably from level to level. The "noise" words represent 3 per cent of the syllables at grade 1, 2 per cent at grade 3, 3 per cent at grade 5, and 4 per cent at adult level.

The analysis of stress patterns involved the identification of syllables bearing major stress vs. those not so stressed. The patterns found in 5 per cent or more of the sentences appeared to be similar at all levels and many kinds of patterns were found, but very few with more than five elements. The corpus analyzed is not large enough to be certain of these findings—perhaps adults will prove to have more long patterns if a sufficiently long corpus is analyzed. But at least the hypothesis that the youngest children produce sing-song speech is disposed of. Their alternating patterns of stressed-unstressed syllables are no more frequent than those of the adults.

The tabulation of frequency of language occurrence of words following substantial pauses (identified by phoneticians) is in process. If this is to test the Goldman-Eisler hypothesis that pauses occur at points of decrease in transition probabilities, then a decision has to be made about the unit which contains the low transition probability. If it is embedded in a phrase, then the word following the pause is likely to represent a very high transition probability. It appears so far that this is the case, but that these following words are about as often stressed as unstressed.

The count of "phonemic units" was based upon at least 31,000 phonemes per level.* Recordings of natural speech were transcribed by phoneticians, who indicated breaks in the sound stream only where they heard a definite pause. The transcription was a restricted phonetic one, but is limited largely to the phonemes of standard American English, the most important exception being the introduction of the glottal stop, which turned out to be a rather frequent phoneme not only among

* This research was conducted jointly with E. C. Carterette. For a full description, see (7).

six-year-olds, but also for adults (about 2 per cent at all four levels). A "word" count was made by computer of the frequency of each unit defined by pauses. These units should be compared with Lehiste's "bounded sequences." Although differently defined, they may prove to have much in common. "Bounded sequences" are often, but not necessarily, coincident with words (35). One can summarize this dictionary easily. Very few lexical words occur as discrete units. There are only a few types which occur with any appreciable frequency,* and these are either "noise" words or function words. For first graders, the first real word is "no" and this among peers! Most of the units occur but once, yet if one examines the print-out, one sees that often long sequences of words have much in common. It appears that there are common forms which take variable suffixes. Examples are: "All the ____ ," "There was a ____ ," "I always ____ ." The program identifies only initial patterns; there are undoubtedly stems which have variable prefixes as well. The pattern of sound is clear, however. Few words stand alone; the phrase and the clause are the obvious encoding units at all levels. In the interests of developmental perception it should be pointed out that six-year-olds have exceedingly mature language skills by many different criteria, so that if they are talking among themselves, as they were in this case, they can be expected to evidence this additional sign of maturity of language, and they did.

Finally we reach the point of relating these findings to the reading process. A child, in the process of perceptual learning, needs all the cues he can get. His spoken language is mature, his visual language skills virtually nonexistent. Any transfer which may occur will be materially aided by making the two languages as similar as possible. ITA will help only in a very minor way, if at all, in making the sound-spelling correspondences more obvious to youngsters (the larger patterns are reasonably regular, in any case), and then only if the spoken

* (Only 20 words occur more than ten times for first graders, only 17 for adults.)

"dialect" is rather similar to the standard. The difference between auditory and visual units, and the relationship suggested between good reading and normal intonation, lead to the implication that something should be done to bridge this gap. There are several simple techniques which might assist: words to be read as one unit could be underlined, primary stress could be indicated by red type or red underlining (often, in adult text, this is done by italics), and there are some circumstances under which pitch changes should be indicated, probably best done by a light blue line going in the proper direction behind the line of type. But pitch and stress are associated and it is possible that the actual intonation pattern will be understood by even a young native speaker, if the primary stress is indicated. It is difficult to say at what point in the learning process these indicators of prosodic features should be introduced, but they should be tried as early as possible. It would be interesting to see whether such bridges between auditory and visual language would speed up the process of learning to read. There are, of course, other possibly more complex differences between spoken and written language, even if both are standard dialects. These have to do with the effects of several sorts of context, which perhaps can be considered to define still different units, but here a good deal more exploratory work will be required before any useful suggestions can be made.

An Exploration of Psycholinguistic Units in Initial Reading

Duncan Hansen and Theodore S. Rodgers

In this presentation the authors report their own quest for viable psycholinguistic units in reading. Using a definition of reading quite different from the previous authors, they identify a unit smaller than the word. The authors offer a glimpse, as they describe a series of studies, into the kinds of research on reading in particular, and curriculum and methodology in general, that the computer can make possible.

Editor

An Exploration of Psycholinguistic Units
in Initial Reading

I. Introduction

Each generation has seen reading theory fall under the ascendancy of the current *Zeitgeist*. In our own time it appears that much of the impetus for new reading research emanates from the similarly new inter-disciplinary field of psycholinguistics. Linguists, psychologists, and educators have been actively collaborating in the formulation of propositions about the way a child's perception and assimilation of orthographic materials are controlled by features of the language, of the immediate stimulus situation, and of the child's behavioral history. Psycholinguistics may be defined as the scientific activity that seeks empirical confirmation or disconfirmation for such propositions. Before presenting the details of our paper, which will report the activities of the Stanford Project on Computer-Based Instruction in Initial Reading, we would like to comment on some recent trends in psycholinguistics, which will, we hope, provide a background to activities of the project.

In any consortium of inter-disciplinary fellows, one comes to expect a wide variation in the units of behavior proposed to describe an activity like initial reading. Linguists, for example, have proposed several such units which customarily coincide with the formal units within the levels of structural analysis. Hence, the forwarding of the phoneme, the morpheme, and the sentence; these being the basic units of linguistic analysis at the phonological, morphological, and syntactic levels, respectively. A scanning of the current linguistic literature, however, reveals a disconcerting amount of disagreement among linguists as to the requirement and definition of the proposed units and levels. There is, if possible, even less consensus as to the explicit inter-relations between the different levels (Chomsky, 7).

Psychologists, in their turn, offer alternative views concerning potential units in language behavior, generally, and in initial reading, specifically (Jenkins and Palermo, 22). Extended S-R associational theories formulated from a tradition of experimentation with N-gram and word associations have been challenged by some psychologists (Miller, 28) who stress the role of recognition and feedback processes. The report of the 1954 Conference on Psycholinguistics (Osgood and Sebeok, 31) is replete with extensive discussions of the relative merits of proposed linguistic-behavioral units. In regard to reading *per se,* scholarly discussions of "the" appropriate reading sub-units, particularly the letter *vs.* the word, date back to the eighteenth century or before (Fries, 11; Morris, 29).

Fully aware then of the sound and fury which has accompanied consideration of linguistic units variously championed by linguists, psychologists, and educators, we timorously offer a new contender to the ranks—a unit we shall call the "Vocalic Center Group." The body of the paper will both define the Vocalic Center Group (hereafter VCG) and substantiate our reasons for considering the VCG a viable unit for initial reading. Our confidence in this new construction rests in the systematic relationship between the VCG, linguistically defined, and the behavioral units one finds necessary to assume in order to account for the specific performance of children in initial reading.

Study of these behavioral units and particularly the mechanism implied in the utilization of such units represents a second facet of our investigations into reading behavior. Here the approach attempts to characterize the child-reader as a device capable of assimilating the systematic structures in natural language, as represented in either speech or reading, when exposed to specific stimulus situations. In this regard we find the work of Liberman and Cooper at Haskins Laboratory illuminating. Liberman, *et al.,* (24) have suggested a rule set and appropriate transmission-reception mechanisms that are sufficient for both production and perception of continuous speech sounds. From another vantage, we note that linguists working on generative and particularly transformational grammars have formulated sets of generative rules which when order-processed by a syntactic mechanism are capable of producing demonstrably proper sentence sequences (Halle and Stevens, 16). Later in the paper we shall present a schema which may hopefully annotate the close relationship observable between speech production, speech perception, and initial reading.

American linguists have been rather outspoken in their criticism of educators who, it has been felt, fail to recognize the high degree of linguistic sophistication which children bring to their initial schooling (Carroll, 9). The considerable language skills possessed by children prior to formal training in language arts has led us to consider the initial reading task as a transfer process that requires the mapping of an orthographic symbol system onto the already extensive language repertoires. This view suggests that the reading task be sequentially subdivided, not only chronologically but methodologically. Traditionally, the first stage consists of teaching the child that the orthographic symbols he sees on the printed page correspond in some way to his spoken language. The immediate task consists of pronouncing letters, words, or sentences aloud as a response to the orthography. This initial skill in decoding the orthography is assumed to be a necessary prerequisite to a higher level response in which the child comprehends the meaning of the segment and makes recall or inferential statements. In this paper we shall restrict ourselves to a discussion only of the first stage.

As theory and implementation have evolved in psycholinguistic research, some parallel developments have been taking place in computer science. The now-working knowledge of programmed learning coupled with the technological advances in computer console instrumentation have opened a bright new area for intensive individualized instruction and perhaps, more crucially, curriculum evaluation. These developments will offer important opportunities to linguists, psychologists, and educators alike. Linguists have here the tools for extensively tracking specific features of language acquisition. Psychologists may look to these developments as providing a promising setting for theoretical studies of such dependent measures as latencies. Educators may here find the means to make valid teacher-independent comparisons between different instructional methodologies. In the latter portion of this paper we will describe a computer-based instructional system that is now coming into existence at Stanford University.

We trust it is in keeping with the purpose of this symposium to have taken this discursive view of some recent developments in psycholinguistics. We shall impose on your good will in two further respects: first, we shall present our project report chronologically and second, we shall initiate our formal presentation with the discussion of a study considerably removed from initial reading. We hope this method of presentation may give you a sense of the way our own thinking has developed in our attempt to isolate the psycholinguistic units and behaviors of initial reading.

II. *The Russian Study*

At the Institute for Mathematical Studies in the Social Sciences, Professors Suppes and Crothers have been conducting a number of studies concerning the optimal list size for learning Russian-English vocabulary pairs (to be reported in Suppes and Crothers (39), in preparation). The term block size refers to the average number of unique pairs intervening between the presentation of pair i on trial n and the re-presentation of that pair on trial $n + 1$. The task for the subject was as follows. A Russian item was pronounced from tape by a native Russian speaker. After five seconds a correct English translation for the item was given. If the subject recognized the Russian word from previous presentations, he was to write the English translation before it was pronounced on the tape. Subjects were called back after a week and given a recall test. In reviewing the primary data from the results of two groups of twenty subjects studying 300 Russian-English vocabulary pairs over a nine-day period, we discovered that some pairs were both acquired and retained with surprising ease by subjects regardless of block size, whereas other pairs were never learned by any subject in any test condition.

The high inter-subject consistency as regards item difficulty encouraged us to attempt to determine those variables about the pair which seemed to facilitate or retard the learning. After investigating a number of possible variables in both the Russian stimulus words and the English response words, we found a form class schema to be the most illuminating. Using a class-frame sentence technique (Fries, 10), we analyzed the 300 words into twelve classes. These results are presented in Table 1. The results indicate a regular monotonically decreasing relationship between the various classes and proportion of correct responses. Independent research has indicated a similar learning hierarchy for the major function classes (Glanzer, 13).

In light of this finding we formulated the hypothesis that functional and possibly semantic properties of the English words provided a mediational linkage to the Russian associates. We then planned a further experiment in an attempt to substantiate this proposition. Selecting the 25 most-learned and the 25 least-learned of the 300 pairs, we reversed the order of the English responses to the Russian stimuli so as to form a set of spurious translation pairs (that is, Russian item 1 was now paired with English item 50, etc.). If our hypothesis concerning the dominating influence of the English response was correct, we expected to observe that the acquisition scores of this new set of 50 pseudo-pairs should be more or less the reverse of what was found in the prior experiment.

The subjects were given exactly the same instructions as in the prior experiment. They were presented the pairs in block sizes of 50 for six trials using the same equipment and procedure as for the earlier experiments. Six randomizations of the 50 items were used. The six trials were given to ten subjects in

Table 1

*Form Class Analysis of English Translations
of the 300 Russian Words*

Form-Class	Number of Words	Mean Proportion Correct per Item	Examples of Russian English Pairs	
Definite pronouns	5	.93	ВЫ	you
Colors	4	.67	БЕЛЫЙ	white
Concrete Nouns	84	.58	ЛОБ	forehead
Possessive Pronouns	3	.42	ОНА	her
Prepositions	11	.42	ЧЕРЕЗ	across
Adjectives	57	.41	ДИКИЙ	wild
Numbers	8	.37	ПЯТЬ	five
Abstract Nouns	34	.36	ВЛАСТЬ	authority
Interrogatives	7	.31	ПОЧЕМУ	why
Adverbs	22	.23	ПОЧТИ	almost
Conjunctions	6	.22	ИЛИ	or
Verbs	59	.21	ДЕРЖАТЬ	to hold

300

one day with a rest break between the third and fourth trials. The results of the experiment are presented in Table 2. Row 1 reports the mean proportion of correct responses in the prior Russian study. Row 2 presents the mean proportion of correct responses in this experiment that reversed the Russian-English pairing. If our hypothesis were to be confirmed, one would expect to find that the means in row 2 would be the reverse of the prior experimental results presented in row 1. To our chagrin the means did not reverse. We were thus forced to shift our attention from the function or meaningfulness of the English responses to factors inherent in the Russian stimuli.

Table 2
Group Statistics for the Russian-English Reversal Study

Group Statistics	Russian Words	
	Low Difficulty	High Difficulty
Mean Proportion of Pair Items Correct in the Suppes-Crother Experiment	.454	.015
Mean Proportion of Pair Items Correct in Reverse Pair Experiment	.299	.118
Number of Syllables in the Russian Words	46	48
Sum of the Consonant Cluster Complexity Scores	22	50

Suspecting that the length of the Russian word might be a critical variable we performed a syllable count, the totals of which are shown in row 3 of Table 2. The number of syllables for the two lists of 25 Russian words are approximately equal.

We then attempted to explore in greater depth a "covert rehearsal" hypothesis which many verbal learning experimenters posit as a necessary condition for success in rote learning tasks. It appeared obvious that rehearsal and pronunciability rating of a Russian word must be highly dependent. How then might one get a pronunciability rating of a Russian word by an American subject? Professors Greenberg and Jenkins (14) have proposed a method for determining structural distance of any given syllable from the syllable canon of English. Unfortunately, the rating procedure is exceedingly arduous, requiring information about English syllable structure which must be hand-generated, and ultimately yields scores only for monosyllabic items. A simpler and more general procedure was obviously desirable. One set of linguistic features which appeared somewhat promising and at the same time relatively easy to isolate was the set of Russian consonant sequences. Using a phonetic transcription of the Russian stimulus words we sought to determine which of the Russian consonant sequences were phonetically and positionally (initially and finally) similar to consonant sequences in English. Having matched those Russian sequences which were phonetically similar to sequences in English, we then determined a consonant complexity score for each Russian word. A Russian word without a consonant sequence (a sequence is defined as two adjacent phonemes of the same type —consonant or vowel) was assigned a complexity score of zero; an item containing a consonant sequence phonetically similar to an English sequence in the same position was assigned a score of one for each such sequence; an item with sequences dissimilar to any found in a comparable initial or final position in English was assigned a complexity score of two for each such sequence.

This rating scheme, you will note, automatically weights complexity scores for length of consonant sequences. The results of this rating yield the values in row 4 of Table 2. The consonant complexity score ranking is observed to be closely correlated with that of the learning score. Apparently English-like consonant sequences are easier to rehearse than non-English consonant sequences. It appears, additionally, that longer consonant sequences, English-like or not, are more difficult to rehearse than shorter consonant sequences.

These two propositions are anticipated by linguistic evidence on the restrictive subset of consonant sequences that occur in comparison to the large combinatorial possibilities. Greenberg (1965) notes in a discussion of consonant cluster universals in 104 languages:

1. For initial and final systems, if x is the number of sequences of length m and y is the number of sequences of length n and $m > n$, and p is the number of consonant phonemes, then $\frac{x}{p} m \leq \frac{y}{p} n$

In other words, the proportion of the logically possible

ambinates utilized decreases or remains the same with increasing length of the sequences. This may be illustrated for English initial clusters as follows: the number of consonant phonemes are 22. All of these except / ž / and / ŋ / occur as single phonemes. The logically possible sequences of length 2 are $22^2 = 484$. Of these, 28 occur. For length 3 the logically possible number of combinations is $22^3 = 10,648$. Of these, only 6 occur . . .

2. For initial and final systems, if x is the number of sequences of length m and y is the number of sequences of length n, and $m > n$ and $n \geqslant 2$, the $x \leqslant y$ . . . syllables containing sequences of n consonants in a language are to be found as syllabic types, then sequences of $n - 1$ consonants are also to be found in the corresponding position (prevocalic or postvocalic) except that $CV \rightarrow V$ does not hold . . .

In general, the validity of 1 and 2, to which no exception was found in the 104 languages of the sample, provides objective evidence of the "difficulty" of clusters. This would seem to correlate with the diachronic tendency towards their simplification, since any simplification automatically reduces the number, both absolutely and proportionally, of sequences of the length subject to reduction and increases the number of shorter sequences.

Encouraged by the linguistic-universal evidence as to the length-difficulty of clusters and by our own evidence as to the role consonant clusters assume in rehearsal difficulty, we entertained the conjecture that some phonemic sequences might be easier for initial readers to rehearse than others. More specifically, that rehearsal difficulty of consonant clustered units may be hierarchically determined, in that each pronounceable subunit of a larger unit is a) permissible in the language, and b) less difficult to rehearse. (Greenberg's evidence suggests that the CV unit may represent a lower bound on this generalization.) One anticipates that there may be evidence of rehearsal or pronunciation "ease" reflected in all of the dominant as opposed to the recessive phonemic patterns in language.

The relationship between the Russian study just discussed and reading research may appear highly tenuous. We have discussed the Russian experiment in this detail because we feel it demonstrates several necessary if not sufficient conditions which we have imposed on our present investigations in beginning reading.

We first examined the Russian data in the light of several inter-dependent hypotheses known to psychologists under rubrics such as meaningfulness, frequency of occurrence, availability, familiarity, concreteness, etc. These "hypotheses" often have appeared as "criteria" in choosing the initial vocabulary and sequence of reading materials. Thus, we find vocabulary chosen on the basis of frequency (McKee, *et al.*, 26), meaningfulness (Fries, 11), and situational availability (Russell and Ousley, 36). In the Russian study these hypotheses appeared intuitively reasonable and, in one instance, gave a fairly accurate account of the initial data. All failed to yield valid predictions as to the results of the follow-up experiment. We will attempt to demonstrate in what follows that such hypotheses also fail to adequately characterize observations of initial reading behaviors.

Secondly we have attempted to indicate, again on the basis of the Russian experiment, some phonetic features of linguistic response which appear to strongly influence the ease or difficulty of language learning tasks. Two such features, composition and length of consonant sequences, which strongly determined the success of pair-learning in the Russian experiment, will be re-examined in our discussion of the sequence of beginning reading material.

In order to understand why certain phonetic sequences present greater difficulty than others, one would like to develop some sort of operational characterization of speech production at the phonological level. We would now like to turn our attention to some relevant research in this area of speech production.

III. *Factors in Speech Production*

Our hypothesis concerning the role of rehearsal in the acquisition of oral reading behavior led us to a serious re-examination of the literature on speech production with particular reference to pronounceability of vocabulary items (see Greenberg and Jenkins (14), or Underwood and Schultz (41), for examples of adult rating of pronounceability). Such an approach seems of limited experimental use in working with children and leaves undefined the principal problem of clarifying the independent variables. A more promising source of information as to the relative difficulty of pronunciation units was found in the experimental research on speech synthesis. Several types of speech synthesizers are currently being explored (see for example, Rosen (35), of Peterson (32). All of these minimally require some set of basic discrete units and some sort of rules for converting these discrete units into a speech-like continuum. We felt that a measure of pronounceability might be deduced from the nature of the base units and the number and type of rules required to synthesize the pronunciation in question.

Rules for synthesis involve considerably more than mere concatenation over phonemes or any other phonetic element. Independent evidence from linguists (Hockett, 21) and acousticians (Harris, 18; Liberman, *et al.*, 24) emphatically suggests that the speech signal can in no way be equated to a string of phonemic beads. Hockett pictures the speech signal as a set of broken phonemic Easter eggs, yolking into one another, if you will. Among the more revealing yolking procedures are those suggested by Liberman, Ingemann, Lisker, Delattre, and Cooper (24) of the Haskins Laboratories in their rules for speech synthesis. There rules are specified in terms of acoustic features, which, when reproduced as a spectographic pattern, can be played back as recognizable speech. The synthesis rules are subdivided into three groups according to the function they play in speech production. The first set of rules specifies the core characteristics of a given phoneme, i.e., the form and freqencies and/or loci which typify the three principal formants of that phoneme. The second group of rules specifies the sequential transitions between core centers necessary to smooth the discrete core characteristics into a speech continuum. The third group of rules called "position modifiers" provide alteration of the core rules for a given phoneme on the basis of adjacent phonemes. In essence, these "position modifiers" determine the allophonic variations of the phonemes in the phonetic string. An example from Liberman, *et al.*, (24) may help clarify the nature of the "postion modifiers." The example is for the syllabic unit /glu/. The formant frequencies, intensities, durations, and transition characteristics for /g/, /l/, /u/, are specified and then the authors note:

> Now a rigid application of the basic rules for the phonemes constituting the syllable /glu/ yields an ultimate acoustic output of less than tolerable intelligibility. A marked improvement is achieved if the basic rules for each phoneme are modified as follows: /g/ before /l/ requires only a burst of specified frequency; /l/ before /u/ has the frequency of its second formant lowered somewhat; /u/ following /l/ has a second formant which first rises from the second formant frequency of /l/ and then, after a specified duration, shifts at a given rate to the normal steady-state frequency for /u/.

Similarly, a successful human rehearsal must operate over units such that the output forms are of tolerable intelligibility. A simple concatenation of phonemes or even allophones will not, as Liberman suggests, produce such a tolerably recognizable output. (It is recognized that additional requirements such as those for syllabic stress are also implied by our intelligibility criterion. Liberman, *et al.*, do suggest a criterion for determining vowel characteristics under primary stress.)

The required detail of the rule specification shown in the example above suggests that speech activity conceived in these terms must require manipulation of a ponderous collection of such rules. Due largely to the overlapping of subphonemic features many of the redundant specifications in phonemic classification can be eliminated in the speech synthesis model. In fact, the Liberman, *et al.*, model utilizes 17 rules for consonantal, and 14 rules for vocalic articulation. This compares favorably with the English phonemic inventory considered to be about 40 phonemes. In order to form connected speech of tolerable intelligibility (not a requirement of phonemic descriptions) twelve position modifiers, a stress modifier, and a meshing routine are also required.

There is a notable isomorphism between the articulation feature sets and the synthetic formant sets. For example, one applies a single articulatory rule for aspiration in initial stop consonants. Similarly, to synthesize aspiration, a single rule specifies 50 millisecond aperiodic second and third formant transitions to steady-state vowel formants. In both cases, the rules apply in the same fashion to the same phonemes.

In terms of our present interest, the categorical nature of rule specification suggests to the linguist economical statements of phonotactic constraints; offers to the psychologist an inference set of complexity measures; and presumably, simplifies for the language-user perception and production of speech sequences. An example of the use to which rule specifications of this type might be put is given by Saporta (37). Saporta has hypothesized that an intermediate number of feature shifts between successive consonants optimizes both speech perception and production. Such a statement is linguistically and psychologically testable.

We interpret this whole line of linguistic and psycholinguistic evidence to suggest that there is a continuum of preference as to pronunciation and perception of speech units and that the learning effects due to rehearsal are directly related to this continuum. The task now becomes one of relating the generic properties of the rules for speech synthesis to an appropriate psycholinguistic perception-production unit and secondly, relating the processes of speech perception and production to the processes of initial reading. We now turn our attention to the first of these tasks.

IV. *Vocalic Center Group*

The psycholinguistic unit for initial reading that we propose in the Vocalic Center Group (VCG) is an elementary structure resulting from the integration of phonemic elements into a minimal pronunciation unit. The VCG is a structure in the sense that it is the optimally minimal sequence within which all necessary rules of phonemic co-occurrence can be stated. Such rules are commonly referred to as phonotactic rules. By integration we refer to the process whereby phonemes are positionally modified so as to form a phonotactically permissible and tolerably intelligible pronunciation. The VCG is marked by one vocalic element (which is not necessarily a vowel). Non-vocalic (consonantal) or semi-vocalic elements may occur preceding or following the vocalic center. The "complexity" of phonotactic rules governing the phonemic combinations within the VCG, we hypothesize, are intimately related to the "difficulty" of speech production, speech perception, and we will claim, initial reading behaviors.

It may have occurred to some of you that our discussion of the VCG thus far is in fact a discussion of that unit which has been traditionally called the syllable. What justification can we offer for adding "the Vocalic Center Group" to the already overloaded lexicon of psycho-linguo-educational neologisms?

In reviewing the literature on the syllable (Haugen, 20), one finds a vast array of definitional diversity and argumentation as to the acceptability of the syllable. Attempts to associate syllables with the breath pauses physiologically observable in the intercostal muscles have been generally successful only in giving quantitative accounts of the number of vocalic nuclei (Stetson, 38). No valid criteria for determining syllable cuts between adjacent consonant groups at the syllabic margins are offered. Definitions based on distributional procedures (O'Connor and Trim, 30) offer little insight as to the classification of these distributional observations and leave unresolved the problem of marking syllable boundaries in polysyllabic units.

Other linguistic theorists have attempted to define the syllable on the basis of higher level, supra-segmental features; thus the attempts to identify syllabic nuclei with stress (Pike, 33) or syllabic boundaries with juncture (Harris, 19). The limitations of these proposals have been discussed extensively in the linguistic literature. Attempts to identify the orthographic syllable have presented similar problems. Contradictions between the phonological, morphological, and historical criteria used in determining lexographic syllabification have been bitterly bewailed by the very lexicographers who perpetuate the system. The unfortunate syllable has fallen heir to the calumny and confusion of its definitions. For reasons then, both political and theoretical, we felt a different terminology advisable.

Perhaps the most valid reason for introducing the new terminology, however, was our intention to assign to the VCG properties of an entirely different nature than those previously defined into the syllable. First, as we have noted, the VCG is the minimal construct defined over a set of phonotactic rules. These rules define constraints not only between continuous elements (consonant-consonant, consonant-vowel, vowel-consonant) but over discontinuous elements (pre- and post-vocalic consonants) as well. Second, ambiguities encountered in syllable cuts at consonantal boundaries are recognized and accounted for in terms of VCG priority rules. These priority rules are used as a basis for discussing individual variations encountered in syllabification of speech. Third, the rule structure of a particular VCG is employed to make predictions concerning the facility of rehearsal of the VCG and, ultimately, the facility for association of the phonotactic to the orthographic pattern. Finally, the structure of the VCG requires us to make both quantitative and qualitative predictions as to the type of errors that initial readers will make in forming pronunciations for a particular graphic segment.

In presenting the rules governing the VCG, we shall refer to the Vocalic Center by the letter V and the consonant cluster by the letter C with superscripts i, m, or f, standing for initial medial, or final positions. Descriptive listings and examples will be held to a minimum as one can find a reasonably complete description of the permissible consonant sequences in English in Bloomfield (2), Whorf (42) and Harris (19). What follows below are examples of the various phonotactic rule types for Monovocalic Center Groups.

Case 1 *Rules Governing Initial Consonant Clusters of the Form C^i ... Where $i = 2, 3$.*

A. Consonants having the same manner of articulation do not occur in the same cluster. The phonemic classes of stop, fricative, nasal, liquid, semi-vowel may be represented no more than once in any cluster. Thus one finds /str-/ but not */sθr-/ or */stp-/ or */slr-/.

Case 2 *Rules Governing Initial Consonant Clusters and Following Vowel of the Form C^iV ...Where $i > 2$.*

Clusters containing the semi-vowel /y/ can be followed only by the vowel /u/. Thus, one has /m y u wt/ *mute* but not */m y a wt/.

Case 3 *Rules Governing Final Consonant Clusters of the Form ... C^f Where $f = 2, 3, 4$.*

Two consonants having the same manner of articulation may cluster only if the second member is articulated in the alveolar region. Thus, one finds /fs, θs, pt, kt, bd, gd, rl, dz, ðz, bz, gz, vz/# but not */sf, sθ, tp, tk, db, dg, lr, etc./#.

Case 4 *Rules Governing Vowel and Following Consonants of the Form ...VC^f.*

A. In VC^f if V = /i, e, æ, u/, then C^f must be greater than zero. Thus we find final vowel /ɔ/ in *law*, /aw/ in *now*, /a/ in *ma*, /ə/ in *sofa*, /iy/ in *me*, /ay/ in *my*, /ɔy/ in *boy*, /ey/ in *bay*, /ow/ in *bow*, and /uw/ in *do* but not *C^i + /i, e, æ, u/#.

B. In VC^f if V $\neq$ /i, e, æ, ə, u, a, ɔ/ (i.e., simple vowels), then C^f can not be of the form liquid (/r,l/) plus any consonant except /d/ and //z. Thus we find /part/ *part*, /help/ *help*, /silk/ *silk*, /mə lč/ *mulch*, /fayld/ *filed*, /fiyld/ *field*,

/feyld/ *failed,* /f ɔ yld/ *foiled,* /fawld/ *fouled,* /fuwld/ *fooled,* /fowled/ *foaled,* but not */fayrt/, */feylp/, */fiylk/, */fuwlc/, etc.

Case 5 *Rules Governing Initial and Final Clusters of the Form C^i and C^f Where i = 2, 3, and f = 2, 3, 4.*

A. All consonants which are members of a voiced-voiceless pair set will be all either voiced or voiceless in the same cluster. Thus one finds /s t u w/, *stew,* /r æ f t s/ *rafts* but not */s d u w/, */r æ v t s/, */r æ f d s/, */r æ f t z/.

B. Any linear partition of a consonant cluster will yield sequences permissible in the same pre- or post-vocalic position as the principal cluster. Thus, initial /s t r-/ is divisible into the permitted initial sequences /st/ + /r/, /s/ + /tr/, /s/ + /t/ + /r; or /— ŋ kθs/ is divisible into the permitted final sequences /ŋ/ + /kθs/ or /ŋ kθ/ + /s/ or /ŋ k/ + /θs/ or /ŋ/ + /k/ + /θs/ or /ŋ/ + /k/ + /θ/ + /s/, etc.

B' Any medial complex consonant cluster (poly-syllabic words where m≧2) is divisible into a permitted final plus initial cluster. For example, /ekstrə/ *extra* must be divisible into at least two simpler initial-final clusters /eks + trə/, /ek + strə/, /ekst + rə/.

Case 6 *Rules Governing Cross-Vocalic Consonant Clusters of the Form C^iVC^f Where i ≧ 2 and f ≧ 1.*

A. Any sonant (/m, n, l, r/) may occur either in initial or final clusters but the same sonant may not occur in both initial and final clusters in the same VCG.

Thus one finds *slit* and *still* but not **slill; bread* and *beard* but not **breard; small* and *slam* but not **smam; snug* and *shun* but not **snun.*

Phonotactic constraints of this type provide the strongest justification for our claim that the VCG is the minimally optimal unit within which rules of phonemic co-occurrence can be stated. This restriction does not apply to form C^iVC^i where i ≦ 1. One does find *lull, rare, mum,* and *none.* We believe other phonotactic constraints apply, less absolutely, to cross-vocalic consonant clusters. We call such forms "un-favored" VCG's. We postulate a broad continuum of such VCG forms that range from "non-permissible" to "favored."

From a psycholinguistic point of view, the ranking of a particular VCG form along this continuum may be inferred from the number and type of speech synthesis rules one must apply to generate a pronunciation. The larger the number of rules required, the more difficult the rehearsal. (The less formal "Principle of Least Effort" has long been a popular explanation for ease of articulation (Zipf, 43).) As the consonant clusters are the only part of the VCG that may vary in phonemic length, we hypothesize that longer consonant clusters will result in more difficult rehearsal and consequently will be acquired with greater difficulty in, say, the context of initial reading. We also speculate that for clusters of equal length the rules for some sequences will be more complex than for others. One apparent form of sequential complexity at this level is measured in terms of the phonetic similarity of adjacent phonemes. This suggests that a sequence of the form *apt*/ æ pt/ containing a consonant-phoneme pair identical in manner of articulation and voiceless-ness would be more difficult, in the sense discussed above, than a form like *art*/art/ where the consonant phonemes share no phonetic features.

Desiring an empirical test of these assumptions, and more specifically, of the viability of the VCG in a reading situation, we designed a learning experiment in which certain complex monosyllabic words and certain simple disyllabic words would be taught as reading units. In an attempt to avoid confounding the results with semantic factors we constructed pseudo-words from occurrent phonotactic patterns. A minimal disyllabic form that avoids adjacent syllabic vowels is the pattern CVCVC. This represented the disyllabic pattern. We assumed stress on the first vowel. The monosyllabic forms consisted of two CCCVC, two CCVCC, and two CVCCC patterns. We also wished to test pre-vocalic and post-vocalic cluster difficulty to see if we could partially replicate the studies of children's

Table 3

*The Mean Total Errors Committed by the Children
on the Twelve English Pseudo-words*

Disyllabic Item	Total Group Mean Total Errors N = 20	Criterion Group Mean Total Errors N = 13
hulig	3.10	1.54
molin	1.85	.62
devan	2.30	.92
renad	3.50	1.69
nateb	2.55	1.23
fegom	2.45	.85
Consonant Cluster Items		
strem	3.25	1.39
splog	2.90	1.46
brind	3.85	1.46
flesk	3.25	1.23
borst	4.05	2.39
vimpt	4.30	3.08

speech perception indicating that post-vocalic errors are twice
as frequent as pre-vocalic errors (Templin, 40). Controlling
for phoneme length and phoneme frequency where possible,
we constructed the list of twelve forms presented in Table 3.
We tested eight-year-old children in order to have subjects who
had only partially mastered the initial reading process (i.e.,
subjects capable of rehearsing words but limited in practice on
the orthographic consonant sequences found in the list).

A paired-associate anticipation method was employed. The
children, tested individually, were shown a 3×5 inch card
on which a given word was printed in ¾ inch letters. A four-
second interval was given for a response. After a response or
at the end of four seconds, the experimenter pronounced the

word and the child overtly rehearsed it once. The cards were reshuffled at the end of each trial (a trial consisted of once through the deck). Twenty children were run for ten consecutive trials.

The mean total errors for each pseudo-word are presented in Table 3. The criterion subjects were defined as children who had two or more consecutive errorless trials. A learning curve for each group of words is presented in Figure 1. An analysis of variance yielded a highly significant difference ($F = 19.67$, $P < .001$) in favor of disyllabic pseudo-words. The summary statistics are presented in Table 4.

Table 4
Group Statistics for Disyllabic and Consonant Cluster Items

	Disyllabic Words	Consonant Cluster Words
Mean Total Errors	2.79	3.60
S.D.	3.24	3.33
Trial of the Last Error	3.06	3.95
S.D.	3.40	3.71
Successes Before the Last Error	.27	.35
S.D.	.67	.89
Mean Errors Before the First Success	2.43	3.04

In regards to individual behavior, the relative difficulty of the consonant clustered monosyllabic words was even more prominent. All subjects initiated errorless sequences earlier for the disyllabic words than for the consonant cluster words (i.e., the first instances of the trial of the last error always had a higher proportion of disyllabic words). There also was a higher proportion of correct disyllabic word pronunciations in the trial of the first success. As evidenced by the item means presented in Table 3, there was not a perfect correlation between syllable length and learning efficiency (i.e., the subjects

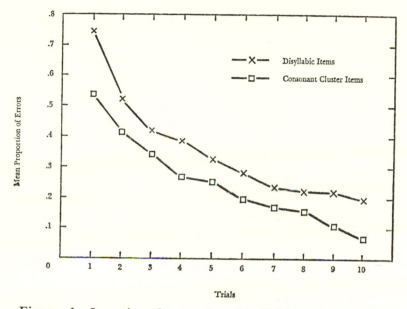

Figure 1. *Learning Curves for Disyllabic and Consonant Cluster Pseudo-Words*

did not learn all the disyllabic words prior to learning the consonant cluster words). As regards the second of our original hypotheses, the results clearly indicate that post-vocalic clustered forms present significantly (P < .01) greater learning difficulties than initially clustered or non-clustered forms. Thus the learning results support the inferences that follow from the VCG conceptualization.

Now if the VCG and the behavioral propositions posited for it have psychological validity, one would wish to provide an account of reading errors as well as of efficient reading behavior. First, we would predict that errors should be intimately connected with failures to handle a unit VCG or a combination of VCG's. Consequently we would expect to find that the frequency of permutation, insertion, and reduction errors would be of the same magnitude as substitution (individual phoneme replacement) errors.

There were, in fact, 809 errors committed by the children. We categorize these as follows, using the items *hulig* and *borst* as examples for each error type:

1) *Omissions:* failure to emit a pronunciation.
2) *Permutations:* shifting a pair of consonants about the vocalic center (*luhig* and *brost*).
3) *Consonant Reductions:* deleting a consonant from the item (e.g., *huli* and *bost*).
4) *VCG Deletions:* deleting an entire VCG from the item (e.g., *lig*). Deletion of the VCG from the single VCG's would be considered an omission.
5) *VCG Insertions:* inserting a phonemic element to form a distinctly new VCG (e.g., *hoglig* and *borsit*).
6) *Familiar Words:* substituting a word (e.g., *holy* and burst).
7) *Vowel Substitutions:* substituting a single vocalic element (e.g., *hulog* and *birst*).
8) *Consonant Substitutions:* substituting a single consonantal element (e.g., *dulig* and *horst*).
9) *Miscellaneous Errors:* errors that we could not categorize or we were unable to analyze due to unintelligibility.

The results are presented in Table 5. We analyzed the data separately for the criterion and non-criterion groups as there were marked differences in total errors and relative percentages of errors in given categories between the two groups of subjects. If the categories of permutations, consonant reductions, VCG deletions, and VCG insertions are combined as representing errors directly related to VCG formation, one accounts for 50 per cent of the results. This is, perhaps, more significant when one observes that single phoneme errors (vowel substitutions and consonant substitutions) constitute only 10 per cent of the errors.

The categories of omissions and familiar words, representing one-third of the errors, suggest a major gap in the formulation to this point. These children, and speakers in general, appear

Table 5
Categorization of the Reading Errors for the Disyllabic and Consonant Cluster Items

Error Categories	Criterion Group (N = 13)			Non-Criterion Group (N = 7)			Total Group
	Disyllabic Items	Consonant Cluster Items	Percentage of Errors	Disyllabic Items	Consonant Cluster Items	Percentage of Errors	Percentage of Errors
Omission	3	2	2%	58	63	21%	13%
Permutations	8	9	10%	8	11	4%	4%
Consonant Reductions	3	30	14%	8	41	8%	10%
VCG Deletions	8	0	3%	23	0	4%	4%
VCG Insertions	30	36	29%	92	97	33%	32%
Familiar Words	4	45	21%	41	91	23%	23%
Vowel Substitutions	11	8	8%	15	9	4%	5%
Consonant Substitutions	8	6	6%	6	8	2%	5%
Misc. Errors	10	5	7%	4	2	1%	4%
Number of Errors	85	147	232	255	322	577	809

to edit potential speech segments in some manner so as to exclude outputs that are not well formed (Loban, 25). The determination of well-formedness, whether in terms of phonological, grammatical, or semantic criteria, is largely a product of prior language experience. It has been suggested that inherent characteristics may also play a part in such determination (Lenneberg, 23). The concept of covert evaluation of potential speech units prior to pronunciation has been formulated into a behavioral feedback process called the "TOTE" by Miller, Galanter, Pribram (27). The "TOTE" process, in essence, requires an internal recognition response prior to the emission of a pronunciation. If there is no recognition response, the would-be speaker re-cycles his processing of the potential output until either a recognition response does occur or the response interval is exceeded so that the potential output is represented as an omission. In terms of our experiment, the familiar word errors occurred, we hypothesize, because certain children required a "TOTE" at the word level and so incorrectly generated a unit that was recognized as a word. Omissions may have occurred through a similar strategy; instead of generating a familiar word that would be obviously incorrect, the "correct" pronunciation was aborted when no lexical match was found.

V. *Heuristic Algorithm for Initial Reading*

At this juncture, we wish to combine the formulations about the VCG and the recognition process into a set of ordered statements that, we believe, characterize a typical behavioral sequence in initial reading. This characterization, for the purpose of specificity, is written as a set of programmatic steps such as one might use for computer instructions. We will, in fact, utilize some of the terminology from computer programming. We disclaim any notion that there is an isomorphic relationship between computational hardware and/or routines and human neurological structure and/or functions known to be utilized in initial reading. We present this "heuristic algorithm" to illustrate how theory can be explicitly implemented but not to claim that either the theory or the implementation is presently a *sufficient* model for characterizing observed reading behaviors. We do contend that initial readers might use a heuristic algorithm of this nature. We have found such characterizations useful in generating hypotheses about initial reading and in planning a set of curriculum materials for initial reading.

We will list the steps in the algorithmic routine and then illustrate the routine by analyzing the words *fasting* and *pasting*.

Step 1. Input the orthographic unit (e.g., that string of orthographic symbols between spaces) into an immediate memory buffer. If the buffer is empty at any point of re-cycling, re-input the orthographic unit.

Step 2. Mark the vowels (e.g., a, e, i, o, u, y) in the unit.

Step 3. Count the vowels not followed by vowels. If the count is zero, branch to Step 1. If the count is one, proceed to Step 4. If the count is greater than one, apply the following syllabification rules to the medial consonants as follows:

> a) ... VCV ... maps into V + CV mATIng → mA +TIng
> ... VCCV ... maps into VC + CV mATTIng → mAT + TIng
> ... VCCCV ... maps into VC + CCV thIRSTY → thIR + STY

If recycled to Step 3, apply these syllabification rules as follows:

> b) ... VCV ... maps into VC + V BUSIng → BUS + Ing
> ... VCCV ... maps into V + CCV tASTY → tA + STY
> ... VCCCV ... maps into V + CCCV pASTRY → pA + STRY

Step 4. Decode each VCG separately and sequentially. Translate the orthographic code onto the code utilized in analyzing and processing individual VCG speech units. (This involves specifying the phonetic components for both the vocalic center and the pre- and post-consonantal clusters according to the constraints specified for any VCG of this articulatory type. In essence, this step translates the orthographic reading code onto the phonotactic speech code.

$$(\text{mA} \rightarrow /\text{mey}/)$$
$$(\text{TIng} \rightarrow /\text{tiŋ}/)$$
$$(\text{mAT} \rightarrow /\text{mæt}/)$$
$$(\text{TIng} \rightarrow /\text{tiŋ}/)$$
$$(\text{thIR} \rightarrow /\theta\text{ər}/)$$
$$(\text{STy} \rightarrow /\text{stiy}/)$$

and so forth.

Step 5. Determine the category in the long-term memory area that is to be searched for a recognition response (that is, decide whether to search the word listings, the listings of experienced VCG forms, or, perhaps, the index of phonotactically permissible VCG forms). If a word listing search is to be performed, assemble the VCG units if there are more than one.

Step 6. Search for a match in the assigned long-term memory area. If a match fails to occur, branch to Step 3 and apply the re-cycling rules for syllabification.

Step 7. Put the matched VCG into the articulation buffer. Assemble the sequence of VCG's. Apply the rules for integration of phonetic units at VCG boundaries. Execute the motor commands for pronunciation.

It would perhaps be useful, before proceeding, to comment in a bit more detail on the notions underlying Steps 3 and 4. We have suggested previously and now state as theorems the following:

Theorem 1: A consonant cluster of length n-1 is simpler to pronounce than one of length n.

Theorem 2: An initial sequence of length n is simpler than a final sequence of length n.

At Step 3 we cut the orthographic string according to the criterion of simplicity. Thus, for orthographic strings of the form $C^iVC^mV \ldots$ where $i = 0, 1, 2, 3$ and $m = 1$, we cut C^iV

$+ C^m V \ldots$ For orthographic strings of the form $C^i V C^m V \ldots$ where $i = 0, 1, 2, 3$, and $m \geqq 2$, we cut $C^i \, V C^F + C^i \, V \ldots$ such that $C^i \geqq C^t$. Note that these are similar to traditional orthographic rules for syllabification based on the "length" of the first vowel and its relative stress. Note also that words containing doubled consonants will be cut between the consonants — *happy* → *hap* + *py*; *running* → *run* + *ning*. Note finally that a single segmentation procedure will not permit us an initially correct solution for, say, both *rather* (*rat* + *her*) and *rathole* (*rat* + *hole*); thus the recycling requirement within the heuristic algorithm.

In Step 4 we speak of the mapping rule for individual VCG. In our examples the strings to the left of the arrow are graphemic inputs while the right hand strings are the VCG outputs of this step. We conceive of the actual processing within Step 4 in terms of a recursive generator which, taking one graphic element at a time, assigns a set of phonetic features to that element. The application is recursive in that as each new element is introduced, the total sequence is reprocessed. This expansion processing continues until no graphic inputs remain. By definition the product of this processing is a well-formed VCG.

Note that this mechanism provides resolution of graphic difficulties of several different types. For instance since neither the full phonetic expansion of kn- → */kn/ (e.g., *knock*) nor -*mb* → */mb/ (e.g., *thumb*)) is tolerated in English phonotactics, the recursive rules yield a phonetic realization of only the element nearest the vocalic center; similarly for doubled final consonants—*tiff, pass, hill,* etc. Re-writes of the form th → */th/, sh → */sh/ ph → */ph/ are similarly prohibited. In these latter cases, however, the realization is phonemically distinct from either member. Phonetically it may be economical to consider that the non-initial graphemic *h* signals manner ("friction") and that its preceding consonant signals place (labial, dental, etc.) of articulation. Exactly what grapheme is to be considered first in this processing and exactly what direction the processing should assume is a matter of some conjecture at this point in our research. We should also point out that these rules are not the ones that will determine which of two well-formed phonetic interpretations is correct for an ambiguous sequence (e.g., *read* → /riyd/ or /red/). One would require, we assume, that the possibility of ambiguity in this string would also be signaled by the generator.

Now let us process the words *fasting* and *pasting* in order to illustrate how the algorithm operates. After inputting the orthographic image for *fasting* into the immediate memory buffer, one marks the two vowels. Step 3 is applied and *fasting* is segmented into *fas* + *ting*. After mapping the orthographic code onto the phonotactic code by Step 4, yielding /fæs + tiŋ/, it is decided to search the word listings for a match. For most adults, a match occurs and the word will be pronounced. The word *pasting*, in the first cycle, yields a partition into the units *pas* + *ting*. At Step 4, this will be given the phonologic shape /pæs + tiŋ/. Obviously this form will fail in the word listing search. If the original unit is re-cycled, the word will now be cut *pa* + *sting* yielding /pey + stiŋ/ at Step 4. This phonologic form will lead to a match, and consequently, a pronunciation.

A direct inference from our heuristic algorithm is that words like *pasting* will show longer latencies in processing than will words like *fasting*. At the moment, no such latency data is available. We do have experimental data from five-year-old children that document the close relationship between speech or orthographic decoding and speech production that we assume in the heuristic algorithm. According to the model, if a child has difficulty in detecting a mispronunciation of a word, then he should have difficulty in learning to read the word since Steps 4 and 5 of the algorithm require a mapping and matching of well-defined pronunciation units.

We pre-trained twenty five-year-old children to accurately point to cells containing pictures of a top, a man, a pair of shoes, and a wall according to which word was pronounced. The children pointed to a blank cell for all words other than top, man, shoes, and wall. We then systematically interspaced

twelve correct pronunciations with tweny-nine mispronunciations that involved a minimal feature shift of either a vocalic
or a consonantal element (e.g., /təp/, /n·en/, /suwθ/, /yɔl/,
etc.). The child had unlimited time in which to point to one
of the pictures or to the blank, depending on his interpretation
of the given pronunciation.

None of the children committeed an error on the twelve
correct pronunciations. Moreover, they committed all of their
errors by pointing to the picture associated with the given mispronunciation rather than to the blank square. As evidenced
in row 1 of Table 6, the children performed significantly better
than chance (P = .20) in detecting mispronunciations.

Table 6
*Mean Results of the Speech Perception-Initial
Reading Experiment*

Group Statistics	top	man	shoes	wall
Mean Proportion of Detection Errors of Mispronunciation	.192	.283	.293	.490
Mean Total Errors	1.45	2.00	2.70	4.50
Coefficient of Correlation Between Perception Errors and Reading Errors.	.73	.60	.75	.85

One week later we taught the same children to read the four
words using the paired-associate anticipation paradigm described earlier in this paper. In row 2 of Table 6, you will find
the mean total errors for each item. Notice the monotonic
relation between the mean perception errors and the mean
reading errors. Moreover the correlation between the mean
error proportions from the perceptual task and the mean total
errors from the reading task are substantial (see row 3, Table
6). We interpret the relationship between the two types of
data to indicate that the children employed common codes and

behavioral algorithms in speech processing and initial reading. This is, of course, the contention of our heuristic algorithm for initial reading.

Let us re-emphasize that the experimental evidence strongly suggests an independent or detachable phonologic processing loop with a VCG-like unit constituting its highest construct. Some contemporary linguistic theorists have claimed that any input perceived as language will necessarily be processed at the highest semantic and syntactic levels; others claim, less extremely, that any such input must be processed at the morphemic level. Postman and Rozenzweig (34) conducted a series of experiments in which nonsense syllables (e.g., *int*), morphemic units (e.g., *ing*), and words (e.g., *ink*), were tachistoscopically shown to a group of adult subjects. In the summary of results, they observed: ". . . the failure of the English words to yield lower thresholds than the nonsense syllables suggests that S is no less ready to use syllables as response units than he is English words of comparable linguistic frequency." This is not to claim that reading should or could be restricted to processing at this level. It is to claim that any reading system which ignores the existence of such processing must fail to efficiently utilize an important language capacity of the child reader.

Even if persuaded of the viability of the heuristic algorithm, one might legitimately inquire if the requirement for the VCG can be justified at psycholinguistic levels presumably higher than that of phonologic decoding and encoding. More specifically, does the evidence on search processes in the long-term memory structure, be it conceived as a word association hierarchy or a conceptual space structure, reveal any manifestation of the VCG?

Recently, Roger Brown and David McNeil (6) have investigated the behavioral nature of near word recall phenomena where a person cannot exactly recall a given word but feels that the word is on the "tip of the tongue." Using low frequency words from the Lorge-Thorndike list, the experimenters read definitions of these words to college students and

asked them to try to recall the words. The subjects were requested to state the number of syllables plus the initial letter
for those words that they couldn't quite recall but felt were
on the "tip of their tongues." For the proven instances of near
recall, the college students were able to give the correct number of syllables with 60 per cent accuracy and the correct initial letter with 57 per cent accuracy. Brown and McNeil interpret these findings as indicating that the structural properties
of a word (number of syllables, etc.) are part of the code the
subjects use in locating words. We maintain that these structural properties can best be characterized by properties of the
VCG. It would appear, in any case, that some VCG-like unit
exists at these higher levels of long-term memory.

A few parenthetical comments about our research strategy
will, perhaps, illuminate our reasons for developing such a
simplified formulation of initial reading. We feel that employ-
ing a minimal amount of theoretical machinery allows one to
be explicit as to the behavioral sequence. Moreover, one has
the added benefit of being able to formulate detailed hypotheses
about sequencing in the reading curriculum. The great dis-
advantage resides in knowing that further theoretical formulations would offer greater scope to the description and application. Thus we know that prior to developing an algorithm for
sentence comprehension we might want to consider at least
three implementations: 1) a prosodic coding system that would
account for intonational information like stress, 2) a syntactic
analyzer in the form of a generative and/or transformational
rule set that would allow for "chunking" of the word units
contained in the sentence, and 3) a semantic processor that
would relate these units to the child's conceptual structure.
Since we concern ourselves here only with teaching children
to "read" words in the pronunciation sense, we consider these
future tasks which we ultimately will attempt to formulate and
resolve.

If one accepts our views about the viability of the VCG and
the heuristic algorithm as psycholinguistic units and processes
in initial reading, one might legitimately inquire if such a con-

ceptualization provides any reasonable implications for specifying the nature and internal sequence of a reading curriculum. We believe there are many direct applicational inferences that, moreover, are empirically testable. First, the VCG provides a new and explicit way of classifying the initial vocabulary of reading according to consonant-vowel-consonant sequences in the vocabulary (i.e., one can classify the words according to the number of VCG's, the structure and position of consonant clusters within the VCG, and the type of phonotactic constraints evidenced in the VCG's). Although consonant-vowel pattern classification schemes are far from novel in reading pedagogy (Bloomfield and Barnhart, 3), our hypothesis about the learning difficulties of a given pattern provides a way of ordering the materials along a continuum of relative learning efficiency.

Perhaps an example treating a within-pattern analysis will illustrate our point. The ubiquitous consonant-vowel-consonant (CVC) pattern dominates the first hundred words of most current materials. How might one order these CVC words in order to maximize transfer effects (i.e., the behavior of generalizing from acquired words to reading new words) while one is commuting seemingly known consonant letters about the five simple vowels? If one happens to start with the words, *tap*, *nag*, and *man*, what commutations would optimize the amount of transfer? We predict that those letter commutations that result in a minimal change in the VCG constraint statements of the acquired words should optimize transfer. Moreover initial consonant-vowel changes should be simpler than vowel-final consonant changes. Therefore we would predict the following orders of difficulty:

Acquired Words	Least Difficult			Most Difficult
tap	tag	nap	gap	Pat
nag →				
man	tan <	map <	mag <	Pam

Tag and *tan* would be least difficult because the children have already mapped orthographic codes onto the CVC forms and the commutation involves only the initial consonant-vowel relationship. *Pat* and *Pam* would be most difficult because the new vocalic-consonant combinations require major relearning or rewriting of the necessary VCG constraints. At the very least, the VCG conceptualization offers a testable hypothesis about optimal sequencing of such forms.

We are now preparing reading lesson materials that are designed to evaluate the hypotheses derived from the VCG conceptualization (i.e., the CVC transfer hypothesis and the consonant cluster hypothesis) and the heuristic algorithm. The experimental work will take place within the confines of a computer-based instructional system. The computer system provides for complete control of the stimulus material (audio and visual) via specified performance criteria embedded in the decision network of the program. A detailed recording of all student responses and response times is made on magnetic tape for off-line data analysis. These fine-grained behavioral histories will be of sufficient number and detail that the proposed hypotheses or alternative hypotheses can be evaluated. Let us for a moment consider some of the present and planned capabilities of this system.

VI. *Description of the Stanford Computer-Based Instructional System.*

This system consists of a medium-sized computer and six instructional booths. Each booth is a small 7 × 8 foot room that contains three input-output devices: 1) an optical display unit, 2) a cathode-ray tube display unit, and 3) an audio system. The main computer controls the presentation of the visual and auditory materials; the students respond with either a light-pen device, a typewriter keyset, or a microphone. The computer evaluates the responses and selects new audio and visual material according to the outcome of the evaluation.

The optical display unit is a rapid, random-access projection device that presents visual material to the student on a 10 × 13 inch screen. The source of the materials (any 8½ × 11 inch page of text) is photographed on microfilm and is stored in a small projector cell that has a capacity of 256 pages. Since each display unit has two projectors, each instructional unit has a total capacity of 512 individual pages. Moreover, additional combinations are possible by constructing composite images from both projectors on the common screen or by using the shutter system that divides the screen into eight equal sections by various masking arrangements. The student responds to the display and sends information to the computer via a light-pen. As the pen is touched to the screen, the coordinates of the position are sent to the computer for evaluation according to pre-defined/redefined areas for correct and incorrect responses. Most of the evaluation operations of the optical display unit will occur in approximately one second.

The cathode-ray tube display unit, commonly called a "scope," can present any of 120 prearranged alpha-numeric characters or line vectors on a 10 × 10 inch screen. A light-pen is available for sending information to the computer for evaluation via the specified coordinate system as described for the optical display device. In addition, a typewriter keyboard is attached to each scope and may be used to send information from the student to the computer.

The random-access audio system can play any prerecorded message to the student. The messages are recorded on a 6 inch wide magnetic tape. Two tape transports are available to each instructional booth. Each transport has a capacity of approximately 17 minutes that can be divided into any combination of message lengths from 1020 one-second messages to one message of 17 minutes duration. The student may record onto the tape and then have the recording played back for comparison purposes or retained as response data. The random-access time to any stored message is less than two seconds.

The various control and switching functions between the

different input-output terminal devices are handled by a medium sized computer that has a 16,000-word core memory. An additional 4,000-word core can be interchanged with any of 32 bands of a magnetic memory drum. All input-output devices are processed through a time-sharing program that services them only when necessary. Two high speed data channels permit simultaneous computation and servicing of terminal devices. Additional back-up in computational power, storage, and increased input-output speed is obtained through connections to a larger computer system located at the Stanford Computational Center.

We are also in the process of developing a similar computer-assisted instructional system that will be located in an elementary school. Sixteen instructional stations will be available on the school site.

Does a sophisticated computer system like the one just described provide the means for answering practical pedagogical questions? The number of repetitions required for mastery of a word represents one of many seemingly simple, direct, but unanswered questions in reading pedagogy. Gates (12) attempted to answer the question in the typical classroom comparison design but the host of uncontrolled variables—teacher competency, student aptitude, etc., now known to affect these experimental situations casts serious doubt on his recommendation of "35" repetitions as the optimal number. Even to attempt an answer to the basic question requires many qualifications and specifications.

One must know the stimulus materials, i.e., the nature and difficulty of the words involved. One must know the nature of the presentation and reinforcement procedures. One must follow the course of acquisition, marking for further study the point of the first correct response and the points and nature of all subsequent errors. One must also account for individual differences in the acquisition process. Thus, one really requires a detailed description of the course of learning.

Mathematical learning models provide a method for concisely describing such a fine-grained sequential learning process. One might ask the practical question, do such models provide a way of telling us how many repetitions a given child will require to reach a given criteria of, say, "one correct cycle through the list of words without an error"? And, more important, can we gain the information about required repetition early enough in the lesson sequence to aid us in our scheduling of presentations?

One must first find a mathematical model that accurately describes the course of learning of a list of words. We hoped that the data from the disyllabic-consonant cluster paired-associate experiment might provide us with an exemplar. We fitted a number of mathematical models to the data and found one, the "one-element model," that yielded a reasonable account of the course of learning. It should be emphasized that the requirement for such models is that they fit the data. There is no suggestion that such a "fit" represents an "interpretation" of the data. Neither is it implied that the model will fit similar experiments with the same degree of accuracy.

The one-element model (OEM) is a special case of the more general models of Stimulus Sampling Theory (Atkinson and Estes, 1). The model (OEM) specifies that the behavioral association between the given orthography of a word and its pronunciation is assumed to be in one of two states, unlearned (UL) or learned (L). Given a word that is in the unlearned state (UL), there is a constant probability, c, that the word is learned during each correction-rehearsal event. While in the unlearned (UL) state, the probability of a correct response is dependent on the number and availability of the set of responses or required pronunciations. In our calculations we set the guessing probability equal to one over the number of VCG's in the word list (i.e., the guessing probability was set equal to $\frac{1}{18}$). The simple all-or-none learning process can be represented by the following transition matrix and response probability vector:

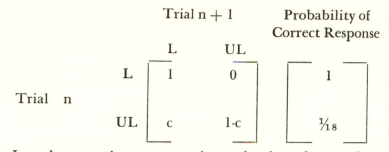

In order to make a comparative evaluation of a number of learning models, an analysis was made of the sixteen possible sequences of correct and incorrect responses that result from considering blocks of four trials. These sixteen possible sequences, presented in the first column of Table 7, encompass a sufficient number of observations to be considered reliable and sensitive to the course of learning. Furthermore, closed theoretical expressions for these sixteen event sequences can be derived for a large number of learning models. A simple method for estimating the parameters for a given model consists of minimizing the χ^2 function associated with the sixteen outcome (0) events. Let $Pr(0_i; c)$ denote the probability of the event 0_i which, of course, is a function of the parameter c. Then one can define the function:

$$X^2(c) = \sum_{i=1}^{16} \frac{[TP_r(0_i; c) - N(0_i)]^2}{TP_r(0_i; c)}$$

where $(N(0_i))$ denotes the observed frequency of outcome 0_i and $T = N(0_1) + \ldots + N(0_{16})$. Using a high-speed computer that is programmed to systematically scan grids of possible parameter values, one selects the estimate of c that minimizes the X^2 function. Under the null hypothesis this minimum X^2 has the usual limiting distribution with the degrees of freedom equal to 16 minus the number of estimated parameters minus one.

The model (OEM) assumes that all items stochastically independent and identical (i.e., all pairs are of equal difficulty and all subjects learn at the same rate). Knowing that the disyllabic and consonant cluster words were significantly different, we performed separate analyses for each list. The results for trials 1 through 4 are presented in Table 7. The X^2 values with 14 degrees of freedom are non-significant so that one accepts the null hypothesis that there is no statistical difference between the observed frequencies and the frequencies predicted by the one-element model. The analyses of trials 5 through 8 yielded even lower X^2 values. The fit of the model is surprisingly good

Table 7

*The Fit of the One-Element Model to the Disyllabic
Consonant Cluster Paired-Associate Data*

Event Sequence	Disyllabic Words		Consonant Cluster Words	
	Observed Fre-quency	Predicted From OEM	Observed Fre-quencies	Predicted From OEM
cccc[1]	38	31.3	21	24.5
ccce	0	.0	0	0
ccec	0	.0	0	0
ccee	0	.1	0	.1
cecc	2	.9	0	.8
cece	0	.1	0	.1
ceec	1	.7	0	.7
ceee	0	1.8	0	2.4
eccc	20	22.2	22	18.7
ecce	1	.1	1	.1
ecec	2	.7	0	.7
ecee	3	1.8	1	2.4
eecc	17	15.8	21	14.3
eece	3	1.8	5	2.4
eeec	6	12.4	12	12.6
eeee	27	30.2	37	40.0
	$\Sigma = 120$ $X = 20.34$		$\Sigma = 120$ $X^2 = 18.65$	
	$c = .250$		$c = .195$	

considering the assumption of no individual differences in the rates of learning. Thus we have at hand a quantitative model that will allow us to predict the necessary amount of repetition required for list mastery.

The appropriate measure for determining the required repetitions is the mean trial of the last error. We predicted the mean trial of the last error for each subject for each of the two types of words by the following procedure:

1) Find the trial of first success (i.e., the trial that first indicated possible learning).

2) Estimate the learning parameter, c, by the equation

$$C = \frac{\text{(Proportion Correct)} - g}{1 - g}$$

(This equation follows directly from the one-element model).

3) Use the estimate of c to predict the trial of the last error by the equation

$$E \text{ (Trial of the Last Error)} = \frac{\frac{(1 - g)}{(1 - c)(1 - g) + c}}{c}$$

(This expectation was derived by Bower (1961) for the one-element model).

4) Calculate the observed mean trial of the last error.

The mean of the absolute value of the difference between the observed and predicted mean trial of the last error yields 1.31 trials for the disyllabic words and 2.65 trials for the consonant cluster words. The item means (see Table 4) indicate the greater heterogeneity of the consonant cluster words; consequently one would expect a poorer fit between the observed and predicted values for these items. Given this reservation, one can predict with reasonable accuracy the number of trials a child will need to cycle through a list of words in order to reach the mean point of mastery, (i.e., the mean trial of the last error).

Now all of these calculations can be performed on-line by a

computer while a child is learning a list of words. If one should use a static optimization scheme that calls for recycling a child through a list until the predicted mean trial of the last error plus one standard deviation of this statistic are reached, would the child attain a criterion of mastery such as one complete errorless cycle of the list? In the disyllabic-consonant cluster paired-associate experiment twelve out of the thirteen criterion subjects would have fulfilled this mastery criterion. Moreover, five of these twelve subjects would have been branched out of the task exactly at the end of the trial where they attained the criterion.

We wish to reiterate that this is only an example of how a computer-based instructional system can be used to solve practical pedagogical questions. Extensive exploration will be necessary before we will have an adequate mathematical model of initial reading that can handle problems of retention over delay periods, interference between differing lists of words, and so on. We remain optimistic, however, that computer-based instructional systems will ultimately provide a setting where practical problems of initial reading can be solved by quantitative methods.

VII. *Summary*

Our lengthy chronicle ceases at this point. If this report appears a bit kaleidoscopic in nature, this ensues from the inter-disciplinary backgrounds and interests of our group. Each of the representatives from linguistics, psychology, and education bestows insights from his particular fund of knowledge. This interaction leads to specific enterprises that range on Hilgard's (17) suggested continuum for educational research from pure scientific discovery to new pedagogical innovations. The substance of the paper reflects these diverse but, we believe, coordinated efforts.

The Russian study provided us with our initial hypothesis about the hierarchy of rehearsal difficulty, resulting from consonant clusters. We then investigated the factors in speech perception and production that might account for this hierarchy of rehearsal difficulty. The Liberman, *et al.*, (24) work on speech perception, provided us with insights into the requirements for "meshing" successive phonemes in order to produce intelligible pronunciations. Using implications of the "rules for speech synthesis" and of our investigations into the phonotactics of English, we formulated the "Vocalic Center Group" as the psycholinguistic unit for initial reading. After investigating an implicit assumption regarding rehearsal and reading performance, we used an analysis of the reading errors observed in this investigation to formulate a "heuristic algorithm" specifying a processing system and an informational flow to stimulate an initial reading performance. Syllabification, orthographic to phonemic translating, VCG construction and concatenation, memory storage, and recognition-matching were assumed operational components in the "heuristic algorithm." We then verified our inference from this schema that speech recognition errors for given words should be monotonically related to initial reading errors for these same words.

After citing some findings from Brown and McNeil (6) suggesting the requirement for VCG-like units in long-term memory processes, we illustrated how the VCG provides some detailed hypotheses about constructing and sequencing the beginning reading curriculum. We described a computer-based instructional system that provides us with an automated pedagogical environment within which to rigorously test our predictions. We concluded by citing an example of how the computer-based instructional system and quantitative models of learning might offer answers to specific questions as to, for example, the amount of word repetition necessary for a specific criterion of mastery.

Our interests and activities do span a number of disciplines but our enterprise retains focus, we feel, by the task we have set for ourselves: the development of the most simple but adequate learning model for initial reading. Just as models of a language learner require less complexity than models of a component language user, so our own model attempts specification of the minimal capabilities of the beginning reader without speculation as to the maximal capacities of the mature reader. The complexity of our theoretical formulation is still several orders of magnitude removed from an adequate "Theory of Reading." But to quote from a philosopher of science, Brodbeck (5), such an approach warrants its user

. . . that instead of helplessly gazing
in dumb wonder at the infinite complexity
of man and society, he has knowledge,
imperfect rather than perfect, to be sure,
but knowledge not to be scorned nonetheless. . . .

Phoneme and Letter Patterns in Children's Language

Edward C. Carterette and
Margaret Hubbard Jones

*Redundancy and linguistic constraint are two
concepts that will soon be widely recognized as
vitally important in the reading process. They
relate to the amount of information that language
conveys and to the ability of the reader to predict
sequential elements in reading. This paper reports
studies that begin the job of charting this largely
unexplored area.*

EDITOR

Phoneme and Letter Patterns in Children's Language*

"The purpose of computing is insight, not numbers." Richard W. Hamming

Numerical methods for scientists and engineers

"Mine is a long and sad tale!" said the Mouse, turning to Alice, and sighing. "It *is* a long tail, certainly," said Alice, looking down with wonder at the Mouse's tail, "but why do you call it sad?" Lewis Carroll relates this encounter in *Alice's Adventures in Wonderland,* and we quote it to remind you and ourselves not to confuse our ends and our means.

Professor Margaret Hubbard Jones and I sought an answer to the question: how do patterns of perception arise? In thinking on ways of pursuing the question it was only natural for us to consider work that had been done by those concerned with communication in the broad sense. Many stochastic processes have had their lids forced up by mathematical levers to reveal an underlying structure. Two well-known instances are Shannon's (36) description of language in the mathematical theory of communication (1951) and the problem of the "genetic code."**

We were concerned, too, about the possible relationship between the new work in structural linguistics and language

* Written in part during Edward C. Carterette's tenure as a Senior Fellow of the National Science Foundation at the Institute for Mathematical Studies in the Social Sciences, Stanford University, 1965.

**Gamow had suggested (1954) that the sequence of amino acids in protein molecules is determined by the sequence of base triplets in molecules of nucleic acid. Eight years later the triplet hypothesis was completely sustained by the experiments of Ochoa and his colleagues Lengyll and Speyer (24) and by Nirenberg and Matthaei (29).

behavior (Chomsky, 9, 10). It did seem impossible, as Miller and Chomsky (1963) have pointed out, that current notions of stimulus-response learning theories could account for how a child comes to master his patois. We remind you that an infant of two years can modulate a stream of sound so that it has a profound effect on the world around him. The string of pearls (as seen by mama) flowing from his mouth is highly structured. The string is grammatical, semantical, and effectual. Here again, we met problems of structure.

Our first thought was to see how the structure of the auditory or visual stimulus input was related to the structure of the output. It quickly became obvious that practically none of the standard materials were useful to us. The Thorndike-Lorge (1937) word statistics were not very useful even as visual stimuli. The statistics on phonemes, diphones, and triphones not only were not based on children's speech, but were taken almost without exception from "phonemic" analyses of written texts, such as phonetic readers (Denes, 11). The most recent example showed up while we were writing this paper. Styled as statistics of the "transitional frequencies of English phonemes" (Hultzén, Allen and Miron, 20), the counts were done on "phonemic" transcriptions of the texts of one-act plays! Rather than cavil because the material required did not exist, we set out to collect and describe it.

There is good evidence that redundancy is a powerful determiner of the learning of verbal materials by adults. Some experiments of ours showed that contextual constraints affect the learning of similar material by children. As part of a larger, experimental program, we wished to compare the redundancy of children's spontaneous language at various ages with that of adults and with that of their books, both classroom readers and free-choice.

As an example, children's graded readers are written on the assumption that a small, initial vocabulary, increasing with a reader and within a series yields texts that become progressively more difficult. If this is true, then sequential constraints should decrease as the difficulty of the reader increases. What of the implied assumption about the spontaneous language of the child? Do linguistic constraints decrease as the child becomes a man, as his grammar becomes syntactically richer, and as his language becomes more complex and subtle?

For exploring these questions we developed a computer program based on the Shannon-Wiener measure of selective information. It calculates the amount of Markovian information over all possible successive pairs and triplets and quartets (i.e., "strings") of symbols in a running text. The measure is very stable for suitably large samples. The symbols may be letters, phonemes, words, or even syntactic units. We shall consider here mainly strings of letters and phonemes. As a string of symbols gets longer there are fewer constraints on what the next symbol can be. Finally, when a string is long enough (about 5 phonemes or 9 letters) the first one in the string has only a random, accidental influence on the last one. We determined such constraints at various distances of the last symbol from the first 1, 2, . . . , 11, 29, 59, and 119, for both letter and phonetic texts. Other useful statistics, such as frequency distributions of symbols, and mean word and sentence length, were byproducts. In addition, the program yields the distributions and statistics of larger units such as phonemic "words," and of words in the ordinary sense. The texts used were two major graded series of readers, and the children's free-choice books at the corresponding levels. Spontaneous speech was collected from freely interacting trios of first, third, and fifth graders in two different public schools, and adults in a public junior college.

We give some results of general interest. The distribution of single letters is about the same for all levels of text. Redundancy of texts decreases with increasing grade in a regular way, while mean word length increases. A third reader has about the same redundancy as simple adult text. The constraints in a first reader are considerable, whereas those in a fifth reader

Table 1

Proportions of Each Letter in Adult and Child Reading Material and Adult and Child Speech.

	First Grade Speech[1]	Third Grade Speech[1]	Fifth Grade Speech[1]	Adult Speech[1]	Adult Text[2]	First Reader[3]	Third Reader[3]	Fifth Reader[3]
A	.0823	.0817	.0808	.0759	.0788	.0811	.0800	.0804
B	.0167	.0158	.0151	.0149	.0156	.0270	.0216	.0156
C	.0180	.0180	.0184	.0193	.0268	.0241	.0214	.0210
D	.0452	.0463	.0430	.0468	.0389	.0412	.0485	.0513
E	.1194	.1176	.1208	.1160	.1266	.1204	.1225	.1310
F	.0131	.0129	.0138	.0144	.0255	.0132	.0195	.0213
G	.0237	.0223	.0234	.0242	.0187	.0186	.0241	.0224
H	.0700	.0711	.0702	.0663	.0574	.0602	.0739	.0745
I	.0647	.0641	.0627	.0697	.0706	.0622	.0590	.0577
J	.0019	.0020	.0023	.0034	.0010	.0025	.0026	.0012
K	.0123	.0153	.0155	.0140	.0060	.0183	.0127	.0110
L	.0334	.0346	.0355	.0411	.0394	.0478	.0431	.0428
M	.0361	.0303	.0258	.0195	.0243	.0250	.0195	.0217
N	.0717	.0709	.0668	.0645	.0705	.0642	.0613	.0648
O	.0809	.0815	.0820	.0880	.0776	.0827	.0802	.0771
P	.0111	.0124	.0127	.0131	.0187	.0149	.0152	.0156
Q	.0003	.0002	.0003	.0004	.0010	.0007	.0008	.0005
R	.0418	.0436	.0444	.0468	.0594	.0462	.0557	.0549

S	.0576	.0597	.0619	.0554	.0631	.0561	.0534	.0583
T	.0967	.0943	.0954	.1004	.0978	.1056	.0947	.0919
U	.0337	.0364	.0362	.0395	.0280	.0270	.0281	.0264
V	.0073	.0068	.0091	.0102	.0102	.0023	.0070	.0070
W	.0316	.0322	.0306	.0290	.0215	.0318	.0306	.0286
X	.0012	.0007	.0010	.0012	.0016	.0011	.0009	.0015
Y	.0291	.0289	.0315	.0361	.0201	.0246	.0228	.0202
Z	.0003	.0003	.0006	.0005	.0006	.0010	.0008	.0009
Total Number of Letters in Sample	72,742	78,065	101,618	61,269	372,729	37,728	43,201	51,005

[1] Our own tape recordings, letter transcription.
[2] Dewey (1923).
[3] Ginn Basic Reader.

approach those in average adult text. However, when free-reading choices are compared with corresponding levels of first, third, and fifth readers, free-reading choices are less redundant than readers. The child apparently prefers reading material which lies closer to the redundancy level of adult text. Mere stylistic differences show little effect, and neither word length nor sentence length is a reliable index of the difficulty of a text. Mean word length increases with level for readers but not for free choices, where it starts high. Mean sentence length is far shorter in readers than in free choices.

The story is rather different for the phonemic analysis of spontaneous speech. Children of grades 1, 3, 5 have the same phoneme inventory as adults with nearly identical frequency distributions. Vowel usage is invariant. The only notable change in consonants is that use of m declines and l rises from the first grader to the adult. By our measure of relative sequential constraint for phoneme strings it is not possible to distinguish children at any grade from adults. The mean phonemic "word" is about 11 phonemes long for children or adults. Yet the mean length in phonemes of a phonemic "sentence" is about 28 for first graders, 37 for third graders, 40 for fifth graders, but falls to 30 for adults.

All of this suggests that children and adults are operating on similar sequences of phonemes but the manner in which they partition the strings changes as children grow up. Hypotheses about partitioning have led us into the fundamental problem of discovering the psycholinguistic units of language use and language perception. We have not been able to avoid the notion that learning to read and learning to hear and speak may be radically different processes.

Some of our findings have clear implications for educators, linguists, and psychologists, or for anyone who works with auditory or visual perception. We proceed now to give details of the method, to characterize the data, which are far too vast to include, and to draw some facts and interpretations from them.

Methods of Data Collection, Data Reduction, and Statistical Analysis

1. Spoken Language

It was desired that the sample should be sufficiently large so that any descriptive measure (with the exception of word counts, which require a vast and expensive sample) would be stable and representative. Likewise, it was desired to obtain adequate language samples at several levels of language competency. The two reasonable extremes were thought to be an adult sample and a first grade (approximately six-year-olds) sample, the latter consisting of children who were just beginning to learn to read and thus have virtually no acquaintance with visual language. To deal with younger children would entail great difficulties in rapport, time, and representativeness. The other two samples were third and fifth graders, judged to be at such positions on the growth curve as to shed some light on development of language to adult status. The adult sample was similar to the child samples in community, origin, and socio-economic status. It was obtained from junior college classes at the Santa Monica City College, Santa Monica, California.

We arranged to use children from two different schools to reduce possible biases of various sorts. Both schools had children drawn largely from the middle socio-economic level. The investigation of the effect of socio-economic status on language development is an important one, but not the subject under investigation here. Moreover it also requires a norm. It was precisely the norm for studies of language development of all sorts that we set out to obtain. We used all children in a grade who were present when called and were not excused by reason of foreign language background, marked non-California dialect, or speech impediments. Since regions of the country differ in the phonemes used in speech, it was judged more in keeping with the aims of the study to include only one type of regional speech. The tribe most convenient for us to study happened to speak Southern Californian.

Table 2

Product-moment Correlation Matrix for Relative Frequencies of 26 Letters from Ginn Readers, General Adult Printed Language, and First, Third, and Fifth Grade, and Adult Speech.

	2	3	4	5	6	7	8
1 First Grade Speech[1]	.998	.996	.997	.97	.98	.98	.98
2 Third Grade Speech[1]		.998	.99	.98	.98	.98	.98
3 Fifth Grade Speech[1]			.99	.98	.98	.98	.98
4 Adult Speech[1]				.97	.98	.98	.98
5 Adult Text[2]					.98	.98	.98
6 First Reader[3]						.99	.98
7 Third Reader[3]							.996
8 Fifth Reader[3]							

[1] Our own tape recordings, letter transcriptions.
[2] Dewey, 1923 (In Reza, 1961).
[3] Ginn Basic Readers.

Several ways of arranging a situation in which natural speech would occur were tried. First, an attempt was made to record unrestricted free speech of children among their peers in the lunchroom or on the playground. This was a complete failure acoustically because the noise exceeded the signal at all times. An attempt to record discussions in the classroom also failed because of excessive noise and poor flow of speech. Next, recordings of speech were made while individual children responded to requests to make up a story about a picture shown them. The speech was impoverished in grammatical constructions, vocabulary, rate, and even phonemes. The speech of a child responding to a request to tell about summer vacation or what he would do during the next vacation was not normal speech either. Next, Strickland's method (39) was tried. This required "props"—a group of objects on a table—and a small group of children (3 or 4) seated around it. The children were asked by the adult moderator to talk about the objects. We got better response in this situation, but even here there appeared to be restriction both of vocabulary and grammatical forms. The normal flow of speech became halting. Finally we tried a simple social situation. Three children were seated around a small table with a young, friendly adult. The adult greeted the children by name, told them she wanted to find out what children in their grade were interested in, and asked them to talk to each other about anything they wanted to talk about. Some groups required somewhat more encouragement; if so, the adult asked a question or two. "What do you do after school?", or "How many in your family?" Thereafter she said nothing. After the initial warm-up period, which was always discarded for the transcription, the speech appeared to be children's normal speech. It was rapid, there were interruptions; it covered every conceivable topic; it was full of slang and noise words; there was give-and-take. This, then, was the situation in which all the speech samples were recorded.

For the adults the situation was structured differently. The participants were from elementary psychology classes, so their knowledge of psychological jargon was flattered. They were told that the experiment was one in small group process and that the situation was to be completely non-directive. Then they were introduced by first names and told they were at a party. The experimenter excused himself (psychologically) to get the snacks. Again groups of three were always used. Most of the adults did not know each other, whereas in the children's group, they did. The 3-person interaction proved as useful for adults as for children, and the language produced was judged to be normal, everyday conversation—as rapid, slangy, and diverse as anyone hears in an unrecorded situation.

The second major problem concerned the quality of the recording. If phoneticians were to be able to transcribe the material with any reliability, the recording had to be very good— better than any speech recordings we had heard. To this end we assembled the following high fidelity components: 1) Ampex 1260 4-track stereophonic magnetic-tape recorder and 2) 2

Altec-Lansing M-20 condenser microphone systems. The microphones were placed 24 inches apart, and about 8 feet from the farthest speaker. New, virgin, *Scotch* (Minnesota Mining and Manufacturing Company) 1.5 mil acetate magnetic tape was used. Recording was at 7.5 inches per second, and each microphone fed a separate channel. Thus only two of the four tracks were used, giving maximum possible channel separation, since an unused channel separated the two used. The cross-talk rejection ratios in the middle frequencies was much greater than 60 db, far more than adequate for our purposes. The recordings were made in the best available room at the three schools. Test tapes were made to disclose the acoustic properties of the room. Where necessary, one section of the room was draped with cloth, felt was applied to chair and table legs, microphones were adjusted and insulated, and gain of amplifiers checked at every tape change. The microphones were always concealed from the elementary school children. To the best of our knowledge, their presence was not suspected. For the case of young adults, the microphones were in plain sight, since they would have deduced their presence in any case. After the brief warm-up period, they lost themselves in conversation and paid no further attention to the presence of the microphones or the experimenter. In fact, it was often hard to get them to stop at the end of the period.

Since the aim was to collect as representative a sample as possible of natural language, we attempted to include as many individuals, and as many groups as possible, in order to reduce the effect of idiosyncracies of vocabulary, topic, sentence construction, pronunciation, and various aspects peculiar to spoken language. However, it was also important to allow sufficient time for each group to warm-up and then become thoroughly engrossed in conversation, for otherwise many aspects of oral language suffer.

We had shown (Jones and Carterette, 22) that at least 6,000 words were necessary for stable statistical results, so the goal was set at 10,000 words per level. It was felt that more than this would require too much time for phonemic transcription, which is very slow. Well over 10,000 words per level were actually transcribed, but more material than that was collected and remains untranscribed. The number of groups and individuals represented in the analysis is:

Level	No. of Groups	No. of Individuals
1	18	54
3	16	48
5	16	48
Adults	8	24

The reason for the discrepancy in groups and individuals is that a control was exercised on the level of number of words produced. First graders did more giggling, interrupting, and drowning each other out, so less usable material resulted per unit time. The total number of characters transcribed is given in the following table.

Level	Total Number of Units				Lexical
	Letters		Phonemes		Words
	A*	B*	A*	B*	
1	94,767	72,742	66,179	58,653	20,030
3	101,285	78,065	70,842	63,029	21,368
5	131,274	101,618	90,471	80,970	27,072
Adult	78,580	61,269	54,478	48,708	15,694

* Column A refers to total number of characters, B refers to this total with word marks and sentence marks removed.

2. Written Language

The sources for written language suitable for the various grades was sought first in standard reading textbooks. Readers of two widely used series were chosen as representative of material of this sort; first, third, and fifth readers were used in both series. The series were the Ginn Readers, and the Sheldon Basic Readers (Allyn and Bacon). In addition the second reader in the Ginn series was used, after it appeared that readers 1 and 3 were too far apart. All material in the given section was used with the exception of foreign words and poetry. Abbreviations were spelled out according to a specially constructed lexicon.

Any story containing a large number of foreign words was omitted. The only punctuation used was word mark and sentence mark. The exact rules are given in Appendix A1.

15. Leave out all speech of an individual with even minor speech pathologies and all with indications of foreign language influence. (This should include British English, Boston English, Southern accents, Brooklynese, etc.)

Appendix A1
*Transcription Rules for Office of Education
Project No. 1877, "The Growth of
Patterning in Children's Language"
Final Revision of 23 November 1963*

1. If you can't understand a word of any part of a sentence, skip the whole sentence.
2. Transcribe the sounds, not what the word should be, or was last time. *Don't normalize the data.*
3. Put in "noise words": "We-e-e-ll," "uhm-m."
4. Don't put in non-phonemic symbols.
5. Watch these pairs that are often neutralized: *and a*
6. Biggest problem: stressed or unstressed or stressed vowel. Listen carefully for this. If you can hear the quality, then use the stressed vowel. If in doubt, use *schwa.*
7. Sentence boundary: Terminal break; rising or falling intonation. Symbol—period.
8. Word boundary: slight phonetic pause between phoneme sequences with no particular intonation pattern. These should be marked as they sound, not as written words would demand. No grammatical definition.
9. Do not put in sheer stammers. (These are infrequent.)
10. *Do* put in word or phrase repetitions.
11. Start transcription only after they are warmed up. Arrow indicates start.
12. Leave out repetition of words when in answer to question like "what."
13. If sentences are spoken at once by several people and are not clear—leave out.
14. Interrupted but continued sentences should be included if semi-equivocal. Leave out the interruption.

Next, material that children like to read was sought. Wilson's Children's Catalog (44 and 46) was used as a guide because of the large number and wide distribution of the judges making the ratings. These books are rated, by a wide sampling of children's literature, as books children should not do without. Each rating is accompanied by a consensus of proper grade level. We chose at random from among those books rated in the top one-ninth and graded K to 2 or 3 as our level 1, those graded 2 or 3 to 5 as our level 3, and those graded 4 to 6 as our level 5. At a single level we used all or part of three or four separate books, drawing equally from them to reduce the effects of idiosyncratic language, aiming at approximately 10,000-word samples. Although there is undoubtedly some adult bias in these ratings due to pedagogical urges, they are also dependent upon circulation and enjoyment in "story hours." It is difficult to believe that a book which is unpopular with children could remain in the list year after year, regardless of adult bias. At least these ratings have the advantage of representing a national sample and a large one.

Written material on the adult level had previously been analyzed by Newman and Waugh (27). Their calculations were used for average adult text (William James sample) and difficult adult text (Atlantic Monthly sample*), but for the easy adult text (the King James version of the Bible), we punched the same passage and computed our own statistics. Figures for the Russian Bible were also taken from *Newman and Waugh* (see Section 5).

3. Transcription Procedures

3.1 Written Language

Since the ordinary alphabetic characters are acceptable to the FORTRAN program to be used in the statistical analysis, transcription of the written material consisted in key-punching directly from the text, according to the rules given in Appendix

---

* An error in their calculation of C_{11} was discovered and is presented correctly here.

A1. Once punched, these were proofread by two people, corrections made, and the corrections proofed. The original keypuncher did not proof her own work alone.

3.2 Spoken Language

Transcription of the spoken language was very much more difficult and time consuming. Each tape was first transcribed by a typist, listening dichotically with stereo earphones on a research quality play-back system (Ampex Model 350–2, two-channel magnetic-tape recorder). This often required many iterations. The instructions were to include all consecutive material, but if some part was incomprehensible to omit the entire utterance. Similarly, if some person was interrupted and did not pick up the thread of his utterance, the whole utterance was to be omitted, but if he did, then the interruption was to be omitted. The purpose of these rules was to preserve the continuous and sequentially-dependent structure of speech.

Ordinary lexical words were used in these letter transcriptions, to make them comparable with the readers and other written material, i.e., words were spelled properly and word marks occurred where they would normally occur in written material. However, normalized spellings were constructed for idiosyncratic words (e.g., "guy," used by many of the children as an exclamation), "noise" words (cf. Strickland) like "er," "um," "uh," and the like.

The placement of sentence marks became a very difficult problem. Since a good deal of the material was agrammatical, the use of a grammatical criterion was nonsense and would conceal any unusual implications of the data. An attempt was made to use tentative pause and final pause, but the two phoneticians could not assign the first of these reliably, so it was abandoned. The sentence mark was placed by the phoneticians and was used whenever an utterance was terminated by a change of speaker or when there was a clear pause of a type the phoneticians were willing to call terminal, judging largely by intonation contours and appreciable silence. The reliability was not high for this aspect of the transcription. Detailed transcription rules are given in Appendix A1. The 38-character phonemic alphabet is exhibited as Table A1.

The second step was to have the letter transcriptions checked

Table A1. *Phonemic alphabet.*
(38 characters plus word boundary and full-stop)

Consonants

	Labial	Dental-Alveolar	Palatal	Velar	Glottal
Stops	vl: p	t	č	k	?
	vd: b	d	j	g	
Fricatives	vl: ɵ, f	s	š		h
	vd: ð, r	z	ž		
Nasals	m	n			
Glides	w	l	y		
		r			

N = 24

Vowels

Front	Unstressed	Back
high { iy (beat) { i (bit)		uw (boot) u (put) ow (boat)
mid { y (bait) { ε (bet)	ə (but)	ɔy (boy) ɔ (bought)
low { ae (bat) { ay (bite)	a (pot)	aw (bout)

N = 14

Also a single primary stress mark (used before stressed syllable) by a research assistant. This always resulted in many changes.

Next the phoneticians took over. When we could get them, there were two working. Because of the volume of material, it was not feasible to have them both transcribe all the text independently. Instead we had to be content with occasional reliability checks together with subsequent ironing out of discrepancies.

Two formal reliability checks were made. The number of disagreements in a passage were counted and this number was divided by the total number of phonemes in the passage. In the first instance there was 6 per cent discrepancy in 2300 phonemes transcribed. In subsequent discussion, agreement was reached. This involved listening together to the taped passage and evolving new rules for transcription. Examples of these are: 1) Don't use *schwa* if you can hear the quality of the vowel, 2) if the sound is genuinely between a "t" and a "d," use the one which is normal for the word. A second check revealed a still greater discrepancy, 16 per cent (1800 phonemes). Much of this was due to insistence by the co-directors that the transcription be as phonetic as possible within the bounds of the phonemic alphabet. Since the phoneticians were not used to this procedure, and also had used different systems in the past, some learning was necessary. The intent, with which everyone concurred, was to represent all the variations possible. There were three very good reasons for not attempting a phonetic transcription: 1) the programming would have been more difficult, 2) the transcriptions would have been very much less reliable, and 3) the import of speech seems to be as much better rendered by the phonemic transcription since this is presumably based upon the contrastive features of the language. The "phonetic" use of the phonemic alphabet with children was intended to permit discovery of lesser redundancy in young children due to inconsistency in pronunciation, if this existed. As an aside we should like to point out that, apparently, most so-called phonemic transcriptions of an individual's speech that appear in the linguistic literature are really pseudo-phonetic transcriptions like ours. That is, a standard phonemic alphabet is used to represent the phonetic character of his speech but the contrastive analysis necessary to establish his phonemic system is never undertaken.

The phoneticians placed word marks only where there were brief pauses. Instructions were to not make printed words a guide, but to indicate natural breaks in the flow of speech.

Sentence marks were likewise placed at natural terminal pauses, defined not by grammar, but by: a) change of speaker, or b) a terminal intonation contour plus a substantial pause. The purpose of these rules was to permit generation of hypotheses about the natural units of language, since it became immediately obvious upon listening to the tapes that the language was quite different from linguistically ideal or written language. The 41-character phonemic alphabet used is presented in Appendix A1.

The problems of reliability of transcription were dealt with as effectively as possible under the constraints of time and availability of phoneticians.

Phonetics is not an area in which linguistic students in America are highly trained. It is therefore difficult to hire phoneticians with any but minimum experience. The turnover was likewise high, with long periods of vacant jobs and retraining. Four phoneticians participated in the final transcriptions and all were interested enough in the project to give it more than mere duty required. There was free interchange and discussion between the members of each pair and some interchange across pairs.

4. Redundancy Measures

Redundancy statistics were calculated by means of a program written for the IBM 7094 computer described earlier by Carterette and Jones (1963) (5). Briefly, contingency tables were constructed showing the number of times each character was followed by every other character, both immediately and at lags of 2, 3, . . . , 11, 29, 59, and 119. From these contingency tables, H_v, the information associated with this k-state stationary Markov chain, was computed from

$$H_v = - \sum_{ij} P(i)P_{ij}\log_2 P_{ij},$$

$$\tag{1}$$

where $P(i)$ is the absolute probability of being in state i and P_{ij} is the stationary transition probability of going to state j on the

$(n + 1)^{\text{th}}$ trial after being in state i on the nth. The relative sequential constraint on the second of a pair of characters when it is the nth member of a sequence n characters long (in which the first character of the pair is the first member of the sequence) is defined as C_n and is given by

$$C_n = \frac{\sum\limits_{k=0}^{n-1} H_k(1{:}2)}{H(1)} \qquad (2)$$

The contingent uncertainty $H_k(1{:}2)$ is defined by

$$H_k(1{:}2) = H(1) - H_v(k), \qquad (3)$$

where the first term of the right side of the equation is the uncertainty without sequential dependency, i.e., the average amount of information in each letter,

$$H(1) = - \sum\limits_{i=1}^{i=28} P(i)\log P(i). \qquad (4)$$

$P(i)$ is the probability of the ith symbol's occurrence. $H_v(k)$ is the Markovian information at lag k. It is formally identical with Equation (1). The index k specifies the forward distance of the transition from symbol i to symbol j. Thus, C_2 gives the relative sequential constraint on the second of a pair of characters in which the second character is contiguous to the first; C_3 gives the relative sequential constraint on the second of a pair in which the second is separated from the first by one character; and so on. Equation (2) makes the subscript of C (that is, n) equal to the lag plus one. We used k's of 1, 2, . . . , 11, 29, 59, and 119, which yielded the constraints between all pairs, of characters in which the second was at the designated step to the right of the first. For a discussion of the restrictions on these computations, see Garner (1962, p. 213 ff). Finally, mean word length and mean sentence length for each text were calculated.[*]

An estimate, H''', of $\hat{H}$ unbiased to terms of order $\dfrac{1}{n^2}$, (Miller and Madow, 1954), was used:

$$H''' = \hat{H} + \log_2 e \left[\frac{a-1}{2n} - \frac{1}{12n^2} + \frac{1}{12n^2} \sum_{i=1}^{a} \frac{1}{P(i)} \right] \quad (5)$$

where a is the alphabet size, and n is the sequence length in symbols. $\hat{H}$ is, of course, the estimate of the theoretical quantity H, and is found from $\hat{P}(i) = \dfrac{f_i}{n}$ and $\hat{P}_{ij} = \dfrac{f_{ij}}{n}$. The quantity f_i refers to the frequency of being in state i on trial s, whereas f_{ij} refers to the frequency of transitions from state i on trial s to state j on trial $(s+1)$. Both estimates H''' and $\hat{H}$ were computed for each P_{ij} and $P(i)$. Apparently the sample sizes used were sufficiently large to give stability, for $\hat{H}$ and H''' differed by only a few thousandths of a bit at most.

No attempt has been made to make statistical tests between the various redundancy functions, e.g., whether the redundancy functions for first and third grade natural speech are different.[**] In view of the correlations among the various constraint measures, it is not clear how they should be made. We point out, however, that the functions are very stable, and there is but one instance of a crossing of two functions which were in any case very similar to begin with.

[*] This schematic development and the equation given are different from those of our earlier papers (Carterette and Jones, (5) 1963, Jones and Carterette, (22) 1963; see also Newman and Waugh, (27) 1960). We are dealing specifically with pairwise sequences of symbols that form a Markov chain and not, as our earlier equations wrongly implied, with pairs formed by sampling from a bivariate distribution. However, the earlier equations and those of the present paper lead to identical numerical results. For an interesting discussion of the different assumptions underlying the two sets of equations, see Binder and Wolin (1964). (1)

[**] For a basic discussion of testing hypotheses based on information measures, see S. Kullback (1959). (22)

5. Analysis of Data and Findings

a. Written Texts

The various outputs from the computer are summarized in Tables 3 through 9. Each table shows the constraints existing between pairs of letters which are adjacent (C_2), pairs which are separated by one (C_3), etc., up to pairs separated by 9 intervening letters (C_{11}). Since all the curves appear to be asymptotic by at least C_9, the data for more distant members are not presented. $(C_{11}) \times (100)$ approximates the usual measure of per cent redundancy, and will be used in comparisons of redundancy in texts. Also presented are: 1) H(1), which gives the average amount of selective information, in bits, contained in the single letters, 2) mean word length, 3) mean sentence length, and 4) sample size.

Table 3
Relative Sequential Constraint in Ginn Series Readers.

	First Reader	Second Reader	Third Reader	Fifth Reader
C_2	.241	.233	.221	.213
C_3	.368	.351	.322	.303
C_4	.427	.413	.363	.339
C_5	.464	.444	.385	.356
C_6	.483	.460	.396	.365
C_7	.496	.471	.403	.370
C_8	.505	.478	.407	.374
C_9	.511	.482	.410	.376
C_{10}	.515	.485	.412	.377
$C_{11}*$	.518	.486	.414	.377
Mean Word Length	3.665	3.748	3.997	4.106
Mean Sentence Length	6.716	7.754	10.617	12.095
H (1)	4.105	4.125	4.131	4.113
Sample Size (No. of words)	10295.	12662.	10808.	12422.

* C_{11} approximates the usual measure of per cent redundancy.

Data for the Ginn Series Readers are presented in Table 3 and Figures 1 and 2. H(1), the average information in the single letters, is characteristic of the language, English, not the particular sample, and will be found to be about 4.1 in all our samples, whereas for Russian text it is higher, 4.55 (Newman and Waugh, 27). Identical H(1) implies identical distributions of frequency of letter usage. It does not imply, however, that the same letter be used with the same frequency in two texts. Table 1 shows the relative frequency for each letter for first, third, and fifth grade speech, adult speech, general adult text (Raza, 30, from Dewey, 12), and for first, third, and fifth Ginn Readers. Children's texts do not differ significantly from adult texts even when individual letters are compared. The correlations (Table 2) among these various sources for individual let-

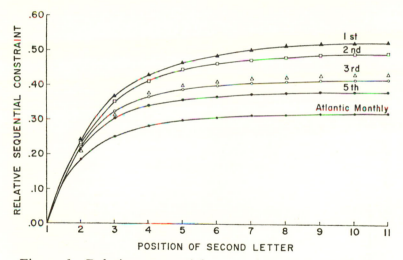

Figure 1. *Relative sequential constraint, C_n, of the letter in the nth position. Four graded readers are shown. The* Atlantic Monthly *gives a lower bound for relatively complex texts. The English Bible is shown by open triangles.*

ters are remarkable; not one is below .97 and several are, for all practical purposes, perfect. In terms of letter frequency distributions, English is English. It will take a more sensitive measure than this to reveal important quantitative differences in language usage. However, see Table 16 and the discussion of it, for a modification of this statement.

Data from the Allyn and Bacon series are shown in Table 4 (see Carterette and Jones, (8)). Differences among reader levels for C_2 are small, but as sequential constraint grows, the differences become greater. Figure 2 shows the regular nature of the growth in sequential constraint in both series of readers. C_{11}, the index of redundancy, shows a regular decrease from first to fifth readers, the first reader being most redundant (52%), the fifth least. Since the third reader lay much closer to the fifth than to the first, the second reader was analyzed. Its curve lies somewhat closer to the first reader than to the third. It is clear

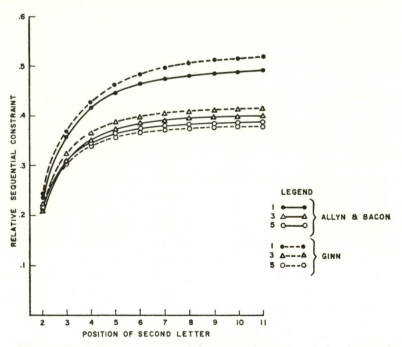

Figure 2. *Relative sequential constraint, C_n, of the letter in the nth position for two series of graded readers. Three levels are shown for each series.*

that there is a much larger jump from first to third than from third to fifth. The two series are not sensibly different. Both first readers are comparable in growth of sequential constraint, as are the two third readers and the two fifth readers. It is apparently possible, using certain limitations on lexicon and sentence length, to produce one text comparable to another, or by modifying these restrictions, to produce another text which will be less redundant. Judged by these particular quantitative measures, the two series of readers are comparable at each level, and show regular growth toward the adult reading level. If we can assume that the redundancy measure quantifies difficulty, then we can say that the greatest growth in reading skills comes in the first two years of reading training.

The argument that redundancy is a quantitative and reliable index of difficulty requires proof. In all cases in which there is some reason for supposing that texts differ in difficulty, there is

Table 4
Relative Sequential Constraint in Allyn and Bacon Series Readers.

	First Grade	Third Grade	Fifth Grade
C_2	.235	.208	.214
C_3	.358	.306	.305
C_4	.416	.349	.345
C_5	.446	.371	.364
C_6	.463	.381	.373
C_7	.474	.388	.378
C_8	.480	.393	.382
C_9	.485	.396	.384
C_{10}	.488	.398	.386
C_{11}*	.490	.400	.387
Mean Word Length	3.736	3.987	4.188
Mean Sentence Length	7.266	9.822	12.038
H (1)	4.094	4.119	4.117
Sample Size (No. of words)	9438.	12768.	12291.

* $C_{11} \times 100$ approximates the usual measure of per cent redundancy.

a difference in redundancy in the proper direction. First, third, and fifth readers can be presumed to differ in difficulty. In these two different series, they also differ in redundancy. Three adult texts of alleged differences in difficulty (a passage from the Bible, from William James, and from the *Atlantic Monthly*) computed by Newman and Waugh (27), differ similarly in redundancy. And three levels of children's free-reading choices rated as suitable for three different ages likewise differ in redundancy. Redundancy, even letter redundancy, is related to difficulty of text in a way in which mean word length and mean sentence length, and even word frequency, are not (see below).

In Figure 1 the Ginn Series data are plotted together with data from Newman and Waugh from adult texts of average (William James) and greater than average (*Atlantic Monthly*) difficulty. They used a passage from the Bible, representative of easy adult text. The points presented in the figure are from our own calculations of the same biblical passage (cf. Table 5), and differ insignificantly from theirs.

Table 5
Comparison of Adult and Child Reading Material in Terms of Information, Constraint, and Mean Word Length.

Source	C_2	C_{11}††	Mean Word Length	Number of Letters in Sample	$H(1)$
*Atlantic Monthly**	.184	.319	4.653	10,000	4.152
William James*	.192	.361	4.556	10,000	4.121
Fifth Reader	.213	.378	4.106	64,454	4.113
Third Reader	.221	.414	3.997	55,027	4.131
Bible	.216	.429	4.014	10,601	4.049
Second Reader	.233	.486	3.748	61,759	4.125
First Reader	.241	.518	3.665	49,556	4.105
Russian Bible*	.245	.472	5.296	10,000	4.549
Russian Phonemes†	.232	—	—	9,000	4.780

* Computed from data of Newman and Waugh.

† Computed from data of Jakobson, Cherry, and Halle.

†† $C_{11} \times 100$ gives the usual measure of per cent redundancy.

It is easily seen in Figure 1 that the *Atlantic Monthly* is less redundant than a fifth reader. The William James data are not plotted because they fall very nearly on the fifth reader curve. The fifth reader is about as redundant as average adult text, and, if this be accepted as an index of difficulty, then the average fifth grader is reading at an adult level, so far as language (not ideas) is concerned. Similarly, the open triangles show the plots for the easy adult text, the Bible. This will be seen to lie close to the data for the third reader. Thus the average third grader is reading at the level of easy adult text.

The data for children's preferred reading are presented in Tables 6 through 9. Table 6 shows the data from several texts at each of the three reading levels. Figure 3 shows the growth of sequential constraint in the three levels of the free-reading choices. It is immediately obvious that levels 3 and 5 are indistinguishable, and are not different from the two fifth readers, all of these lying at the level of average adult text. But level 3 of the free-reading choices is less redundant than the two read-

Table 6
Relative Sequential Constraint in Free Reading Choices.

	Level 1	Level 3	Level 5
C_2	.217	.209	.206
C_3	.313	.302	.298
C_4	.358	.337	.336
C_5	.382	.355	.355
C_6	.396	.363	.364
C_7	.406	.368	.370
C_8	.414	.372	.373
C_9	.419	.373	.376
C_{10}	.422	.375	.377
C_{11}*	.425	.376	.379
Mean Word Length	4.120	3.992	4.029
Mean Sentence Length	10.142	12.222	16.481
H (1)	4.133	4.091	4,100
Sample Size (No. of words)	12384.	11440.	14981.

* $C_{11} \times 100$ approximates the usual measure of per cent redundancy.

ers at this level, and level 1, though more redundant than level 3, is still considerably less redundant than either of the first readers.

Children's free-reading choices are, in the early years, less redundant than their readers. It seems probable that, at least at level 1 and perhaps to some extent at level 3, these books are read to the child. The point is not whether he can read them, given our current techniques of language teaching, but rather what he enjoys. He appears to prefer language which is

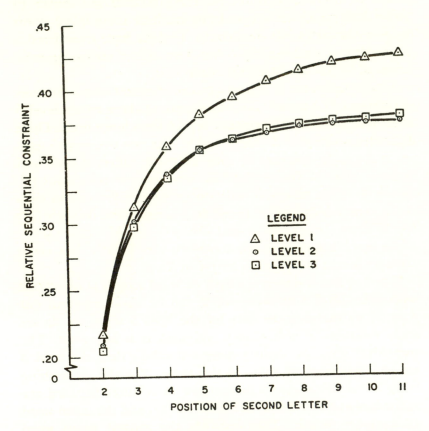

Figure 3. *Relative sequential constraint in three levels of children's free-reading choices.*

less redundant than that presented to him in his readers. Writers of readers assume that a very high level of redundancy (as evidenced by a large amount of word, phrase, and sentence repetition) is optimal. The child himself prefers less redundant language.

It was of some interest to investigate the effect of sample size on these measures. One long level 5 free-choice text (*Alice in Wonderland*) was used. Random samples of approximately 1,400, 3,000, 6,000, 12,000, and 18,000 words were taken. The results of the computations on these samples are shown in Table 7. All measures appear to be stable at about 6,000 words (approximately 24,000 characters). This we have considered a minimally acceptable sample, but have always used samples in excess of 10,000 words (40,000 characters).

Another question of interest is to what extent style influences redundancy. To answer this, we compared three entire level 5 free-choice texts and three entire level 3 free-choice texts. These data are presented in Tables 8 and 9. The first two level 5 texts are not greatly different in spite of vastly different style and lexicon. *Alice in Wonderland* is, however, less redundant (cf. Figure 4). This may well reflect a genuine difference in difficulty, comparable to that found by Newman and Waugh (27) for William James (36%) and the *Atlantic Monthly* (32%). Mean word length does not appear to vary greatly, but mean sentence length is very much longer in *Alice*.

Whether mean sentence length or word length is correlated with difficulty is a question which can be answered from our data. If we examine the data for the level 3 texts, we do see some variation in redundancy, although it is not great. The individual texts are slightly more redundant than the level 3 sample, composed of parts of the three. But the astonishing thing about these results is the lack of relation between the redundancy of *The Emperor's New Clothes* and the mean word an sentence length. This text has the longest mean word length and longest mean sentence length we have ever computed. They are longer than those in the more difficult level 5

Table 7

Relative Sequential Constraint in Free Reading Choices Effect of Sample Size**

	1400 words	3000 words	6000 words	12000 words	18000 words
C_2	.202	.204	.204	.206	.207
C_3	.288	.291	.291	.298	.297
C_4	.327	.327	.327	.336	.335
C_5	.346	.344	.344	.353	.353
C_6	.355	.352	.352	.362	.362
C_7	.362	.358	.358	.367	.362
C_8	.364	.360	.360	.370	.367
C_9	.366	.362	.362	.372	.370
C_{10}	.366	.363	.364	.373	.372
C_{11}*	.366	.363	.365	.374	.373
Mean Word Length	4.037	3.991	3.977	3.998	.374
Mean Sentence Length	17.885	16.062	17.597	17.116	4.006
H (1)	4.091	4.086	4.083	4.089	18.054
Sample Size (No. of words)	1395.	2859.	5719.	11314.	4.090
					18000.

* C_{11} × 100 approximates the usual measure of per cent redundancy.

** Alice in Wonderland—random sample.

Table 8

Relative Sequential Constraint in Three Third-level Texts.

	The Courage of Sarah Noble	Winnie the Pooh	The Emperor's New Clothes
C_2	.219	.208	.224
C_3	.325	.308	.329
C_4	.372	.351	.376
C_5	.396	.373	.407
C_6	.410	.378	.422
C_7	.418	.390	.434
C_8	.423	.395	.441
C_9	.426	.398	.444
C_{10}	.428	.400	.445
C_{11}*	.430	.403	.446
Mean Word Length	4.023	3.979	4.198
Mean Sentence Length	10.430	11.976	19.313
H (1)	4.082	4.117	4.071
Sample Size (No. of words)	6748.	21462.	1970.

* $C_{11} \times 100$ approximates the usual measure of per cent redundancy.

text, *Alice in Wonderland.* The calculated redundancy agrees with the ratings of difficulty in Wilson's *Children's Catalog.* It is apparently quite possible to write fairly easy books using long words and long sentences.

The secret, we believe, in writing easy but interesting books is to use a limited lexicon, as in *The Emperor's New Clothes,* but not to limit it to the few thousand most frequent words in adult language. Rinsland (31) has shown that, although a single first grader's vocabulary is limited to 5,000 words (active vocabulary), the total sample of first graders use all the words the eighth graders use. The ones they use depend on their experience, not on the frequency in the adult written language. They can use any word, and they can read any word; they just can't handle too many at one time in either area. A

Table 9
Relative Sequential Constraint in Three Fifth-level Texts.

	Doctor Dolittle	Mary Poppins	Alice in Wonderland
C_2	.217	.210	.207
C_3	.322	.308	.297
C_4	.368	.352	.335
C_5	.394	.375	.353
C_6	.407	.388	.362
C_7	.415	.397	.367
C_8	.420	.404	.370
C_9	.424	.409	.372
C_{10}	.426	.412	.373
C_{11}*	.428	.415	.374
Mean Word Length	3.966	4.150	4.006
Mean Sentence Length	15.384	14.454	18.054
H (1)	4.087	4.140	4.090
Sample Size (No. of words)	8246.	9930.	18000.

* $C_{11} \times 100$ approximates the usual measure of per cent redundancy.

book they like tells them about something interesting and uses the necessary lexicon to do so. Sentence length in *The Emperor's New Clothes* is phenomenal. We have not analyzed the relationship between sentence length and grammatical complexity, but it is obvious that there is some relationship. It is equally obvious too that the relationship is not simple. Cases in point are: the tremendous sentence length in the level 3 text cited above; the *decrease* in sentence length from level 5 to adult speech (see below); the fact that Strickland (40) found no regular development of grammatical complexity in readers; and the large differences in mean sentence length (without other statistical differences) between the two schools in the fifth grade and there only.

b. Natural Speech

The analyses of natural speech are presented in Tables 10

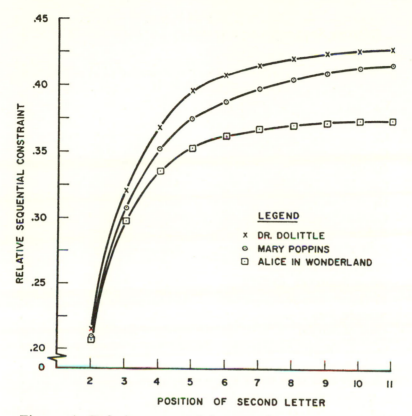

Figure 4. *Relative sequential constraint in three texts of children's free-reading choices at Level 5.*

through 12. Table 10 shows the relative sequential constraints for both the letter and the phonemic transcriptions. There is very little change in redundancy from first grade to adult speech in the letter transcription data. For the phonemic data, as Figure 5 shows, the two growth curves are indistinguishable. In terms of sound pattern redundancies, therefore, six-year-old speech is adult; there is no change after age six. Figure 5 also shows the relative sequential constraints for a first reader, and for a letter transcription of first grade speech. Here the difference is sizable, the reader being the more redundant. Hence, the differences between natural speech and written material may be more important in learning to read than has been previously considered.

In Table 10, H(1) is seen to be characteristic of the language, with the added proviso that the number of characters used is also revelant.* Mean word length (letters) increases from 3.6

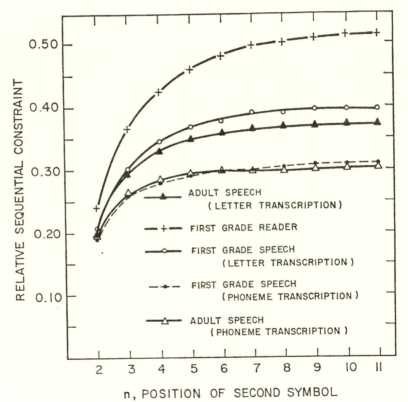

Figure 5. *Relative sequential constraint in letter or phoneme transcriptions of the speech of first graders and adults and in a first reader.*

* Phonemic coding, using a 41-character alphabet, yields more information per letter, than the ordinary English alphabet. Jakobson, Cherry, and Halle (21) obtained H(1) = 4.78 bits for Russian speech, using 42 phonemes.

letters for first grade speech, to 3.8 letters for fifth grade speech. Word length for first readers is 3.7, rising to 4.1 for fifth readers. Word length (letters) for adult speech is not very different, 3.9 (Table 11). Thus it appears that word length is somewhat greater in readers than in speech. For free-reading choices, there does not appear to be a difference between level 1 (4.1) and level 5 (4.0), but both are closer to fifth than to first readers. For adult speech, word length (letters) is similar to that of fifth reader and all free-reading choices. The shorter mean word length in speech as compared to written texts may be due to the frequent use of "yes," "no," and personal pronouns, especially in children's speech, and need not give any information about the length of lexical words. This hypothesis can and should be checked.

Phonemic "words" increase proportionately about the same amount with level, adult phonemic "words" being somewhat longer than six-year-olds' "words." It should be remembered that a phonemic word was defined in such a way as to aid in the discovery of the novel features of spoken language. Great caution is necessary in interpretation. A phonemic word, then, is not the same as a lexical word, and is not intentionally related to word classes or syntactical units. It was defined only in terms of prosodic features, specifically a pause in the flow of sound. These units, phonemic "words," are three times as long as lexical words,* and represent a grouping that occurs between pauses. In terms of length, they appear to be more like phrases than words. In any event the pauses do not occur at the same places as the gaps in written language. This discussion raises the important question of the nature of the decoding (auditory) units of language. Insofar as the units of spoken language and written language are different, the learning of written language (reading) will be more difficult.

---

* A sentence from a reader is about 40 letters long, whilst a sentence of speech is about 30 phonemes long. However, the 40 arises from $3.8\overline{w} \times 10.5\overline{s}$, but the 30 arises from $10.5\overline{w} \times 2.9\overline{s}$, where $\overline{w}$ is mean word length in symbols, and $\overline{s}$ is mean sentence length in words.

Table 10

Relative Sequential Constraint in the Letter and Phoneme Transcriptions: Grade 1, 3, and 5 and Adult Speech.

	Grade 1		Grade 3		Grade 5		Adult	
	Letter	Phoneme	Letter	Phoneme	Letter	Phoneme	Letter	Phoneme
C_2	.211	.192	.208	.189	.201	.191	.198	.196
C_3	.305	.257	.303	.252	.295	.255	.291	.264
C_4	.345	.280	.342	.274	.333	.276	.328	.286
C_5	.366	.289	.363	.280	.353	.283	.348	.294
C_6	.374	.293	.372	.284	.362	.286	.357	.298
C_7	.381	.296	.378	.286	.367	.288	.363	.299
C_8	.384	.297	.382	.287	.371	.289	.366	.300
C_9	.387	.298	.384	.287	.373	.289	.368	.300
C_{10}	.388	.299	.386	.288	.374	.290	.370	.300
C_{11}*	.389	.299	.387	.288	.375	.290	.370	.300
Mean Word Length	3.632	2.746	3.653	3.212	3.754	2.772	3.903	2.540
Mean Sentence Length	10.040	10.631	11.538	10.579	10.477	11.276	9.705	11.765
H (1)	4.083	4.834	4.084	4.842	4.104	4.872	4.124	4.882
Sample Size (No. of characters)	94,767.	66,179.	101,285.	70,842.	131,274.	90,741.	78,580.	54,478.

* $C_{11} \times 100$ approximates the usual measure of per cent redundancy.

Table 11
Mean Word Length for Two Series of Graded Readers, Free-reading Choices, and Letter Transcription of Speech at Four Levels.

	First Grade	Third Grade	Fifth Grade	Adult
Ginn	3.7	4.0	4.1	–
Allyn and Bacon	3.7	4.0	4.2	–
Free-reading Choices	4.1	4.0	4.0	–
Letter Transcriptions	3.6	3.6	3.8	3.9

Table 12
Mean Sentence Length for Two Series of Graded Readers, Free-reading Choices, and Letter Transcriptions of Speech at Four Levels.

	First Grade	Third Grade	Fifth Grade	Adult
Ginn	6.7	10.6	12.1	–
Allyn and Bacon	7.3	9.8	12.0	–
Free-reading Choices	10.1	12.2	16.5	–
Letter Transcriptions	10.0	11.5	10.5	9.7

Turning now to Table 12, we see that mean letter sentence length behaves peculiarly: it is higher in the grades, especially third grade, than in adult speech. The letter transcription data for speech can be compared with data from written materials because of the similarity in alphabet and word definition. In making such a comparison, we find that in first and third grade speech, the mean sentence lengths (10.0 and 11.5) are similar to those found in free-reading choices (10.1 and 12.2), but higher than in first and third readers (6.7 and 10.6). But the mean sentence length of the free-choice material at level 5 is much higher (16.5) than that for fifth grade speech (10.5) and fifth reader (12.1). The most difficult individual level 5 text had an even higher mean sentence length (18.0). Yet adult speech, on the contrary, shows a drop in mean sentence length (9.7).

There are several possible explanations of this strange state of affairs. In the first place, formal language has a literary norm which places value upon long sentences for avoidance of monotony in both sentence length and grammatical construction. Informal speech, on the other hand, has at least two other tools for use in avoiding monotony—all the several aspects of prosody, and the natural community of interest that sustains the conversation. Speech thus has no need for varied sentences. Furthermore, long sentences in formal language virtually demand complex grammatical forms. This can be coped with in writing, because it is possible to start over again when one becomes entangled in the construction. In speech there is no retracing unless the listener interrupts with "what?" and after a few instances of that, the speaker simplifies his discourse, or the listener walks away.

Secondly, the definition of a phonemic sentence was based, not upon grammatical structure, but upon certain features of the prosody: intonation contour, terminal pause, change of speaker, whereas in written language a sentence is usually a certain type of grammatical unit. Linguists, when pressed, cannot really define a sentence. Indeed, Fries (16) found different kinds of utterances, some that start a conversation, some that can only be responses, some that produce action responses, and they all have different structures. Many are not in themselves complete grammatical structures of the sort grammarians discuss. Fries' sentence patterns more nearly describe our spoken patterns, because he used a speech corpus, although ours appear to be more fragmentary and less structured than his, even at the adult level. A grammatical analysis has not been attempted with this material yet, so any comments upon this aspect are based upon an impression of the material as a whole. In any event, since our spoken "sentence" was largely determined by a terminal pause, it may be more closely related to vital capacity than to grammatical structure, although one would expect a pause where a natural unit of comprehension occurs. The drop in mean sentence length with adults lends some credence to this supposition. The hypothesis is that the childen string together simple syntactic structures with "and" connectors as long as their breath lasts, in part to avoid interruption. Adults, on the other hand, with more mannerly companions, can afford a syntactic pause. We also find that adults use "and" much less frequently, using more complicated syntactic structures to convey the more complex relations in their conversations. This hypothesis was checked by a count of the "ands" at level 3 and adult. A count was made of those phonemic words involving "and" (e.g., "and," "an," "anum") that occurred three or more times in the third grade and adult corpuses. It was found that the total number of occurrences of such words, after correction for sample size, was approximately twice as great in third grade as in adult speech.

The main point to be made here, however, is that spoken language and written language are again shown to be different, the spoken language tending toward shorter sentences, and presumably, simpler forms. Insofar as they are different, the problem of learning to read is increased.

The relative frequency for each letter for each level of natural speech is shown in Table 13. Again there are no great differences among the spoken samples. Table 14 shows the relative frequency of phonemes for each level of natural speech, where the differences among levels also is small. Reference to Table 15 will show the minor changes. Table 2 shows that the correlations between the letter frequencies used in adult speech and those used at the other three levels are all .99 or better. This is another indication that certain features of speech do not change from six years of age to adulthood. The differences reflected in some aspects of language are more likely to be due to complexity of thought than to genuine language differences.

The stability of phoneme distributions from age 6 to age 20 may be noted in Tables 15A and B which give the rank order of vowel and consonant phonemes by relative frequency of occurrence. Vowels change rank in only five cases (out of eleven) from first graders to adults, the percentage changes being $+47$ (/uw/), -22 (/æ/), -20 (/a/), $+8$ (/e/), and -7 (/ey/). From an articulatory view the major changes are an increase in the closed vowel /uw/ and decreases in the open vowels /æ/ and /a/.

Proportionately fewer consonants change rank (7 out of 25), but only four show large changes (greater than about 15 per cent). From first graders to adults the changes in per cent are: $+ 128$ (/y/, $- 45$ (/m/, $- 30$ (/g/ and $+ 28$ (/l/). These are all voiced consonants, but /l/ and /y/ are both (alveolar) approximants, whereas /g/ is a velar stop, and /m/ is a bilabial, nasal consonant.[*]

We have not considered whether these relatively slight changes reflect physiological and structural changes of the vocal mechanism. An interesting speculation may be based on a statistical study of the larger units of speech that we now have in progress. Prelimary data show that the most frequent phonemic word for first graders is "um" whereas the two most frequent phonemic words for adults are "yeah" and "y' know," with "you know" not far behind. This change is consistent with the increase in relative frequencies of /y/, /uw/ (as in boot), and /e/ (as in bet), and with the decrease in /m/. (It is interesting that the most frequent single "lexical" word is "yeah" for adults and "no" for first graders!).

Table 16 displays the correlation matrix for 22 consonant phonemes from 15 (actually, it will turn out, 14) sets of data. Data sets 1 to 10 are taken directly from the study by Wang and Crawford (44). They omitted vowels from their comparisons because consonants are relatively simple to compare, but vowel systems are difficult because of transcription problems and the relative complexity of dialectical differences.

The nature of the sources and sample sizes of the consonant phonemes used in these computations is listed here inasmuch

[*] Further details will be found in a forthcoming monograph now in preparation, "Alphabetic and Phonetic Texts of Informal Speech with Statistical Analyses."

Table 13
Proportions, p, of Letters in Natural Speech.

of Grade 1			of Grade 3			of Grade 5			of Adults		
letters	f	p	letters	f	p	letters	f	p	letters	f	p
e	8683	.11936	e	9180	.11759	e	12273	.12077	e	7109	.11603
t	7032	.09667	t	7362	.09430	t	9693	.09538	t	6150	.10037
a	5987	.08230	a	6376	.08167	o	8329	.08196	o	5390	.08797
o	5886	.08092	o	6362	.08149	a	8211	.08080	a	4652	.07592
n	5213	.07166	h	5552	.07112	h	7139	.07025	i	4271	.06971
h	5089	.06996	n	5536	.07091	n	6791	.06682	h	4062	.06630
i	4706	.06469	i	5007	.06414	i	6375	.06273	n	3952	.06450
s	4190	.05760	s	4663	.05973	s	6290	.06189	s	3394	.05539
d	3289	.04521	d	3613	.04628	r	4517	.04445	r	2870	.04684
r	3039	.04178	r	3406	.04363	d	4371	.04301	l	2520	.04113
m	2623	.03606	u	2842	.03640	u	3679	.03620	u	2418	.03946
u	2451	.03369	l	2705	.03465	l	3611	.03553	d	2213	.03612
l	2431	.03342	w	2511	.03216	y	3179	.03146	y	2210	.03607
w	2301	.03163	m	2362	.03026	w	3111	.03061	w	1780	.02905
y	2119	.02913	y	2253	.02886	m	2623	.02581	g	1482	.02419
g	1721	.02366	g	1740	.02229	g	2381	.02343	m	1196	.01952
c	1312	.01804	c	1407	.01802	c	1868	.01838	c	1181	.01928
b	1214	.01669	b	1236	.01583	k	1574	.01549	b	912	.01488
f	955	.01313	k	1197	.01533	b	1537	.01512	f	885	.01444
k	892	.01226	f	1005	.01287	f	1406	.01384	k	860	.01404
p	809	.01112	p	968	.01240	p	1293	.01272	p	804	.01312
v	530	.00729	v	533	.00683	v	925	.00910	v	627	.01023
j	137	.00188	j	159	.00204	j	237	.00233	j	206	.00336
x	90	.00124	x	52	.00067	x	101	.00099	x	71	.00116
q	24	.00033	z	23	.00030	z	58	.00057	z	31	.00051
z	19	.00026	q	15	.00019	q	28	.00028	q	23	.00038
Total	72,742		Total	78,065		Total	101,618		Total	61,269	

Table 14
Proportions, p, of Phonemes in Natural Speech.

	of First Graders					of Third Graders				
	Vowels		Consonants			Vowels		Consonants		
	f	p		f	p		f	p		f	p
e	7490	.12770	n	4791	.08168	e	8064	.12794	n	5095	.08083
i	2615	.04458	r	2884	.04917	i	2884	.04576	r	3305	.05243
iy	2235	.03810	t	2783	.04745	iy	2502	.03969	t	2943	.04669
ae	1900	.03239	m	2633	.04489	ae	1933	.03067	s	2831	.04491
e	1725	.02941	s	2438	.04157	e	1914	.03037	d	2473	.03923
ow	1196	.02039	d	2218	.03782	ow	1383	.02194	m	2383	.03781
ey	976	.01664	w	1959	.03340	ey	1020	.01618	w	1976	.03135
a	900	.01534	l	1745	.02975	a	976	.01548	l	1910	.03030
⊃	843	.01437	k	1648	.02810	⊃	875	.01388	ʔ	1862	.02954
uw	711	.01212	z	1609	.02743	uw	785	.01245	k	1802	.02859
u	244	.00416	ʔ	1580	.02694	u	314	.00498	ð	1729	.02743
			ð	1553	.02648				z	1619	.02568
			h	1186	.02022				b	1184	.01878
			b	1117	.01904				h	1162	.01844
ay	2179	.03715	g	1021	.01741	ay	1997	.03168	g	953	.01512
aw	451	.00769	f	776	.01323	aw	477	.00757	p	887	.01407
⊃y	35	.00060	p	747	.01274	⊃y	50	.00079	f	827	.01312
Total Vowels	20,835	.35523	v	576	.00982	Total Vowels	22,650	.35936	y	713	.01131
			y	496	.00846				v	599	.00950
			ŋ	368	.00627				ŋ	450	.00714
			θ	363	.00619				θ	363	.00576
			š	296	.00505				š	356	.00565
			ǰ	187	.00319				č	217	.00344
			č	179	.00305				ǰ	216	.00343
			ž	0	0				ž	0	0
			Total Consonants	35,153	.59933				Total Consonants	37,855	.60060

144

Table 14 (continued)

Proportions, p, of Phonemes in Natural Speech.

of Fifth Graders

Vowels	f	p	Consonants	f	p
ə	10593	.13082	n	6118	.07556
i	3693	.04561	r	4379	.05408
iy	3348	.04135	t	3738	.04616
e	2463	.03042	s	3549	.04383
ae	2209	.02728	d	3309	.04087
ow	1823	.02251	m	2637	.03257
ey	1359	.01678	l	2591	.03200
a	1330	.01643	w	2451	.03027
ɔ	1163	.01436	k	2342	.02892
uw	1079	.01333	z	2243	.02770
u	418	.00516	ð	2198	.02714
			ʔ	1772	.02188
			h	1478	.01825
			b	1430	.01766
			g	1245	.01538
ay	2261	.02792	y	1228	.01517
aw	578	.00714	p	1211	.01496
ɔy	74	.00091	f	1115	.01377
Total	29,478	.36406	v	1030	.01272
Vowels			ŋ	668	.00825
			š	647	.00799
			θ	505	.00624
			č	360	.00445
			ǰ	335	.00414
			ž	0	0
			Total	48,579	.59996
			Consonants		

of Adults

Vowels	f	p	Consonants	f	p
ə	6325	.12985	n	3464	.07112
i	2489	.05110	r	2806	.05761
iy	1835	.03767	s	2264	.04648
e	1551	.03184	t	2248	.04615
ae	1229	.02523	l	1850	.03798
ow	1139	.02338	d	1827	.03751
uw	869	.01784	k	1414	.02903
ey	755	.01550	w	1397	.02868
ɔ	737	.01513	ð	1354	.02780
a	596	.01224	m	1199	.02462
u	230	.00472	z	1107	.02273
			ʔ	988	.02028
			y	941	.01932
			b	877	.01800
			h	793	.01628
ay	1555	.03192	v	738	.01515
aw	367	.00753	p	694	.01425
ɔy	43	.00088	f	692	.01421
Total	17,755	.36451	g	598	.01228
Vowels			ŋ	516	.01059
			ǰ	397	.00815
			θ	388	.00796
			š	221	.00454
			č	215	.00441
			ž	0	0
			Total	28,988	.59514
			Consonants		

Table 15

Rank Order of Vowel and Consonant Phonemes by Frequency of Occurrence for First, Third, Fifth Graders and Adults.

A. Vowels

Rank	First		Third	Fifth	Adult	Denes*
1	ə	(the)	ə	ə	ə	ə
2	i	(hit)	i	i	i	i
3	iy	(beat)	iy	iy	iy	ay
4	æ	(bat)	æ	e	e	e
5	e	(bet)	e	æ	æ	iy
6	ow	(boat)	ow	ow	ow	ow
7	ey	(may)	ey	ey	uw	ʌ
8	a	(pot)	a	a	ey	ɔ
9	ɔ	(bought)	ɔ	ɔ	ɔ	a
10	uw	(boot)	uw	uw	a	ey
11	u	(put)	u	u	u	uw

* = rank according to Denes (1963).

as some apparent anomalies will be easier to understand if the character of the source material is known. We have consulted all the original sources except for Carroll (2) but Carroll's original data are given by Hultzén, Allen, and Miron (20).

1. Trnka (42) dictionary—15, 459 phonemes—"Nearly all the words used in this work are taken from the *Pocket Oxford Dictionary of Current English* (London, 1928)." Analysis was restricted to words consisting of one morpheme and containing at most two vocalic phonemes.

2. Fowler (13) modern prosa—10,194 phonemes—(5000 phonemes each from a narrative and an essay by Graham Greene, *Concepts of the Calculus* by Boyer, and the entire 501 phonemes from *The Story of a Fierce Bad Rabbit* by Beatrix Potter. Apparently the data from Boyer and the 501 phonemes from Potter were not used by Wang and Crawford).

3. Carroll (2), juvenile plays—10,784 phonemes (taken from Wang and Crawford).

Table 15 (continued)
Rank Order of Vowel and Consonant Phonemes by Frequency of Occurrence for First, Third, Fifth Graders and Adults.

B. Consonants

Rank	First	Third	Fifth	Adult	Denes*
1	n	n	n	n	t
2	r	r	r	r	n
3	t	t	t	s	s
4	m	s	s	t	d
5	s	d	d	l	l
6	d	m	m	d	m
7	w	w	l	k	ð
8	l	l	w	w	k
9	k	?	k	ð	r
10	z	k	z	m	w
11	?	ð	ð	z	z
12	ð	z	?	?	b
13	h	b	h	y	v
14	b	h	b	b	p
15	g	g	g	h	f
16	f	p	y	v	h
17	p	f	p	p	j
18	v	y	f	f	ŋ
19	y	v	v	g	g
20	ŋ	ŋ	ŋ	ŋ	š
21	θ	θ	š	ǰ	θ
22	š	š	θ	θ	j
23	ǰ	č	č	š	č
24	č	ǰ	ǰ	č	ž
25	ž	ž	ž	ž	

* = rank according to Denes (1963).

4. Hayden (19) lectures—41,412 phonemes.
5. Whitney (46) "modern prose"—6,371 phonemes: from five poems (Shakespeare, Milton, Gray, Bryant, Tennyson) and five prose passages (Bible, Samuel Johnson, Goldsmith, Carlyle, and Macauley).

Table 16

Product-moment Correlation Matrix for 22 Consonant Phonemes from 15 Sets of Data.[1]

| | 2 | 3 | 4 | 5 | 6 | 7 | 8 | 9 | 10 | Natural Speech | | | | |
| | | | | | | | | | | First | Third | Fifth | Adult | Hultzén |
										11	12	13	14	15
TRN 1	.58	.42	.75	.67	.73	.75	.72	.72	.71	.63	.66	.68	.71	.41
FOW 2		.92	.83	.80	.81	.82	.86	.74	.82	.76	.80	.83	.86	.92
CAR 3			.63	.56	.58	.62	.71	.54	.72	.60	.62	.64	.66	.999
HAY 4				.95	.98	.97	.97	.88	.88	.89	.91	.93	.94	.62
WHI 5					.98	.97	.92	.86	.80	.88	.91	.93	.94	.56
DEW 6						.98	.96	.90	.87	.89	.91	.94	.94	.58
VOE 7							.96	.91	.88	.91	.93	.95	.96	.62
FRE 8								.89	.94	.89	.90	.92	.93	.71
FRY 9									.90	.90	.92	.92	.90	.55
TOB 10										.81	.81	.83	.82	.72
1st 11											.99	.98	.93	.60
3rd 12												.99	.96	.62
5th 13													.98	.64
A 14														.66

[1] Sample sources: 1, dictionary; 2, modern prose; 3, modern plays; 4, lectures; 5, modern prose; 6, newspapers; 7, radio announcements; 8, telephone conversations; 9, phonetic readers; 10, telephone conversations; 11, 12, 13, 14, phonemic transcriptions of our own data; 15, modern plays (same data as CAR, 3). See discussion in text for details.

6. Dewey (12) newspapers—235,025 phonemes.
7. Voelker (43) radio announcements—different announcers, 409,506 phonemes.
8. French, Carter, and Koenig (14) long-distance telephone business conversations, a different part of speech sampled on successive days—135,548 phonemes.
9. Fry (17) phonetic readers, short simple anecdotes for foreigners learning English—10,305 phonemes.
10. Tobias (41) telephone conversations; a different phonemic coding of material from Study 8—133,460 phonemes.
11–14. Carterette and Jones (8) phonemic transcriptions of natural speech from the present study, number of phonemes: first graders, 35,153; third graders, 37,855; fifth graders, 48,579; adults, 28,988.
15. Hultzén, Allen, and Miron (20) same data as Carroll (Study 3)—10,657 phonemes.

The correlations among items 1–10 were recomputed using the distributions of Wang and Crawford (44) and the values of r obtained are identical with those calculated by them.

The most salient and important features of this table are: 1) the very high correlations (.88 and greater) among our data (first, third, fifth grades, and adult speech), HAY, WHI, DEW, VOE, FRE, and FRY; 2) the relatively low intercorrelations between these sets of data and TRN, FOW, CAR, and HULTZÉN. The correlation of 1.0 between the Carroll and Hultzén data comes about because Hultzén, Allen, and Miron used Carroll's data as the basis for their study of transitional frequencies of English phonemes. It appears that the highest correlations occur between phonemic systems derived from material closest to natural speech, whereas the lowest correlations occur with phonemic systems based on material furthest from natural speech. To illustrate, third grade speech has the highest correlations (.90 or higher, accounting for 81 to 85 per cent of the variance) in decreasing order, with VOE (radio announcements), FRY (phonetic reader), HAY (lectures), WHI ("modern prose"), DEW (newspapers, and FRE (telephone conversations), but the lowest correlations (.80 to .62, accounting for 64 to 39 per cent of the variance) with FOW (modern prose), TRN (dictionary) and CAR (modern plays), r being least for the last. The Hayden corpus is more nearly like speech than any of the others. Since her system of transcription was virtually identical with ours, we were able to correlate the proportions of phonemes for her data with our adult data for 38 phonemes, *consonant and vowel*. In spite of the transcription difficulties and dialect differences for vowels, the correlation is relatively high: .88.

6. The Larger View—Diphones, Triphones and Tetraphones as Protoplastic Phonemic Words

It is impossible to exhibit here the huge volume of material* that we have obtained by means of computer programs from the phonemic and letter transcriptions. We shall merely adumbrate the results. One general conclusion will be stated now: In spite of the statistical similarity among the four levels, there are clear differences in the fine structure. We believe that these data are a rich source of hypotheses about psycholinguistic behavior.

Let us give a wee taste of the pudding. Suppose that a first grader were a Markovian generator of concatenated strings of diphones. (You who shudder at the thought that this might be true, take comfort. Chomsky (9) appears to have proved its impossibility). The most likely 10-diphone word he could speak is "ənədəmænwəðətəindəen." When he became an adult (were he to live so long) his tune would have changed to "ərəniniŋəmələs stenæm."

---

* The running texts, singlets, doublets, and triplets, as well as the distributions in both letter and phonemic transcription, is being prepared for publication by the University of California Press. We gratefully acknowledge a grant from the Hope for Hearing Foundation, Los Angeles, to defray the cost of preparing the phonemic transcriptions for letterpress.

6.1 Diphones

Table 17 shows the rank order of the ten most frequent diphones for each of the four levels of speech. The sounds common to different levels may be seen from the following abstraction of the table.

a)

Diphone	Grade 1	Grade 3	Grade 5	Adult
ən	1	*	1	2
əd	2	1	*	*
əm	3	*	5	5
æn	4	*	*	*
wə	5	3	3	*
ðə	6	2	4	*
tə	7	4	7	*
in	8	*	*	3
də	9	5	6	*
ɛn	10	*	*	9

* not in the first ten ranks relative to Grade 1

b) Number of diphones in common among the 10 most frequent at each level:

	Grade 1	Grade 3	Grade 5	Adult
Grade 1	10	5	6	4
Grade 3		10	5	2
Grade 5			10	4
Adult				10

From a) and b) there is at least the hint that the grades are more closely related to each other than to the adults. The most notable features of Table 17 with respect to changes from first grade to adult speech are 1) /ər/ has become most frequent and has displaced /əd/, 2) /iŋ/ has moved from 9th place in third and fifth grades to 4th place for adults, 3) /s/ appears at grade 5 and becomes more frequent for adults, 4) /æn/ occurs only at grade 1, 5) /wə/, /ðə/, /tə/ and /də/ which are common to grade 1, grade 3, and grade 5, do not appear in the adult top ten, 6) diphones combining with *schwa* decrease in absolute number and proportion from the grades (G1: n = 7, p ≅ .106; G3: n = 8, p ≅ .092; G5: n = 8, p ≅ .113) to adults (A: n = 5, p ≅ .068).

Without more analytic study of a larger segment of the diphone population, it would be foolish to draw many conclusions or hypotheses from these data. There are a few reasonable suggestions, though. As one example, remark (5) indicates that highly confusable diphones, /wə/, /ðə/, /tə/ and /də/ are being replaced by sounds less confusable by virtue of a "new" vowel /i/, a differentiation of the nasal /n/ into two classes, /m/ and /n/, as well as an increase in sibilance and liquidity.

There are exactly 1521 logically possible diphones (39 × 39, excluding word boundary and full stop) of which about 400 do not occur in the sample. The ten most frequently occurring diphones make up about 11 per cent of the total for adults (Table 17). Our count includes both /nt/ and /tn/ but only /nt/ is *produced* as a sound with any finite frequency. The occurrence of such diphones impossible to produce inflates the number "observed." If we assume that about half the entries do not occur as productions (and might not be heard as perceptions) we may estimate that about 11 per cent of the total number of diphones are accounted for by about 1.8 per cent of the inventory of different diphones. Roughly the same may be said of the children's speech.

However, by considering larger units more insight into the structure of psycholinguistic units may be had. For example, as a diphone, /ər/ occurs about as often as /ən/ (1157 times vs 1083 times, respectively), in the adult sample of 48,707). On the other hand /ən/ occurs 145 times as the leading unit in phonemic words two or more phonemes long, whereas in the same setting /ər/ occurs only 35 times. Thus one might be led to the hypothesis that 1) /ər/ is more often at the end or 2) more often in the middle of a phonemic word than is /ən/. A random sample taken over 500 different phonemic words gave 23 end occurrences of /ər/ to 20 of /ən/, from which it is reasonable to reject hypothesis (1). Thus we conclude that 1)

Table 17

Proportions, p, of the Ten most Frequently Occurring Phoneme Pairs from the Natural Speech of First, Third, and Fifth Graders, and Adults.

First Clover n = 31,094

Rank	Diphone	f	* p **	
1	ən	754	.02152	.02426
2	əd	647	.01846	.02081
3	əm	433	.01236	.01393
4	æn	419	.01196	.01348
5	wə	390	.01113	.01254
6	ðə	377	.01076	.01212
7	tə	368	.01050	.01183
8	in	294	.00839	.00946
9	də	281	.00802	.00904
10	ɛn	380	.00799	.00900
			.12109	.13646

Fifth Clover n = 42,454

Rank	Diphone	f	* p **	
1	ən	1066	.022379	.025109
2	ər	987	.02072	.023248
3	wə	533	.011609	.013025
4	ðə	523	.010979	.012319
5	əm	517	.010854	.012177
6	də	467	.009804	.010999
7	tə	423	.008880	.009963
8	dn	388	.008145	.009139
9	iŋ	331	.006949	.007796
10	sə	318	.006676	.007490
			.11699	.13038

/ən/ begins a phonemic word far more often than /ər/, 2) /ər/ is far more often an interior diphon than /ən/, and 3) /ən/ and /ər/ are terminal diphons about equally often.

It will not be difficult to think of and test a variety of hy-

Table 17 Continued
Third Clover n = 32,437

Rank	Diphone	f	* p **	
1	əd	722	.01972	.02226
2	ðə	472	.01289	.01455
3	wə	429	.01172	.01323
4	tə	358	.00978	.01104
5	də	338	.00923	.01042
6	nə	269	.00735	.00829
7	əl	224	.00612	.00691
8	wiy	223	.00609	.00687
9	iŋ	211	.00576	.00650
10	əf	210	.00574	.00647
			.09440	.10654

Adult n = 48,707

Rank	Diphone	f	* p **	
1	ər	1157	.02124	.02375
2	ən	1083	.01988	.02224
3	in	475	.00872	.00975
4	iŋ	455	.00835	.00934
5	əm	378	.00694	.00776
6	əl	363	.00666	.00745
7	əs	354	.00649	.00727
8	st	345	.00633	.00708
9	ɛn	332	.00609	.00682
10	æm	331	.00608	.00679
			.09679	.10826

* Proportions based on all symbols.

** Proportions based on phonemic symbols only; i.e., word boundary (/) and full stop (.) omitted.

potheses about the phonological or grammatical structure of psycholinguistic units using the materials that we have gathered.

6.2 Triphones, Tetraphones, and Phonemic Words

Our program provides all sequential units up to tetragrams, and with a listing of all phonemic words (that is, the sequences between word boundaries) not more than 45 phonemes long. The printout provides the frequency distribution, cumulative distribution, a listing of items by frequency, and an alphabetical listing. There are too much data to present here, and so we give only a hint of its character.

Table 18A shows some examples of frequency of occurrence of phonemic trigrams (triphones) transcribed from the free speech of first graders. Note that triphones containing a word boundary (/) or full stop (.) have not been included. The counts have *not* been adjusted to reflect this fact. For example, the most frequent triphones of all is /æn/ which occurred 417 times in the total sample of $T = 66,253$ phonemes. The second most frequent triphone /wən/ occurred 321 times in T, as may be seen in the first line of the table. Thus the two most frequent triphones account for a proportion $738/T = .0111$ of the total. Similarly /nwə/ occurs $60/T$ or about one fourth as often as /əðə/ which occurs 242 times in T.

Only 34 different triphones make up $\frac{1}{10}T$; 164 different triphones account for $\frac{1}{4}T$; and 704 different triphones account for 33,136, or about $\frac{1}{2}T$. Said another way, 50 per cent of the sample is made up of only about one-fourteenth of the different triphones, i.e., $(704/9876)T = .0713T \cong \frac{1}{14}T$.

Table 18B shows some examples taken from less frequently occurring triphons. It is quite obvious that on the average the infrequent triphons are more difficult to pronounce than those in part A. This may reflect merely the fact that the computer counts every possible triphon. Whether triphons more difficult to pronounce also occur less frequently is an experimental matter. These data do provide a test of this or similar hypotheses. As an example, do the most frequent triphones require less energy of production than that required by a randomly chosen (pronounceable) set?

We mention that naturally some of these triphons (/wən/ or /səm/, say) are also phonemic "words" as shown by our com-

Table 18

Examples of Phonemic Trigrams (triphones) Occurring with Various Frequencies in the Sample of T = 66,253 Triphones, Transcribed from the Free Speech of First-grade Children. (Triphones containing a full stop (o) or word boundary (1) are not included, nor have counts been adjusted to reflect this fact.)

Part A shows the 79 most frequent triphones (column one), each with its frequency (column two), the cumulative number of triphones (column three), and the cumulative number of *different* triphones (column four).

Part B gives some arbitrary exemplars selected from among those triphones occurring 50, 40, 30, 20, 10, 5, 4, 3, 2, and 1 times each in the sample of T triphones. For example, /ang/, /aygɛ/, /bik/ and /gown/ designated by 30 (15) are a selection of four triphones from the 15 which occurred exactly 30 times each in the sample of T triphones.

A. The 19 most frequent triphones.

Triphon	frequency	Cumulative no. triphones	Cumulative no. *different* triphones
wən	321	738	2
əðə	242	1799	6
ðər	241	2040	7
ɚɛŋ	212	2931	11
wəz	202	3338	13
tər	183	3902	16
səm	179	4491	19
wɛn	168	5154	23
stə	163	5287	24
taym	152	5747	27
nðɛ	150	5897	28
nðə	128	6952	36
ænd	117		
hæv	117		
layk	117	7708	43
wər	116	7896	44

Triphone	frequency	Cumulative no. triphones	Cumulative no. *different* triphones
ənə	108	8228	47
ðɛr	107	8335	48
plɛy	103	8544	50
ænð	102	8646	51
hæd	101	8474	52
ənə	100	8847	53
nwiy	94	9039	55
θiŋ	92		
ðæʔ	92		
ðis	92		
ənt	92	9407	59
ʔæn	91	9498	60
ərd	88		
iywə	88	9853	64
əns	87	9940	65
ərz	86		
iyhæ	86		
dəl	86		
vər	86	10,284	69
məð	82	10,617	73
kəm	81	10,779	75
brə	80		
idə	80		
məyɛy	80	11,099	79
ərs	79		
inə	79	11,257	81
əmt	78		
əniy	78		
ɛnay	78	11,491	84
əzə	77		
howm	77	11,645	86
kəz	75	11,870	89
ðæt	74		
aymz	74		
down	74		
zən	74	12,240	97

Table 18A Continued

Triphone	frequency	Cumulative no. triphones	Cumulative no. *different* triphones
ayhæ	73		
big	73		
græ	73	12,459	97
frə	72		
mtay	72	12,747	101
ənd	71	12,889	103
gɛt	70		
inð	70		
nnə	70		
ʔwə	70	13,169	107
ənow	68		
dən	68	13,374	110
əgow	66		
ædə	66		
its	66	13,639	114
əbaw	65		
ənn	65		
dər	65		
əin	65	13,899	118
nəð	64	13,963	119
aykə	61		
ɛybiy	61		
gat	61		
ist	61	14,207	123
aymə	60		
fowr	60		
nwə	60	14,507	128

plete computer analyses. In fact, the complete triphone tables show all phonemic words that are singlets, doublets and triplets. Tetraphones have been computed, but that analysis is only touched on here.

It is well known that the intelligibility of speech depends almost entirely on the presence of consonants. In our analysis of single phonemes, only a few phonemes showed any appreciable change over age levels; the analysis of diphones in Section 6 gave clear indication of changes in diphone distribution. We might expect triphones to reflect these changes even more. Tables 19A, 19B and 19C show, respectively, the first 15 triphones by rank by age level; a comparison of the relative ranks of grades 3 and 5 and adults with grade 1; and the number of triphones in common for the four levels. The major and obvious implications are 1) that the grades have more triphones in common with each other than with the adults (Table 19C); 2) /wəz/ increases its rank from first grade to adult while /wən/ drops from rank 1 (grades 1, 3, and 5) to rank 13 for adults; 3) /layk/ has rank 15 for grade 1 and grade 3 but rises to rank 3 (grade 5) and 4 (adult); 4) /θiŋ/ is not in the first 15 for grade 1 and grade 3,

B. Some examples of less frequent triphones. The number of different triphones at frequency f is shown in parentheses.

Triphone	frequency	Cumulative no. triphones	Cumulative no. *different* triphones
ænn	50 (10)	18,070	194
iyst			
ərg			
ænz			
ðəb	40 (13)	21,301	267
ənz			
ərð			
rəv			
əng	30 (15)	26,100	408
aygɛ			
bik			
gown			
əsiy	20 (49)	33,136	704
æmp			
ɛykə			
wowk			
owgz	10 (158)	44,541	1,552
ðɛm			

Table 18B Continued

Triphone	frequency	Cumulative no. triphones	Cumulative no. *different* triphones
aywow			
rfr			
ayir	5 (452)	54,131	3,024
bla			
iŋay			
ris			
ayhə	4 (602)	56,539	3,626
gəs			
lɛyh			
rks			
owti	3 (931)	59,332	4,557
ætə			
ʔayθ			
šap			
əbu	2 (1602)	62,536	6,159
rfow			
skow			
æsk			
ačf	1 (3717)	66,253	9,876
dyv			
pwiy			
sfiy			

has rank 11 for grade 3 and rank 1 for adults; 5) approximants and sibilants in combining form increase from grade 1 to adults. We note, finally, 6) that there is a strong tendency toward equalization in the use of the most frequent triphones. For example, the relative frequency of rank 1 triphones to rank 15 triphone is about 3 for grade 1, 2 for grade 3, and grade 5, and 1.7 for adults; the type-token ratio is somewhat greater for adults—.17 compared to .15, .15, and .13 for grade 1, grade 3, and grade 5, respectively.

There is an interesting observation to be made here on redundancy. We might expect that adult speech would be less redundant than children's speech, since the distribution of triphones is becoming more uniform in adult speech. Furthermore, that tendency should be enhanced by a greater use of the most frequent triphons (shown by the higher type-token ratio). Yet, the amount of redundancy measured as relative sequential constraint for pairs of phonemes is not sensibly different from first grade to adult. The paradox may be resolved by anticipating some remarks to come: it is quite likely that intra-word constraints are more important than inter-word

Table 19
A. Ranks and Frequencies of Triphones

Rank	First Grade f triphone		Third Grade f triphone		Fifth Grade f triphone		Adult f triphone	
1	321	wən	291	wən	355	wən	185	θiŋ
2	242	əðə	285	ʔəm	299	wəz	151	ðæʔ
3	241	ðən	239	wəz	294	ðər	150	wəz
4	212	ðɛn	234	ðər	248	layk	147	ðɛr
5	202	wəz	207	əðə	225	əðə	132	layk
6	183	tər	203	wɛn	218	ənow	125	ərs
7	179	æəm	194	ðɛn	213	yən	125	wər
8	168	wɛn	168	tər	199	wər	119	wɛl
9	163	stə	162	ðis	195	stə	115	jəs
10	152	taym	160	stə	193	wɛn	112	ənow
11	150	nðɛ	157	nðə	189	θiŋ	112	səm
12	128	nðə	154	ʔæn	172	ðɛn	112	vər
13	117	ænd	162	ənə	170	tər	110	wən
14	117	hɛv	140	dər	169	vər	110	yən
15	117	layk	137	layk	167	səm	109	hæv
$n$total	66,253		70,912		90,919		54,620	
$n$different	9,876		10,532		11,628		9,242	
Ratio $\left(\dfrac{n\text{different}}{n\text{total}}\right)$	.1491		.1485		.1278		.1692	

constraints. Thus a measure based on phoneme pairs will be insensitive to the positive and negative interaction terms. To the extent that these do not cancel each other out the pairwise measure will be in error (see Garner, 1962).

We are hardly surprised that /wən/, /ðɛn/, /səm/ and /tər/ sound very familiar, or that /zsk/ and əbu/ sound rather less familiar, or that /kəz/, /big/ and /əzə/ sound moderately familiar. Neither should we be surprised that when the letter transcriptions of these are *seen* their familiarity may change drastically, as with *tur, big,* and *cuz* (or kuz). These data will make it possible for us to equate auditory and visual stimuli for use in perceptual experiments, since there are both letter and phonemic transcriptions of the speech, as well as letter transcriptions of written texts.

As a last word we mention that one of the dangers of estimating "phoneme" redundancy from a phonemic transcription of written material while using what is probably too small a sample, is illustrated by the work of Hultzén, Allen, and Miron (20). They found transitional frequencies of phonemes transcribed from the text of written plays. The corpus consisted of 20,032 symbols, including juncture. They calculated the Markovian information up to blocks of length 4. In Table 13 we compare the relative sequential constraint reported by them with the values we found. The values they obtain are the largest estimates which we have seen reported in the literature. If one uses an exponential equation offered by them as fitting C_k for k = 1, 2, 3, and 4 (see Table 20) to extrapolate to C_5 and C_6, the redundancy estimate becomes unrealistically large. No doubt it is unfair to extrapolate from their equation, but it does make clear how rapidly redundancy appears to increase in their sample with k-gram length. The most convincing evidence of the paucity of their sample is contained in the fact that of the possible 79,507 3-phoneme states (43^3), only 3,083 of them occur, whereas in our data with even fewer possible states ($41^3 = 68,921$) the number occupied is 9,876, or more than three times as many. It is quite reasonable to assume that their

B. *Relative Ranks of Triphons in Third grade, Fifth grade, and Adult Speech Compared to First Grade Speech.*

Triphone	Grade 1	Grade 3	Grade 5	Adult
wən	1	1	1	13
əðə	2	5	5	*
əðr	3	4	3	*
ðɛn	4	7	12	*
wəz	5	3	2	3
tər	6	8	13	*
səm	7	*	15	11
wɛn	8	6	10	*
stə	9	10	9	*
taym	10	*	*	*
nðɛ	11	*	*	*
nðə	12	11	*	*
ænd	13	*	*	*
hær	14	*	*	15
layk	15	15	4	5
vrə	*	*	14	12
ðiŋ	*	*	11	1
yən	*	*	7	14

*did not occur in first 15.

C. *Triphones in Common Among 15 Most Frequent.*

	Grade 1	Grade 3	Grade 5	Adult
Grade 1	15	10	10	5
Grade 3		15	9	3
Grade 5			15	7
Adult				15

sample size was too small, and that the very high redundancy arises both from this fact and from the special character of the material. One-act plays simply do not have the structure of free speech, even under a "phonemic" transformation. We have discussed the matter of style and minimum sample size elsewhere (Jones and Carterette, 21) and merely reiterate that a minimum sample of about 6,000 words appears to be required for stability of redundancy estimates.

One important fact is clear from the comparison of the relative sequential constraint, as computed from sequential pairs of symbols separated by 0, 1, . . . , or k symbols, (Column 1), and as computed from k-grams. The latter measure C_k for $k \geq 3$ appears to be substantially larger. The reason is no doubt that internal constraints within k-grams cannot be assumed to have positive and negative interaction terms which cancel each other (see Garner, 1962, 213–46, especially), as has been implicitly assumed in the measures of C_k presented in tables earlier than 12. Neither does the measure of C_k based on pairs take into account interword constraints which at least begin to operate

Table 20

Relative sequential constraint, C_k as found by Hultzén, Allen and Miron (1964) from a 20,032 character phonemic transcription of written texts, and as found by us for the phonemic transcription of the free speech of first graders based on a sample of 66,253 phonemes. They report C_k computed with $H_{max}(1) = \log_2 43 = 5.43$, assuming equi-probable occurrences of any phoneme. Our data are shown computed for the base $H_{max}(1) = \log_2 41 = 5.36$ (the equi-probable assumption) as well as for $H_{max}(1) = 4.84$ (each phoneme weighted according to its estimated probability of occurring in the entire sample). C_k based on $H_{max}(1) = 5.36$ is of course the appropriate comparison value.

C_k	Phoneme pairs	$H_{max}(1)$ $= 4.84$	K-grams $H_{max}(1)$ $= 5.36$	$H^{*}_{max}(1)$ $= 5.43$
C_1	–	–	.10	.15
C_2	.19	.19	.19	.36
C_3	.26	.36	.43	.55
C_4	.28	.42	.53	.70
C_5	–	–	–	.88*
C_6	–	–	–	.92*

Values for C_5 and C_6 (indicated by asterisks) were extrapolated from the equation given by them as an adequate fit for $C_k(k = 1, 2, 3, 4)$.

* Hultzén *et al.*

in a k-gram analysis. The relative weights of these two factors is not easy to estimate. Garner states (1962, p. 240) that the "really important constraints in printed English are those which exist within words, and not constraints which operate across words." Either the situation is different for phonemic transcriptions of free speech, or the constraints within phonemic trigrams and tetragrams are considerable, and the positive interaction terms are greater than the negative. This latter alternative seems the more attractive and reasonable. The dynamic constraints of the speech production inherent in the movements of tongue, lips, jaw, and glottis, taken together with the great mean length of a phonemic word, incline us to believe that the important constraints in spoken English are to be found within the word.

Acknowledgments

1. The work reported in this paper was supported in large part by the Cooperative Research Program of the Office of Education U.S. Department of Health, Education and Welfare (Project No. 1877). Other sources of support were the National Science Foundation (Grant GE-6139), National Institute of Mental Health (MH-07809) and the Office of Naval Research (Nonr-233(58)).

2. Computing assistance was obtained from the Health Sciences Computing Facility, UCLA, sponsored by NIH grant FR-3.

3. We owe thanks to many people for their assistance in arranging for subjects and space, and especially to Mr. Kyle Esgate, Mr. William Haley, Mrs. Esther S. McGinnis, Dr. John D. McNeil, Mrs. Marjorie M. Rohrbough, and Mrs. Genie Swinney.

4. Thanks are due also to our psychology research assistants over the course of the project: Janis Stone, Dolores D. Kluppel, and S. Joyce Brotsky, and to our phoneticians: Elite Ohlshtain, Robert Chamberlin, Jane Chamberlin, and Herman Pevner. In addition, a number of people have spent many tedious hours transcribing tapes, punching IBM cards, typing tables, coding phonetic texts into Fortran symbols and proofing. To all of them we owe thanks for a job well done, but especially to Lori Bohlmann, Judith Hayward, Mary Ann Nakagawa, and Gudrun Ulman.

Language and Cognition
in the Young Child

Moshe Anisfeld

As evidence accumulates on the acquisition of language by children it becomes increasingly perplexing that young children use language with far greater sophistication than they display in dealing with concepts. How can this seeming anomaly in the cognitive development of children be explained? Dr. Anisfeld here reports experiments designed to probe this mystery. His answers bear directly on the understanding of the psycholinguistic nature of the reading process. Is the child really so advanced in his language development when he begins to learn to read? Does his conceptual ability really lag behind in development? Reading method and material should be vitally affected by the answers.

EDITOR

Language and Cognition
in the Young Child*

This paper is concerned with a disparity between descriptions of linguistic and of cognitive functioning found in the developmental literature. Investigators agree that the young child has mastered a complex and highly abstract system of rules underlying language behavior. In contrast, descriptions of his other cognitive capabilities leave the impression of a rather limited and primitive level of development. It is hoped that an experimental attempt to resolve this "cognitive lag" can contribute to the understanding of the level of mental development of the child whom we teach to read.

Related Literature

An analysis of the lawfulness of language behavior has frequently led observers to conclusions similar to that reached by Whorf (23, p. 258) when he said:

> . . . the higher mind deals in symbols that have no fixed reference to anything, but are like blank checks, to be filled in as required, that stand for "any value" of a given variable, like . . . the x, y, z of algebra.

Students of language who subscribed to the Watsonian behaviorist position (Watson, 23) were reluctant, in explaining language, to ascribe to the "higher mind" any characteristics of function not found in the "lower mind." They attempted to explain phenomena of grammar in terms of the specific words that make up utterances, thus avoiding the postulation of abstract categories of the sort referred to by Whorf. According to

* The research reported herein was performed pursuant to a contract with the U.S. Department of Health, Education and Welfare, Office of Education.

the strict behaviorist view, the construction of a sentence can be understood as a chain of associations where the nth word is determined by the $(n-1)$ word in the sequence. While it is true that associative processes play a role in the selection of words in speech, it is equally true that such processes have no hope of accounting for the phenomena of syntax. An expert speaker of English will perceive as grammatical the utterance "Colorless green ideas sleep furiously" even though its individual words are not likely to have been linked with each other in his past experience with the language (Chomsky, 8). Any given word can occur in immediate temporal contiguity with more than one other word, which directly leads to the conclusion that words "can have no intrinsic temporal 'valence' " (Lashley, 14). In speech, grammatical order "must therefore be imposed upon the motor elements by some organization other than direct associative connections between them" (Lashley, 14).

It is clear now that any theory which endeavours to explain the generative aspect of language, i.e., the speaker's creative ability to produce and understand novel sentences, cannot operate on the level of words, or other elementary units of speech, but must postulate abstract symbols or categories. The most elementary theories with serious claims of generative power are phrase structure grammars (Chomsky, 8). In these grammars, sentences are described in terms of a hierarchical system of superordinate and subordinate categories. Such a system for a small fraction of English sentences might have the form depicted in Figure 1. On the top of the structure of categories is the Sentence which branches out into a Noun Phrase and a Verb Phrase. The Noun Phrase in turn splits into an Article, an Adjective, and a Noun, and the Verb Phrase into a Verb and a Noun Phrase, and so on down to the word level. The defining criteria of these grammatical categories are by no means simple or immediately given in observed speech. Membership in the noun category, for instance, is not determined by commonality of sounds or by physical similarity of referents but

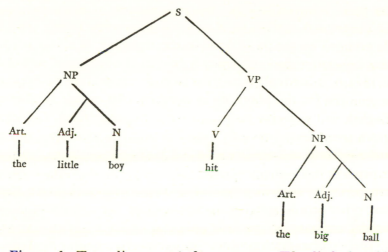

Figure 1. *Tree diagram of the sentence: The little boy hit the big ball.*

rather by such extraneous features as "having plural and possessive inflections," "being preceded by articles," and by other
privileges of occurrence (Francis, 12, pp. 237–44). Examining
the nature and complexity of these concepts, it must be acknowledged that anyone who has acquired grammatical categories has attained an intellectual achievement of the highest
order. This achievement, however, is not restricted to an intellectual elite, but must be considered the minimum granted any
person, including the young child, who is able to produce and
comprehend sentences he has not heard before. This is a minimum, because the transformational theory of language, origi-
nated by Chomsky (8, for a nontechnical exposition, see Postal,
20), increases the degree of abstractness of mental operations
required of the language user. In transformational theory,
grammatical categories have the status of scientific hypothetical
constructs; they are set up to facilitate the development of a
generative system of rules. Individual words are assigned membership in the categories by consideration of the totality of their
functions and behavior in the language, rather than solely on

the basis of environments of occurrence. The increased complexity introduced by transformational theory is not limited to linguistic categories; it is even more apparent in the transformational system of generative rules.

These rules go far beyond the statements of prescribed order of grammatical categories for different types of sentences ordinarily found in grammar books. It can readily be shown that the order of categories in a sentence is not directly relevant to its interpretation. Active and passive sentences manifest different orders but are interpreted similarly. On the other hand, two sentences may have the same order of grammatical categories and not necessarily be interpreted in parallel fashion. For instance, the phrases *the growling of lions* and *the raising of flowers* have an identical sequence of grammatical categories (article, gerund, preposition, noun) but in one the noun is the agent of the action described by the gerund (lions growl) and in the other it is the object (somebody raises flowers). To account for such divergent interpretations of seemingly similar utterances, transformational grammar postulates two levels of representation of sentences: a surface level which is close to, although not identical with, the sentence as it is heard or produced, and a deep level which contains an analysis of sentences into their component propositional content. For instance, the sentence *the little boy hit the big ball,* contains the propositions expressed by a) the boy was little (X), b) the ball was big (Y), and c) X hit Y. The combination of these three separate propositions into one sentence is accomplished by rules of transformation.

These few remarks about transformational theory should suffice to convey the level of mental operations entailed in language use. In view of the enormous intricacy and abstractness of the linguistic system revealed by transformational analysis, it is not surprising that workers in this framework have been tremendously impressed by the linguistic achievement of children. Lees (15, p. xvi), for instance, has stated:

Perhaps the most astounding aspect of human behavior . . . is the young child's ability to acquire in a short time, and with no special tuition, complete mastery of an immensely complex apparatus for constructing and understanding grammatical sentences.

Psychological work carried out in the spirit of uncovering children's generative rules of grammar (e.g., Braine, 2; Brown and Fraser, 5; Miller and Ervin, 18; Menyuk, 17) has generally supported the notion that the child's acquisition of language cannot be understood solely in terms of imitation and retention of utterances heard, for these processes could not account for the child's creative ability to use new but grammatically correct utterances. One has to assume that the child utilizes the linguistic data he receives from his speech community to abstract rules and regularities which in turn guide his productive use of language. One writer has been so fascinated by the child's mastery of rules as to assert that:

> . . . almost all the basic syntactic structures used by adults that we have thus far been able to describe are found in the grammar of children as young as 2 years 10 months (Menyuk, 17, p. 429).

The phenomenal achievements of the child in the linguistic sphere lead one to expect comparable achievements in other mental spheres. But the picture that emerges from descriptions of the child's cognitive capabilities is so primitive in comparison, that it seems hard to believe that the same child is being referred to in both cases. While the recent literature on child language is replete with positive statements relating to what the child can do, the literature describing child problem solving and concept formation is characterized by negative statements of what he cannot do. An insightful reviewer (Wallach, 22) of the work of Piaget and his collaborators reaches the conclusion that the cognitive development of the child is slow and far from the adult level even at the age of seven.

This conclusion can perhaps be best demonstrated by reference to the "conservation" experiments of the Geneva school. Conservation refers to a perception of invariance of object qualities in face of irrelevant transformations. The conservation studies revealed the difficulties children face in conserving quantity, weight, volume, length, area, number, and other properties. In a typical study of conservation of quantity, a child would be shown two equal-sized beakers filled with water to the same level. The water of one beaker would then be poured, in the sight of the child, into another, narrower or wider, container. In this situation the preschool child will usually say that the amount of water to drink in the new beaker is not equal to that in the one that remained filled.

A similar view of the crude level of intellectual development of the preschool child arises from Vigotsky's (20) reports of children's modes of categorizing. He found that in object-grouping tasks, young children tended to form complexes and pseudo-concepts rather than genuine analytic concepts. Overall similarity and momentary impressions played a greater role in their performance than commonalities of features. And yet the same child can form and manipulate the high-level analytic categories of language.

Another example of the unevenness in the child's cognitive functioning appears when his skills in the use of his natural language are compared with his behavior in experimental situactions involving language. While the preschool child uses language in a way that implies categorization of words with respect to part of speech and he can learn quite readily the class membership of new words (Brown, 3), he does not frequently employ these grammatical categories in free association tasks. When a child is presented with a stimulus word and asked to respond with the first other word that comes to his mind, he will characteristically produce a response that bears a sequential relation to the stimulus (e.g., nice-doll) in contrast to adults who frequently give responses that belong to the same grammatical category as the stimuli (Brown and Berko, 4; Ervin, 10).

The discrepancy between what the child can do and what he

actually does in the free association task points to the possibility that certain experimentally induced behaviors underestimate the child's capabilities. If all we knew about the child's language was based on his responses in free association tasks, we would have no reason to assume that he possessed grammatical categories. But since his normal use of natural language makes the postulation of such categories unavoidable, the reasons for failure to exhibit them in the free association task must be sought in the child's interpretation of the instructions or in the interfering effects of other factors. The general lesson to be gained from this is that when a child does not do something it is not always safe to infer that he cannot do it. The importance of distinguishing between observed performance and inferred mental competence was only recently brought to the fore (Chomsky, 9) with regard to the study of language, but it parallels the standard psychological distinction between performance and learning (e.g., Hilgard, 13, pp. 4–5). It thus appears that any experimental manipulation of the child's behavior that does not provide optimal conditions for the manifestation of the particular conceptual abilities searched for should be suspected of underestimating the child's cognitive competence.

This guideline leads one to question interpretations of the Piaget studies that deprive the child of the possession of the logical rule of conservation. In fact, a variation on the Geneva procedure (Bruner, 6) suggests an interpretation more favorable to the child. In the procedure reported by Bruner, the new beaker was covered from the child's view while he watched the pouring operation. When this design was employed preschool children rarely failed to state that the two beakers contained the same amount of water "because you just poured." But if, following this, the screen were removed, many five-year-old children would change their minds and insist that the two beakers could not contain the same amount of water because the water came to different levels. It thus appears that the child does have the relevant logical rules, but when their dictates conflict with the tendencies induced by momentary stimuli, the latter win out. Piaget (19) himself also believes that preschool children do possess the logical concept of invariance and attributes the observed nonconservation to the children's inability to reconcile the logical rule with the contradictory perceptual evidence. Only when the child can coordinate height and diameter and recognizes that an increase in one dimension compensates for a decrease in the other, will he be guided by the logic of invariance and ignore the seemingly contradictory appearance. Thus it is the child's difficulty in explaining the facts of appearance, rather than lack of logic, that is responsible for his nonconservation responses.

Vigotsky's studies can be interpreted in a similar fashion. In what Vigotsky called a chain complex the child puts together a green triangle with a blue triangle and then adds to it a circular blue block. This manner of grouping does not necessarily reflect an inability on the part of the child to group according to features abstracted from the whole, but may rather be due to his difficulty in staying under the control of a constant basis of classification in the face of varying constellations of stimuli. Thus, in the example mentioned, the child first classifies by shape (triangles together) and then switches to another attribute momentarily more prominent, but in both cases he uses abstracted features as bases for grouping.

More evidence can be adduced, especially from the work reported by Luria (16), to support the general proposition that, in guiding the child's behavior, ideational processes (rules, plans, sets, etc.) have to contend with heavy competition from immediate internal and external stimuli, which continually change and demand the child's attention and response.

Objectives for Research

Our general hypothesis then asserts that the behavior of the young child is governed more intensely by immediate sensory input than by ideational processes such as sets, plans, and rules. With the aid of this hypothesis, it is possible to grant the child the possession of the necessary competence for successful performance on such tasks as conservation and object grouping, and to attribute his failure to fully manifest this competence to the power of momentary stimuli.

Assuming this interpretation to be valid, the question arises whether the child's linguistic competence is subject to similar limitations. Could linguistic rules withstand interfering effects from immediate stimuli or would they also give in?

In order to answer this question, it is necessary to examine the realization of linguistic and other cognitive rules in a wide range of situations including some with minimal interference from environmental stimuli and some with more interference, and to observe how different rules react to the various situations. Such research would provide evidence relevant to our general hypothesis and yield suggestions for resolving the observed discrepancy between linguistic and cognitive development. This discrepancy can be resolved in one of two ways: a) by assuming that the discrepancy is only apparent and due to an underestimation of the level of cognitive development of young children and/or to an over-estimation of their linguistic development or, b) by granting that there is a real difference and providing a justification for it. Although we favor the first alternative as a working hypothesis, the latter can not be completely discounted. For if linguistic development turns out to be truly ahead of other cognitive functions, this could be explained by assuming either that language is relatively autogenous and not as dependent on environmental nourishment as other systems, or that a greater supply of environmental input is available for linguistic growth, since children are exposed to language for a large portion of their waking hours.

Let me now sketch briefly two experiments inspired by these considerations. These experiments do not answer the questions raised here, but I believe that they provide the kind of information about the child's mental capacities that is needed before such answers are attempted.

It was decided to start the program with an investigation of the concept of singularity-plurality, since tasks for studying both the linguistic aspect and the conceptual aspect of this dichotomy could be quite readily designed. Our interest lies in assessing whether preschool children have the concept of "one vs. more than one" and in the nature of their morphological rules for distinguishing between singular and plural nouns.

Our procedure for testing concept formation departed from the standard design used in such tasks. In standard concept formation experiments, the child is required to find out through trial and error what differences among the stimulus items were chosen by the experimenter as relevant for the particular task at hand. To put it crudely, the child has to guess what the experimenter has in mind. In contrast to this method, we tried to make it clear to the child what the relevant distinguishing feature was and then tested his ability to be guided by this feature in his responses to new instances.

The concept formation experiments, carried out by Eileen Studd for her honors thesis at McGill University, were designed to explore the validity of our theoretical and methodological approach. They were only preliminary in nature, and one experiment will suffice to convey the flavor of the method and results. Twenty-four kindergarten pupils, ranging in age from 5 years 3 months to 6 years 6 months, from an English-speaking public school in Montreal participated in the experiment. The task was to sort pictures of everyday-life objects, drawn on cards, according to the singularity-plurality dichotomy. There were twenty pairs of cards. One member of each pair was a singular item and the other a plural item. In ten pairs, to be referred to as the Non-Embedded stimuli, the singular card depicted a single object and the plural card two or more exemplars of the same object. For instance, in one pair the singular card depicted one tree and the plural card four trees, in another pair, one card showed a single car and the other two cars. Size of objects was varied so that within any pair the space occupied by the singular picture would sometimes be equal to or larger than that of the plural picture. This was done to avoid confounding number with mass. In the other ten pairs, to be referred to as the Embedded stimuli, plurality was represented by number of features in an object rather than by number of objects. Examples: a) a singular picture showed an ice-cream cone with one scoop of ice cream and its plural counterpart an ice-cream cone with two scoops, b) another pair contrasted a one-pane window with a 16-pane window, c) in a third pair the singular card depicted three rings with one stone each and the plural card three rings with two stones each. Thus, in the Embedded pictures the relevant and varying attribute was the number of multiple features rather than number of objects; the number of objects was the same for both the singular and the plural cards. Five of the Embedded pairs had a single object on both the singular and the plural cards and the other five pairs had more than one object on both cards.

By way of introducing the child to the task, the experimenter showed him a pair of cards and placed the singular card on one side of the table and the plural card on the other side. After several examples, the child was asked to take over. He was informed after each sorting whether his response was correct or not and the next pair was handed to him. The subject proceeded in this way through all twenty pairs, arranged in random order.

There was virtually no difference between the five one-object pairs and the five more-than-one object pairs. Both kinds of Embedded stimuli were therefore pooled for the comparison with the Non-Embedded stimuli. This comparison revealed that the mean number of correct responses for the Non-Embedded stimuli was 7.38 and for the Embedded stimuli 5.92. The t value (2.58) for the difference between these two means is significant beyond the .02 level. Classification by a feature constituting part of an object thus appears to be harder than by the object as a whole. Although this finding can perhaps bear alternative interpretations, it seems to be favorable to the stimulus-binding hypothesis. When a card depicts one object, the unity of the object seems to cause the child difficulty in classifying by the multiplicity of its features. Similarly, the presence of several objects on a card seems to impress plurality on the child and interferes with its classification as singular on the basis of the oneness of the feature. In other words, it is assumed that the total configuration of a familiar object competes with its classification on the basis of partial characteristics.

Results are also available concerning the linguistic aspects of singularity-plurality from studies conducted by Dick Tucker for his master's thesis, also at McGill. The standard rules of English provide three allomorphs for plurality: /s/ for words ending in unvoiced phonemes, /z/ for words ending in voiced phonemes, and /ɨz/ for words ending in sibilants and affricates, both voiced and unvoiced. Berko (1) studied these rules in preschool children by assigning a nonsense name to a singular animal drawing and asking the child to provide the plural form for two instances of the same referent. She found that while the percentage of errors did not exceed 32 for names requiring a /z/ ending, it went as high as 86 for those requiring /ɨz/. Tucker replicated Berko's production task and added to it a recognition task in the hope that the two together might reveal more about the child's competence than either one alone. (Actually, each child had either three production or three recognition tasks, but only one of each type will be discussed here.) In all, 36 kindergarten pupils from an English-speaking school in Montreal participated in the experiment. Their mean age was 5 years 11 months. Half of the Ss were tested on a production task and half on a recognition task. The production task followed Berko's procedure, in main outline. It employed twelve nonsense syllables of the CVC shape as names for animals. In half of the items, the experimenter assigned a name to a single animal and requested the child to name several animals, and in the other half of the items, the child was provided with the name for several animals and requested to name a single animal. In the recognition task, the child was shown twelve pictures, six depicting a single animal and six a plural number of animals. For each picture the child was asked to choose the best of two names suggested by the experimenter, one singular (e.g., Pesh) and the other plural (e.g., Peshes). The nonsense names for both the production and recognition tasks were so chosen that four required an /s/ for pluralization, four a /z/, and four a /ɨz/. The Ss had therefore an equal opportunity to err with each of the allomorphs on each task. The distribution of the errors they actually made on the average is as follows:

	/s/	/z/	/ɨz/	Total
Production	.61	.44	1.51	2.56
Recognition	.78	.34	.66	1.78

On each row, the values joined by lines differ from each other beyond the .01 level of confidence; the other comparisons are not significant. The total recognition score does not differ significantly from the total production score ($t = 1.29$), but, as can be seen in the table, the patterns of errors for the two tasks do differ. In production, /s/ and /z/ are easier than /ɨz/, but in recognition, /z/ is easier than the other two. The greater difficulty of /ɨz/ in production is in accord with Berko's findings and can readily be explained by the smaller frequency of this form in the child's everyday experience with English. The ease of /z/ in recognition, however, seems to reflect an aspect of the child's competence not expressible in production. English has very few words ending in /consonant + z/ which are not plurals. Also, /z/ is more frequently used to mark plurality than the other suffixes. It is suggested that in the recognition task, children drew on these characteristics of English and therefore performed better in the choice involving /z/ than in the other choices.

Summary

The literature on intellectual development appears to attribute to the child a high level of linguistic development and relatively low level of development in other cognitive spheres. Even the preschool child is credited with a very abstract and complex linguistic system which is not essentially different from that of the adult. Yet on such tasks as conservation and object grouping, he is thought to function at a considerably lower and qualitatively different level than the adult.

In an attempt to resolve this discrepancy, a hypothesis was advanced that the descriptions of language development are based on an analysis of the child's competence as it is reflected in optimal performance conditions, while the unfavorable descriptions of his cognitive development arise from experiments that place obstacles in the way of the actualization of his competence. The immediate stimuli the child has to deal with were hypothesized to constitute the major factor interfering with the child's manifestation of his competence. In general, it was postulated that immediate stimuli compete forcefully with ideational processes in guiding the child's behavior.

To explore the possibility of dealing experimentally with this problem, we conducted two experiments involving the singularity-plurality dichotomy. In the first experiment children had to sort objects according to this dichotomy. The children performed better on a task where singularity-plurality was expressed in terms of objects than in a task where it was expressed in terms of number of duplicate features embedded in an object. This finding suggested that the imposing presence of the object as a whole interferes with responses based on the characteristics of its parts.

Another experiment tested the pluralization rules of kindergarten pupils using nonsense CVC syllables as names for cartoon animals. It was found that in a production task where they were given either a singular name and requested to produce its plural counterpart or vice versa, the children made significantly more errors with names pluralized by addition of /ɨz/ than with names having /s/ and /z/ as plural suffixes. But in a recognition task where the task was to decide which of two names was singular and which was plural, Ss made fewer errors in choosing as plurals the names ending in /z/ than the names ending in /s/ or in /ɨz/. This was taken as an indication that the children abstracted the generalization that in English a noun ending in /consonant + z/ is much more likely to be plural than singular. This is so: a) because there are very few singular nouns having this ending, and b) because /z/ is the most common allomorph of plurality. There is no way children could reveal this knowledge in the production task. In this case therefore, recognition procedures cannot be considered as merely more sensitive tests of the same underlying competence as is measured by production procedures, but must be recognized as tapping different aspects of competence.

Spelling-to-Sound Patterns

Ruth H. Weir*
Richard L. Venezky
University of Wisconsin

Much has been written, under the general heading of phonics, on the relationships of English spellings to the sounds of the language as it is spoken. Much teaching of reading has been based on what these relationships are supposed to be. But the teaching is only as good as its base and in the case of phonics it has been a weak and shaky one. This paper is the report of a careful, scientific, linguistic study of spelling-to-sound patterns. It shows that these relationships are both more consistent and more complex than they were thought to be.

Editor

* Ruth H. Weir's untimely death came just a few months after the completion of this manuscript.

English Orthography—
More Reason Than Rhyme*

The introduction and ordering of vocabulary for the teaching of reading is controlled primarily by the spelling-to-sound regularities, or lack of such regularities, in common English words. Reading programs, whether based upon phonemic or whole word strategies, generally present words with highly regular spelling-to-sound correspondences first, saving the so-called irregular forms for later lessons. The most common criterion for forming the regular-irregular dichotomy is the direct spelling-to-sound correspondence. That is, when a letter or letter string in a word has its most common pronunciation, then it (the letter or letter string) is classed as regular. Otherwise, it is irregular. Exceptions to this procedure are made occasionally for environment, as for example, in the rules for pronouncing the letter *c* or for the vowel spellings before a single consonant plus final *e*, but seldom for any other modifying factor.

While schemes based upon such definitions of regular and irregular may be the best available processes for teaching reading, the question still remains whether or not, through a thorough analysis of English spelling-to-sound correspondences, better techniques can be developed. The purpose of this paper is to present some of the results of a two-year investigation of English orthography and its relationship to sound, with the hope that these results will lead to the development of a linguistically sound basis for the initial teaching of reading. Major emphasis will be placed upon the type of patterning which exists in the current orthography, that is, upon the factors which can be utilized to predict sound from spelling. The first object here is to show that even if the direct spelling-to-sound view is assumed, more types of relationships must be

* The work reported here was supported by the U.S. Office of Education under Projects S-039 and 2584.

considered than the simple regular-irregular classes that bisect the traditional approach to this subject. Furthermore, it will be shown that the concepts of regular and irregular are far more complex than is generally assumed, and, indeed, require quite sophisticated notions for adequate definition. For the present, however, the terms *regular* and *irregular* will be used in a loose sense, meaning simply, high frequency and low frequency, without careful enumeration of what objects are to be counted to arrive at such statistics.

The research reported here began with a computer-aided tabulation of the grapheme-phoneme correspondences in the most common 20,000 English words.[1] It proceeded over the past two years with an analysis of these correspondences and the words in which they occurred, to determine the types of relationships which are reflected in the orthography. Although the first goal of this work is to obtain a structural description of the correspondence between spelling and sound, the ultimate goals are to develop a theoretical model for this structure, and then to apply these results to the improvement of reading instruction.

This research at present deals only with the one-way mapping of spelling into sound. While many of the results apply also to mappings in the other direction, that is, to spelling, no consideration of this area will be given here. Words in the 20,000 word corpus were selected on the basis of the frequency counts given in the *Thorndike-Century Senior Dictionary*, which in turn were based upon the word counts in running text accumulated through the Thorndike-Lorge studies. Proper nouns, abbreviations, and contractions have been omitted for the present study. Pronunciations are drawn chiefly from John S. Kenyon and Thomas Knott, *A Pronouncing Dictionary of American English*, with modifications based upon current Dialect Atlas results.[2]

Phonological Patterns

Phonological patterns have been classed rather arbitrarily as either regular phonemic, irregular phonemic, or phonotactical.

Unless otherwise stated, phonological correspondences apply
to single morpheme words. "Word" in this discussion will be
defined graphemically, that is, as anything that commonly occurs between blank spaces in print. While the complete stock
of graphemes includes the punctuation marks, letters, and possibly a few more general items like *capital,* only the letters will
be intended here through the use of the term *grapheme.* (While
grapheme may appear to be a needless technical obfuscation of
letter, it does have structural implications which *letter* lacks.)

In the regular phonemic class are, first: invariant patterns,
based upon those graphemes which have a single, high frequency pronunciation regardless of the environment in which
they occur. *v,* for example, is always pronounced /v/, regardless
of where it occurs. *f,* except for the word *of* and its compounds
is also invariant, *k, m, n, y* (as a consonant spelling), and *z*
are nearly invariant. (There is a general process for handling
geminated consonants like *-mm-* as in *dimmer* and *lemma.*
These may be spelling problems, but they are regular from a
reading standpoint.) Many of the so-called irregular pronunciations of these graphemes become considerably less aberrant
when morphemic and graphotactical patterns are considered.
For example, the final *n* in *hymn* is an exception to *n*'s invariance. But this does not mean that the *n* here is irregular. Its
chief function is to preserve a morphemic pattern, as revealed
in the word *hymnal* where the *n* is pronounced.

Whether to pronounce or not pronounce *n* in these cases can
be based upon phonotactical processes. If the *n* is pronounceable, pronounce it; otherwise, don't. In the meantime, the
graphemic shape of the stem *hymn* is preserved through the
retention of the *n,* regardless of its phonemic value. (Patterns
similar to this one will be discussed in a later section of this
paper.)

In the second subdivision of the regular phonemic class are
variant correspondences—correspondences that are still regular,
but that relate the same spelling to two or more pronunciations, depending upon regular graphemic, phonological, or
grammatical features. The letter *c,* as an example, corresponds

to /s/ when it occures before *e, i, y* plus a consonant or juncture as in *cent, city,* and *cycle;* in most other positions it corresponds to /k/.* The spelling *k* corresponds to zero in initial position before *n,* e.g., *knee, know, knife.* In all other positions, *k* corresponds to /k/. This is graphemic conditioning from the letter-sound standpoint. Yet, just as with the *n* in *hymn,* the silent initial *k* is explained more adequately by phonotactical rules. The cluster /kn/ does not occur at the beginning of a syllable in English; where such prohibited consonant clusters would otherwise occur in initial position, the first consonant is dropped. Compare *knee, gnat, pneumonia, psychology.* Or, as in the previous case, if it's pronounceable, pronounce it; otherwise, don't.

Position alone may determine the correspondence of a spelling unit. For example, initial *gh* always corresponds to /g/: *ghost, gherkin, ghoul* (but never to /f/ as assumed in the spelling reform creation *ghoti*), but medial and final *gh* have pronunciations besides /g/. Stress may also be a conditioning factor for regular, variant correspondences. The most prominent role that stress plays in spelling-to-sound correspondences is in the pronunciation of unstressed vowels. While the reduction of unstressed vowels to a neutral vowel (called *schwa*) is not entirely regular, it can still be predicted in some cases. The patterns, however, are highly complex and are beyond the scope of this paper. Another example of stress conditioning occurs in the correspondences for intervocalic *x,* which generally corresponds either to /ks/ or /gz/, depending upon the position of the main word stress. If the main stress is on the vowel preceding *x,* the pronunciation is /ks/ as in *axiom* and *exercise.* Otherwise, the pronunciation is /gz/ (cf. *examine, exist*). While this rule is similar to Verner's Law for the voicing of the Germanic voiceless spirants, it is not a case of pure phonological conditioning. Words like *accede* and *accept* have the identical phonetic environments for /gz/, yet have /ks/.

* In *social, ocean,* etc., where *c* is followed by *i* or *e* plus another vowel, the sibilant /s/ is palatalized by the following vowel to /š/.

Stress is also important in the palatalization of [sy, zy, ty, dy] to [š, ž, č, ǰ]. This form of palatalization occurs when [sj, zj, tj, dj] are followed by an unstressed vowel, as in *social, treasure, bastion,* and *cordial.* Compare stress placement and palatalization in the following pairs: *credulous:credulity, cynosure:pursuit, capitulate:institute.* The retention or deletion of medial /h/ in most cases also depends upon the position of the main word stress. Compare *prohibit:prohibition, vehicular:vehicle.* In each pair, the first member, which has the stress on the vowel following *h,* has a fully pronounced *h,* while the second member, with an unstressed vowel after *h,* has no /h/. This rule also holds for *vehement, shepherd, philharmonic, annihilate, rehabilitate,* and *nihilism,* all of which generally have no /h/. (Some forms like these may have /h/ occasionally preserved by over-correct pronunciations.)

The other major subdivision of phonological correspondences is the *irregular class.* This class, though accounting for only a small portion of the total phonological category, receives the greatest attention in educational and popular writings on the general subject of orthography. There are two and possibly three seemingly natural categories for this class. The first contains frequent spellings that have various pronunciations which can only be predicted by knowing the whole word. Most occurrences of the digraph *ch* fit into this class. While the most common pronunciation of *ch* in high frequency words is /č/, there is no procedure for predicting in an unfamiliar word whether the pronunciation is /č/, /k/, or /š/, other than in the few cases where a French or Greek origin is evident from other graphemic characteristics of the word.*

The second subdivision of the irregular class is composed of such nonce forms as *debt, doubt, thyme* and *island.* As a general

---

* It is difficult to decide what would be a correct generalization about the pronunciation of *ch.* Should a child be expected to pronounce all unfamiliar occurrences of *ch* as /č/? Should he pronounce most of them as /č/, but a few as /š/ and /k/, or should he just be confused and refuse to respond?

description of this class, "rare-irregularities" should suffice. Number of tokens is what distinguishes this subdivision from the first one mentioned. The *b*'s in *debt* and *doubt,* in spite of their rare-irregularity label, are not without some redeeming social or linguistic merit, in that they preserve a morphemic identity to the stems in *debit* and *indubitable.*

Irregular spelling-to-sound correspondences, while classed together here, also show important differences. *Arcing* and *cello,* for example, both have irregular correspondences for *c,* yet there is an important distinction between these two irregularities. *Arc,* from which *arcing* is derived, has the expected correspondence for *c.* When suffixes beginning with *e, i, y* are added to words ending in *c,* a *k* is normally inserted after the *c,* as in *picnicking* (cf. *picnic*) and *trafficked* (cf. *traffic*). The irregularity in *arcing,* therefore, is in the irregular formation of the derivative. *Cello,* on the other hand, contains a rare correspondence for *c,* paralleled only by a few other Italian borrowings.

Morphemic and Morphophonemic Patterns

The most commonly mentioned morphemic elements in the orthography are the final -(*e*)*s* used as, among other functions, the regular noun plural marker, and the regular past tense marker -(*e*)*d.* Both of these graphemic forms represent single morphemes. There are simple phonotactic rules in English for predicting their pronunciations, once their morphemic identity is ascertained. Without this information, there is little regularity in their behavior.

The final consonant clusters in the words *paradigm, damn,* and *bomb,* can be viewed as morphophonemic spellings. In a pure and direct spelling-to-sound analysis, one is forced to the conclusion that the *g* in *paradigm,* the *n* in *damn* and the final *b* in *bomb* are functionless graphemes. When viewed, though, from a morphophonemic standpoint, the pairs *paradigm:paradigmatic, damn:damnation, bomb:bombard* reveal a regular morphophonemic alternation that is preserved in the orthography. This consonant pattern is quite common in English. Besides the three examples given, there are, for example, *malign:malignant, design:designate, sign:signify, autumn:autumnal, condemn:condemnation, hymn:hymnal, column:columnal.* Without the retention of the full consonant cluster in final position, the identity of the common morphemic element in such pairs would be obscured on the graphemic level.

Another fairly regular pattern is a voiced-voiceless morphophonemic alternation as is reflected in *house:houses, north: northern, south:southern, worth:worthy.*

Overall Description

It should be evident from the foregoing material that attempts to describe spelling-to-sound correspondences must account for phonemic, morphemic, and morphophonemic patterns. An adequate description must also handle irregularities, that is, it must show on what level the irregularity occurs. For example, given the irregular forms *arcing* and *facade,* it is necessary to distinguish the different types of irregularity which are reflected in the pronunciations of the grapheme /c/ in these words. The irregularity in *arcing* enters with the irregular formation of the graphemic allomorph *arc-* before a suffix beginning with *i.* This is an exception to a general orthographic rule that requires a *k* to be inserted in this environment, as in *trafficking. Facade* is irregular in the basic graphemic word—*c* before *a* is pronounced /s/ instead of the usual /k/. This is an exception to a basic environmentally conditioned graphemephoneme correspondence.

From this research on spelling-to-sound correspondences, we have found that the best descriptive approach to the spelling-to-sound relationship is the morphophonemic approach; that is, to assume that English spelling is basically a morphophonemic system. We are not saying that English spelling *is* a morphophonemic system—it should be evident from the foregoing that English spelling is a complex of graphemic, morphemic, and phonemic patterns with sound playing the dominant role—

but rather, that if we view this system as a morphophonemic one, more regularity will emerge than will under any other view.

Using this approach, a model has been constructed for describing spelling-to-sound relationships in terms of spelling units, morphophonemic units, and phonemic units. Rules for mapping from the spelling level to the morphophonemic level, and then from the morphophonemic level to the phonemic have been formulated for the majority of the correspondences found in the initial 20,000 word corpus. Working from this model, we have found that many of the traditional ideas about spelling units are in violation of the basic patterning of the system.[3] Some of the results of our work on spelling units is contained in the next section.

Selection of Spelling Units

The selection of spelling units is determined chiefly by the spelling-to-morphophoneme rules. For the most part, these choices are dictated by the morphophonemic forms which are derived from the spelling units in question. Thus, *ch* is treated as a single unit because the morphophonemes [č], [k], and [š] which are derived from it, are single units. For the same reason *ai, oi,* and *ow* are treated as single units as are *gh, ph, sh, th* and various other clusters, including *ck, dg,* and *tch.* All of these unit clusters thus far agree with the traditional divisions made by orthographers. Where the system presented here deviates from tradition is in the treatment of such grapheme clusters as *qu, ng, rh,* and the geminate consonants.

While *q* occurs almost invariably in the combination *qu,* there is no reason to treat this cluster as a unit. If we did so, then we should for the same reason treat final *-ve* as a cluster since *v* does not occur in word-final position except in rare borrowings. And there is no reason to stop here. *gu* could also be taken as a cluster in *guest* and *guess* since the *u* functions as a buffer between *g* and *e.*

Most of these clusters demonstrate facts about English

graphotactics only and our purist instincts require that such facts be placed in their proper place. To include *qu* as a single unit would be inconsistent with the general form of the spelling-to-sound model which has been adopted here. Invariably *q* is mapped into /k/, and *u*, when preceded by *q*, is mapped into /w/ with some exceptions. Graphotactical rules are treated independently of the mapping rules since the majority of them account for the various spellings of the same morpheme and have no place in the mapping rules. To write a single rule for *qu* would, therefore, be inconsistent with the model and uneconomical. This argument also applies to *-ve* and *gu* where the *e* and the *u* are properly parts of the environments of *v* and *g* and not components of unit forms.

Traditionally, *ng* has been treated as a unit cluster, in word-final position, representing the phoneme /ŋ/.

Consider the adjective *long*. Under the traditional view the positive form has the mapping $l \rightarrow /l/$, $o \rightarrow /ɔ/$, $ng \rightarrow /ŋ/$. But the comparative and superlative forms require that *ng* be split to account for both /ŋ/ and /g/: /lɔ́ŋ gə r/, /lɔ́ŋ gɪ st/. In the parallel cluster *mb* as in *bomb*, however, the traditional view considers *b* as a silent grapheme which comes to life in *bombard* because of the syllable division.

"*b* is usually silent after *m* in the same syllable, as in *climb, thumb*, etc." *Webster's New Collegiate Dictionary*, p. XI.

While the syllable divison criterion is meaningless on the graphemic level in forms like *bombing*, the silent grapheme approach, nevertheless, is sound and should be extended to *ng*.

By treating *ng* as two units one gains not only consistency but generality. The rule that transforms /n/ before the velar stops /g/ and /k/ to /ŋ/ that must be written for words like *ankle* and *congress* can now be applied to *long* as well as *sing* and to the other forms which end in *ng*. The initial morphophonemic forms become /lɔŋ g/, /sɪ ŋ g/, etc., and a single rule for dropping the final /g/ except before the regular comparative and superlative endings accounts for the final phonemic forms.

As a final note, we consider it crucial to distinguish between spelling units that function purely as *markers* and those that are *relational*. A marker serves solely to indicate the correspondences of other graphemes—it has no proper morphophonemic correspondence itself, although for systemic purposes it can be mapped into zero. The final *e*'s in *have, mate,* and *chance* are markers, although the marking-functions they perform are distinct. The *e* in *have* preserves a graphotactic pattern since *v* is not allowed in final position in English words. In *mate,* the *e* marks the complex pronunciation of *a* (*a* → /e/ as opposed to *a* → /æ/ as in *mat*), and in *chance* the *e* marks the correspondence *c* → /s/ as opposed to *c* → /k/.

In *rage* the terminal *e* serves two marking functions: *a*—/e/ (rather than *a*—/æ/ as in *ran*) and *g*—/ǰ/ (rather than the *g*—/g/ as in *rag*). To treat the vowel spelling in *rage* and in similar words as *a . . . e,* as is commonly done by both linguists and educators, is to create inconsistencies and confusions.[4] *a* is the vowel spelling. *e* is part of the environment, just as is the *g* in *rage,* the *nn* plus the following *a* in *annals,* and the *g* plus juncture in *rag*. The vowel spelling *a* has two major pronunciations in stressed positions: /æ/ and /e/. Both are marked by distinct environments of which the most important elements are the consonants and vowels that immediately follow *a,* or a suffix if it occurs, as in *sanity* (compare *sane*).

What must be realized is that the vowel spellings in *rate* and *anal* (first syllable) are the same, viz. *a,* and not two different spellings, *a* and *a . . . e*. Environments differentiate the pronunciations, and in all cases these environments are more complex than the presence or absence of final, silent *e*. Compare, for instance, the following pairs: *axe:ate, chance:bathe*. One *a* spelling in each pair is pronounced /æ/ and one is pronounced /e/, yet all words have the ill-posited unit *a . . . e*. Furthermore, both words in the first pair have one consonant *letter* between the *a* and the *e,* and both words in the second pair have two. Therefore, neither the presence of the final *e* nor the number of consonants between the *a* and the *e* is a reliable indicator of the pronunciation of *a*.

The rule that applies here requires a knowledge of the distinction between functionally simple and functionally complex consonant units.* The complex units either correspond to two different consonants, like *x* and *wh,* or function as geminates, like *ck, dg,* and *tch.* All other units are simple units, including *th, ch, sh, gh,* etc. A single vowel spelling (*a, e, i, o, u, y*), followed by a functionally simple consonant unit (regardless of the number of letters the unit contains), and then another vowel spelling, corresponds to its free (long) pronunciation. Otherwise, it has its checked (short) pronunciation.

To state the rule as a *vowel* plus *consonant* plus final *e* is misleading, in that the number of consonants between the *a* and the *e* does not matter; what is important is whether or not *a* is separated from a following vowel spelling, any vowel spelling, silent or not, by a functionally simple consonant unit. Therefore, the isolation of *a . . e, e . . e,* etc. as separate spelling units is meaningless as a complete device for indicating pronunciation. In addition, it is misleading in that the final *e* in words like *chance* does not mark the vowel pronunciation, but rather the final consonant pronunciation. And in words like *race* and *rage* it marks both a vowel and a consonant pronunciation. That is why the concept of markers is important for an understanding of how English orthography functions, and the a . . e business confuses the issue by combining a marker with the

---

* Exceptions to this rule—and there are more than a few—result chiefly from prohibitions against doubling certain consonant units (e.g., *v* and *th,* as in *river* and *mother*) or from borrowings from the Romance languages. The doubling of a final consonant before a suffix beginning with a vowel is in compliance with this rule. Furthermore, three digraphs were introduced into late Middle English orthography to replace geminate consonants that the scribes and orthoepist felt should not or could not be doubled. These are *ck, dg,* and *tch.* No corresponding units have evolved for *th* and *sh,* thus there is no way to mark the pronunciation of a single vowel spelling which occurs before these units.

unit it sometimes marks, without reference to the other marking features of the vowel environment.

Numerous markers are employed in the current orthography, and for a proper understanding of spelling-to-sound correspondences, they must be distinguished from those units that are primarily relational—that is, those units which have proper morphophonemic correspondences. Relational units are those units that appear as the first elements on the left-hand side of spelling-to-morphophoneme rules. Some relational units, like the *i* in *city* and *u* in *argue* perform marking functions, but since their primary function is relational, they are classed as relational units.

Conclusions and Implications

The results presented in this paper contain a number of implications for the teaching of reading. We hope to have demonstrated above all that simple grapheme-to-phoneme correspondences are not only unproductive for the prediction of sound from spelling, but also are in conflict with the underlying system of the orthography. If the function of the teaching of reading is to establish productive habits which relate to the underlying patterns of the orthography rather than to impart instruction on statistical correlations, then both morphology and syntax must be considered in the development of reading materials. This should not be constructed as a suggestion to teach morphology and syntax in the first three of four grades where reading is normally taught, but rather as a recommendation for the selection and arrangement of words to be used in the design of teaching materials. It has been shown that the child entering the primary grades has a good command of the basic morphological and syntactic patterns of his native language.[5] To teach, therefore, the pronunciations of *hen, cat, match,* and also *hens, cats, matches* as whole units is superfluous; the child has already learned the correct plural allomorph to be used with each stem. What he has to learn, however, is the graphemic shapes of the noun plural marker so that he does not confuse such pairs as *hens* and *hence* in reading.

Some work still remains to be done before the ideas presented in this paper can be adapted to the teaching of reading. Some general notions, however, can be advanced at present. The most important one is that the major emphasis in teaching the relationship between spelling and sound should center on the spelling-to-morphophoneme patterns. These represent totally new habits which must be obtained in order to read; the morphemic and syntactic patterns are, in general, already part of the child's language habits. The spelling-to-morphophoneme patterns should not be viewed as rules to teach as such, but rather as indicators of regularly and irregularly spelled words, that is, of words which have high transfer value and words which have low or negative transfer value for reading or other words. Obviously, words that are included in rules (e.g., *ee* (been) → [ɪ]) have low transfer value because they contain either exceptions to general patterns or rare and mostly unproductive correspondences.

The traditional view of spelling recognizes only one level of graphemic units, namely, the 26 letters of the alphabet, which are combined in various ways to correspond to phonemes. In the research reported here it has been found that among the many distinctions built into the orthography, one of the most important is that between *relational units* and *markers*. We feel that these distinctions are important for the teaching of reading and should be considered in the design of reading materials. Markers are an integral part of the English orthography; they are used specifically to point out the correspondences of other spelling units and do not, themselves, correspond to sounds. To neglect this distinction is to neglect much of the patterning in the spelling-to-sound relationship. In short, we suggest that the entire graphemic basis of spelling, down to even the term *grapheme,* be reconsidered in light of the results presented here.

An Instrument for the Syntactical Analysis of Children's Compositions

Eldonna L. Evertts
University of Illinois

Writing and reading are highly interrelated processes. Dr. Evertts describes a unique approach, based on linguistics, to the study of children's written compositions. The instrument and techniques she discusses may be applicable to the study of a wide range of language phenomena.

EDITOR

An Instrument for the Syntactical Analysis
of Children's Compositions

Introduction

Scholars and educators who attempt to analyze the status of composition at the elementary level, indeed at all levels, and to report on the theoretical and practical basis for composing find all too often a scarcity of quality materials related to composition at this level. Although all of us who work with children have definite ideas, theories, insights, or mere hunches concerning the nature of composition, we fail to validate our assumptions by research and by the utilization of newer methods of investigation. Teachers especially must know more about how children learn to write, in what stages, and under what legitimate pressures. They must be aware of more than a single method of evaluating the completed compositions of their pupils.

Though a considerable number of studies have investigated the writing abilities of children, little has been done with written compositions of young children. Nothing analogous to the work of Piaget and Inhelder[1] has been tried with children's compositions. But fortunately at the present time there is, throughout the nation, among both teachers of English and scholars in the field, an interest in the composing process and in a desire to improve instruction in this field.

Two excellent studies concerning the development of language by children, *The Language of Elementary School Children: Its Relationship to the Language of Reading Textbooks and the Quality of Reading of Selected Children* by Dr. Ruth Strickland[2] and *The Language of Elementary School Children*[3] and *Problems in Oral English* by Walter Loban[4] have recently appeared. These studies utilize the newer linguistic research instruments. Similar studies describing the syntax and content of children's written language have been lacking.

Psycholinguistics, which presents new approaches to the study of language and methods of inquiry, holds promise for the identification of objective methods of analysis of written composition for both young writers and recognized authors. This paper suggests one research technique and method of analysis of language which might be pursued and explored further.

This scheme of analysis, an exploration of the use of an objective measure to describe children's use of language in written communication, was funded by a grant of nearly $65,000 from the Louis W. and Maud Hill Family Foundation of Saint Paul, Minnesota, with support from the University of Nebraska. Initial support for this investigation was given in part by the Nebraska Curriculum Development Center (United States Office of Education, Project English) directed by Paul Olson.

The writer designed this *instrument* as part of the larger study, *A Longitudinal Study of the Syntax and Content of Children's Compositions (Grades 2–6)*. Valuable assistance was given by Dudley Bailey, Vance Hansen, Albert Marckwardt, and Donald Nemanich. During the period of development, this *instrument* was revised several times. The children's writing collected as part of this study contributed to the revision process. Since it is based upon an analysis of a given corpus of pupil writing, only those features of language which children actually used, even rarely, were included in the revised draft presented here. Examples of these uses of language are given in the *instrument* to illustrate the meaning of each symbol used in the scheme of analysis.

The scheme includes a description and identification of fixed slots and movable elements which serve as complete subjects, verbs, objects, complements, and other fixed and movable structures on Level I. Since many of these elements or structures contain two or more words, they can also be analyzed on Level II thus giving a description and identification of what is contained within a given slot. Wherever phrases and clauses are nested within one another, the resulting description may contain several levels of analysis, i.e., Levels II, III, etc.

A close examination of the *instrument* will reveal that verb-headed structures are not treated as completely as noun-headed structures, since it was believed that a more detailed study of children's use of this structure needed to be made from a corpus of pupil writing. At the present time verbal negation is considered as part of the verb.

One who uses the *instrument* looks closely during the process of analysis at the sentence structure. He attempts to operate independent of semantics; nevertheless he is working with the child's piece of writing in its entirety. Thus ambiguous sentences are capable of being analyzed with this *instrument*. No distinction is made between surface and deep grammar.

The *instrument* concludes with an analysis of sample sentences having more than a single level of structure and which illustrates how the scheme can be applied.

An Instrument for the Syntactical Analysis of Children's Compositions

LEVEL I

0. Overview of the instrument's structure: two levels
    0.1 Level I
        0.1.1 Adapted from Strickland, Ruth G. *The Language of Elementary School Children: Its Relationship to the Language of Reading Textbooks and the Quality of Reading of Selected Children;* Bloomington, Indiana, *Bulletin of the School of Education,* Indiana University, 1962.
        0.1.2 Purpose: Level I is a description and identification of fixed slots and movable elements which serve as complete subjects, verbs, objects, complements, and other fixed and movable structures.
        0.1.3 Identification of a sentence: Many of the students have not mastered the conventions of English punctuation; therefore the researcher must use a uniform system of division to identify what

is to be considered a sentence. Criteria similar to those of Hunt and Loban are used.[5] The punctuation of pupils is followed whenever possible; however, each independent clause is considered a separate sentence. Compound sentences are divided into two or more communication units for the purpose of analysis. Each subordinate clause is joined to the independent clause which seems most closely related to it.

0.1.4 Example of elements considered at Level I:

	Once	my big brother Tom and I	had seen
Level I	movable element	complete subject	complete verb

a goat that wanted to eat everything in the world.
complete object

0.2 **Level II**

0.2.1 Purpose: Level II is a description and identification of the individual grammatical items which serve as fillers in sentence level slots whenever the slot on Level I consists of more than a single element. It will be necessary to have more than two levels of analysis when syntactic structures consisting of phrases and clauses are nested within one another. These additional levels will be identified as Levels III, IV, etc.

0.2.2 Analysis to indicate further levels of subordination

Example:

	Once	my big brother Tom and I	had seen
Level I	movable element	complete subject	complete verb
Level II		poss. pron. adj. noun appos. connective pron.	

a goat that wanted to eat everything in the world.
complete object

Level I

Level	deter-head				
II	miner noun clause				
Level					
III		subject	verb	object	
Level				head	
IV			pronoun	prep. phr.	
Level					deter- head
V					prep. miner noun

1.0 Description of items for analysis at Level I, including notational devices and examples.

1.0.0 Notational device: W

Definition: a question word occurring in the initial position in an interrogative sentence.

Examples:

Why did the children put beans in their ears?
W

How did the children get the dog on the roof?
W

1.0.1 Notational device: W / 1

Definition: A question word which occurs in the initial position in an interrogative sentence and which also functions as subject.

Examples:

Who tied the cans to the tail of the dog?
W
1

What is the matter here?
W
1

1.0.2 Notational device: W / 2

Definition: The verb or part of verb shifted to the position in front of the subject in an interrogative sentence.

Examples:

Is John here yet?

$$\frac{W}{2}$$

Did John go to play baseball?

$$\frac{W}{2}$$

1.0.3 Notational device: $\dfrac{W}{3t}$

Definition: A question word which occurs in the initial position in an interrogative sentence and also functions as the object of the prepositional phrase transform of the indirect object.

Examples: Who did John send the flowers to? [child's
$$\frac{W}{3t}$$
own words]

Who did she give the money to?
$$\frac{W}{3t}$$

1.0.4 Notational device: $\dfrac{W}{4}$

Definition: A question word which occurs in the initial position in an interrogative sentence and which also functions as direct object.

Example: What do you want?
$$\frac{W}{4}$$

1.0.5 Notational device: $\dfrac{W}{5}$

Definition: A question word which occurs in the initial position in an interrogative sentence and which also functions as predicate complement.

Examples: What were the results of the investigation?
$$\frac{W}{5}$$

Who were the victims of the attack?
$$\frac{W}{5}$$

1.1   Notational device: 1
Definition: The subject slot of a sentence, the filler of which may be a word, a phrase, a clause, or a combination of these.

Examples: $\underline{\text{John}}$ shot my dog.
$$1$$

$\underline{\text{John}}$ is a very good boy.
$$1$$

$\underline{\text{Mr. Brown and Mr. Jones}}$ live near me.
$$1$$

$\underline{\text{That this dog could sing}}$ was an unusual fact.
$$1$$

$\underline{\text{Mr. Brown, who delivers mail on our block,}}$ is kind to
$$1$$
children.

$\underline{\text{My boy Max}}$ is a mouse too.
$$1$$

$\underline{\text{You}}$ tell him to stop that.
$$1$$

1.1.1 Notational device: (1)
Definition: The standard absence of the subject slot is the imperative sentence. (Should a filler for the subject slot be present in an imperative sentence, 1 would be used to make it, as in the last example above.)

Example: $\underline{\hspace{2cm}}$ Help me to do this.
$$(1)$$

1.1.2 Notational device: 1s
Definition: In discontinuous subjects, the part of the subject which contains the continuation or supplement.

Examples: $\underline{\text{They}}$ were $\underline{\text{all}}$ going home.
$$1 \qquad 1s$$

We were both very happy.
$$\overline{1}\qquad\overline{1s}$$

1.1.3 Notational device: T-1

Definition: Subject position filled by expletive "there."

Examples: Once there were three dogs.
$$\overline{\text{T-1}}$$

Actually there was no choice in the matter.
$$\overline{\text{T-1}}$$

1.1.4 Notational device: T-2

Definition: Subject position filled by expletive "it."

Examples: It was nice that she offered to help.
$$\overline{\text{T-2}}$$

1.1.5 Notational device: 1p4

Definition: The "by" prepositional phrase which, in a passive transform, expresses the subject of the sentence in the active voice.

Examples: My dog was shot by John.
$$\overline{\text{1p4}}$$

This house was haunted by an old man's ghost.
$$\overline{\text{1p4}}$$

1.1.6 Notational device: x

Definition: The omission of an obligatory slot or filler. This does not include the (1) in an imperative sentence. This symbol combines with other symbols.

Examples: (Note: additional examples will appear on Level II).

And about fifty times _____ to my mom and
$$\qquad\qquad\frac{x}{1}\qquad\frac{x}{2}$$

and dad that I wish he was my brother.

But they are both O. K., so the boy threw ___ away.
$$\frac{x}{4}$$

1.2.0 Notational device: 2

Definition: The verb slot of a sentence, the filler of which may be a single-word verb, a verb phrase, or a compound verb. The slot may be discontinuous. Negation expressed by *not* is considered a part of the verb phrase.

Examples: John <u>thinks</u> I am right.
             2

John <u>will play</u> baseball next Saturday.
      2

John <u>left</u> and <u>returned</u> later.
      2   +   2

John <u>ought to try to stop smoking</u> cigarets.
                 2

John <u>doesn't want to have to keep on helping</u> his
                       2

mother

John <u>was not going to go</u> with us.
           2

John <u>wanted to play</u> baseball.
          2

John <u>went to play</u> baseball.
          2

1.2.1 Notational device: 2n

Definition: In discontinuous verb phrases, the part of the phrase which contains the nucleus (or headword).

Examples: The coach <u>has</u> already <u>awarded</u> the letters.
                    2   2n

We <u>ought to try</u> hard <u>to formulate</u> a good system.
        2   2n

He <u>must</u> always <u>keep on turning</u> the lights out.
       2   2n   (2)

1.2.2 Notational device: (2)

Definition: A word which is not of the verb form-class

but which provides a structurally and semantically necessary completion of a verbation. Its distinctive feature is movability to either of two positions: immediately following the verb or after the complement. (However, if the complement is a personal pronoun, the word *must* follow the complement.) The structural necessity may be a feature of the standard language or may be dialectal.

Examples: John took the trash out.
$$\underset{2}{\underline{\text{took}}} \qquad \underset{(2)}{\underline{\text{out}}}$$

He blew up the ship.
$$\underset{2 \;\; (2)}{\underline{\text{blew up}}}$$

I'll phone you up when I get home.
$$\underset{2}{\underline{\text{phone}}} \;\; \underset{(2)}{\underline{\text{up}}}$$

1.2.3 Notational device: -2-

Definition: A word which is not of the verb form-class but which provides a structurally and semantically necessary completion of a verbation. It always follows the verb immediately and, if omitted, would either change the meaning of the sentence or render the sentence meaningless. The structural necessity may be a feature of the standard language or may be dialectal.

Examples: One of my brothers is going on six.
$$\underset{\text{-2-}}{\underline{\text{on}}}$$

He came across the facts.
$$\underset{\text{-2-}}{\underline{\text{across}}}$$

This story took place in 1491.
$$\underset{\text{-2-}}{\underline{\text{place}}}$$

1.2.4 Notational device: 2b

Definition: The equational or copulative verb.

Examples: The results of the study were satisfactory.
$$\underset{2b}{\underline{\text{were}}}$$

He became president of his class.
$$\underset{2b}{\underline{\text{became}}}$$

You look sleepy.
$$\underset{2b}{\underline{\text{look}}}$$

They seem frightened of something.
        2b

1.2.5 Notational device: 2bn

Definition: In discontinuous equational or copulative verb phrases, the part of the phrase which contains the headword.

Example: He had always been good.
        2   2bn

1.2.6 Notational device: 2p

Definition: The verb in the passive voice.

Examples: My dog was shot by John.
        2p

The game was played last Saturday.
        2p

1.2.7 Notational device: 2pb

Defintion: A verb in the passive voice which takes a predicate complement.

Example: He was made president of his class.
        2pb

1.3.0. Notational device: 3

Definition: The indirect object slot of the sentence, the filler of which may be a word, a phrase, a clause, or a combination of these.

Examples: Coach Jones is teaching John the funda-
        3
mentals of the game.

Coach Jones is teaching the team the fundamentals of
        3
the game.

Coach Jones will teach whoever tries out for the team
        3
the fundamentals of the game.

Coach Jones will teach the boys who try out for the
        3
team the fundamentals of the game.

1.3.1 Notational device: 3t

Definition: The *to*-prepositional phrase transform of 1.3.0

Example: Coach Jones is teaching the fundamentals of the game <u>to John</u>.
   3t

1.4.0 Notational device: 4

Definition: The direct object slot of a sentence, the filler of which may be a word, a phrase, a clause, or a combination of these.

Examples: John spends <u>money</u>.
    4

John spends <u>what his mother gives him</u>.
    4

John spends <u>the allowance his mother gives him</u>.
    4

1.4.1 Notational device: 4s

Definition: In discontinuous objects, the part of the object which contains the continuation or supplement.

Example: And <u>what</u> do you think <u>he saw</u>?
    4   4s

1.5.0 Notational device: 5

Definition: The complement slot for an equational or copulative verb, the filler of which is substantive in nature and which may be a word, phrase, clause, or combination of these.

Examples: John is <u>the boy next door</u>.
    5

That book is <u>what I want</u>.
    5

John seems <u>a boy who enjoys life</u>.
    5

John was elected <u>president of his class</u>.
    5

1.5.1. Notational device: 5a

Definition: The complement slot for an equational or copulative verb, the filler of which is adjectival in nature and which may be a word, phrase or combination of these.

Examples: John is cheerful.
$\qquad\qquad$ 5a

The milk turned sour.
$\qquad$ 5a

The work proved exhausting to the children.
$\qquad\qquad$ 5a

1.6.0. Notational device: 6

Definition: The objective complement slot, the filler of which is substantive in nature and which may be a word, phrase, clause, or combination of these.

Examples: They elected John president of his class.
$\qquad\qquad\qquad$ 6

You made me what I am today.
$\qquad$ 6

They thought him a man who spoke hastily.
$\qquad$ 6

1.6.1 Notational device: 6a

Definition: The objective complement slot, the filler of which is adjectival in nature and which may be a word, phrase or combination.

Examples: They painted the house red.
$\qquad$ 6a

They declared him unfit for office.
$\qquad$ 6a

The board ruled the activity too exhausting for the
$\qquad\qquad$ 6a (and following line)

children to engage in.
$\qquad$

1.7.0. Notational device: M

Definition: Those syntactic segments which do not fit

into the slots already named and which by comparison with these slots are freely "movable," i.e., have greater degrees of freedom of order and placement. Note: this group does not include the movable verb particle (see section 1.2.2). Movability will be determined according to apparent freedom of movement, either in respect to the core sentence or in relation to fixed elements or other movable elements. The filler may be a word, phrase, clause, or combination of these. The same word or phrase may be fixed in one sentence and movable in another, depending on its environment. Whenever the movable in any of its positions causes an inversion of other elements, it is marked with an asterisk. This is a group designation by position subdivided as follows:

1.7.1 Notational device: M_1 (2) (3) (4) (5)

Definition: A movable which precedes everything else in the sentence. This position may be filled by more than one movable. The number in parentheses indicates the number of positions possible without changes of meaning.

Examples: <u>Soon</u> the little boy will be down to breakfast.
    M1 (3)

<u>On the way</u> John met his friend.
    M_1 (2)

<u>Happy to be going,</u> John packed his suitcase.
    M1 (3)

<u>Speeding down the highway,</u> John began to get sleepy.
        M_1 (3)

<u>When he got the flower in his mouth,</u> the bee stung
            M_1 (2)
him right in his mouth.

<u>Then with a fanfair</u> the ceremony began.
    M_1 (3) M_1(2)

1.7.2. Notational device: M2

Definition: A movable which occurs between the subject and verb slots, or between the expletive and verb slots.

Examples: She never was bad.

$$\overline{M2\ (2)}$$

John, happy to be going, packed his suitcase.

$$\overline{M2\ (3)}$$

John, speeding down the highway, began to get sleepy.

$$\overline{M2\ (3)}$$

There once was a tiger, who lived in a cave.

$$\overline{M2\ (5)}$$

It usually is a good idea to look before you leap.

$$\overline{M2\ (5)}$$

1.7.3 Notational device: M3

Definition: A movable which occurs within the verb slot.

Examples: The little boy will soon be down to breakfast.

$$\overline{M3\ (4)}$$

He had, like any other horse, been given a halter.

$$\overline{M3\ (4)}$$

1.7.4 Notational device: M4

Definition: A movable which occurs after the verb slot. It may be followed by an object or complement. This position may be filled by more than one movable.

Examples: There was once a horse who talked.

$$\overline{M4\ (4)}$$

Then a fox came out of the forest looking mad.

$$\overline{M4\ (3)} \qquad \overline{M4\ (2)}$$

The farmer had only his three horses.

$$\overline{M4\ (3)}$$

He worked every day hauling logs until five o'clock.

$$\overline{M4\ (2)} \quad \overline{M4\ (2)} \qquad \overline{M4\ (2)}$$

The man came out bouncing with suds coming out of

$$\overline{M4\ (2)} \quad \overline{M4\ (2)} \qquad \overline{M4\ (3)}$$

his ears.

It was for us a very difficult decision.

$$\overline{M4\ (3)}$$

She left <u>right after the game.</u>
M4 (2)

1.7.5 Notational device: M5

Definition: A movable which occurs after an object, a complement slot, or a fixed slot following the verb. This position may be filled by more than one movable.

Examples: John met his friend <u>on the way.</u>
M5 (2)

He got an A <u>on his paper.</u>
M5 (2)

So Billy was nice <u>then.</u>
M5 (2)

They called him a pig <u>because he was always dirty.</u>
M5 (2)

So they went home <u>sadly.</u>
M5 (3)

They never went to the city <u>again.</u>
M5 (2)

Timothy went on a vacation <u>with his family.</u>
M5 (3)

1.8.0 Notational device: F

Definition: Those syntactic segments which do not fit into the slots already named, but are relatively "fixed," or not easily "movable"; i.e., their placement within the sentence appears to be obligatory. The filler may be a word, phrase, clause, or any combination of these. This is a group designation subdivided as follows:

1.8.1 Notational device: F1

Definition: A fixed segment which comes first in the sentence.

Examples: <u>When Henry didn't have to go to school, he</u>
F1
said that he would play a trick on his mother.

<u>After the barber cut my hair,</u> he gave me some candy.
F1

So was the other one, too.
<u>F1</u>

1.8.2 Notational device: F2

Definition: A fixed segment which comes between the subject and the verb in a sentence, or before an imperative verb.

Examples: He <u>never</u> goes out with girls.
        F2

<u>Never</u> do that again.
  F2

The princess <u>never</u> knew it.
     F2

My grandfather <u>almost</u> caught a Northern Pike.
       F2

One day he <u>really</u> got into trouble.
     F2

1.8.3 Notational device: F3

Definition: A fixed segment which occurs within the verb slot.

Example: I might <u>as well</u> go.
      F3

1.8.4 Notational device: F4

Definition: A fixed segment which follows the verb. This position may be filled by more than one fixed element.

Examples: Then he came <u>to a house that was being</u>
                    F4
<u>built</u>.

The bees were buzzing <u>around</u>.
         F4

He never goes <u>out</u> <u>with</u> girls.
    F4   F4

They lived <u>happily</u> <u>ever after</u>.
    F4   F4

1.8.5 Notational device: F5

Definition: A fixed segment which follows an object or complement. This position may be filled by more than one fixed element.

Examples: She put it in the trunk of the car.
<u>   </u>
F5

He got ready <u>for Christmas.</u>
                F5

My mother kept me <u>home.</u>
                   F5

They took it <u>home</u> to have it <u>for dinner.</u>
          F5   F5

She left it <u>where she couldn't find it.</u>
                 F5

1.9.0 Notational device: V

Definition: A segment which selects constructions traditionally described as "direct address."

Example: Give me the book, <u>John.</u>
                         V

1.10.0 Notational device: Y

Definition: A segment which selects such absolute elements as interjections and exclamations which do not occur as separate utterances.

Examples: <u>Why</u> this is the lost baby.
          Y

<u>Well</u> he tried to stop him but he couldn't.
 Y

1.11.0 Notational device: Z

Definition: A segment which selects words, phrases, clauses, or combinations which are parenthetical.

Examples: It was, <u>of course,</u> an excellent idea.
                  Z

It was, <u>I thought,</u> an excellent idea.
         Z

1.12.0 Relating words and phrases

1.12.1 Notational device: +

Definition: A coordinator used to connect elements within a sentence or utterance.

Examples: He always kicks or screams when I try to give
$$+$$
him a bath.

I neither can nor shall tolerate that.
$$+ \qquad +$$

1.12.2 Notational device: —

Definition: A symbol to mark the linking of items in a structure of coordination which are not joined by a coordinator.

Example: The children played, sang, and danced.

1.12.3 Notational device: &

Definition: A sequence marker between independent structures or utterances.

Examples:

Both knights were mounted and each held a lance.
$$\&$$

And she could dance.
$$\&$$

But one day this dog died.
$$\&$$

And so they had to find another dog.
$$\&$$

So the cat was in show business.
$$\&$$

1.13.0 Notational device: U

Definition: A short utterance—one or more words, structured if multiword, lower than sentence level—conveying meaning and usually marked by 3 1 intonation contour.

Examples: Will you do it?—All right.
$$U$$

He swallowed the torpedoes. A job well done.
$$U$$

1.14.0 Notational device: [   ]

Definition: An element of any length which is extra-structural in the sentence and usually unstructured in itself. It expresses a maze, hesitation, false start, primer, or onomatopoeia.

Example: [Our uh] our dog [well he] got away.

1.15.0 Notational device: ʌ

Definition: A symbol to indicate a syntactic completion between independent structures or utterances when the student has not indicated the completion with a sequence marker or an end-mark of punctuation.

Examples: One day Tommy was going to his grandpa's ʌ his grandpa lived across the sea.

Once I went on a Boat ride ʌ We went in side to eat our breakfast.

1.16.0 Notational device: "

Definition: A symbol used in pairs to indicate the enclosure of a direct quotation. When the tag phrase, i.e., *he said*, is a simple 1 2 pattern as such, the tag phrase is not analyzed. If, however, the tag is more complex than the simple 1 2 pattern, it will be analyzed on Level I and the quoted segment will be a 4 on Level I and will be analyzed at higher levels. (See 3.0.4 and 3.0.5.)

Examples: He said, "Henry, brush your teeth."
              "   "

The innkeeper would say, "No, sorry no room
                                "

available."
       "

One day Mr. White said, "We just have to get rid of
                                  "

that horse."
        "

And then a little duck said, "I know where the sea is."
                        "   "

An Instrument for the Syntactical Analysis of Children's Compositions

Level II

2.0 Description of the Level II analysis

Subject and complement slots, M's and F's where applicable, as in structures of predication or structures of complementation, use whatever Level I symbols are appropriate. The following additional symbols may also be used. All of the items apply on the third, fourth, and all additional levels beyond the second, as well as to Level II.

2.1. Notational device: d

Definition: a noun indicator or determiner, specifically articles and demonstrative or quantitative adjectives. This grammatical item appears at the beginning of a nominal slot. Note: although frequently classified as determiners, the possessive pronouns will be identified by another symbol in this study. See 2.10.

Examples: The blue dress looks very nice.

I	1
II	d

Do you have any money?

I	4
II	d

This book is overdue.

I	1
II	d

You should have some ideas.

I	4
II	d

2.2 Notational device: pd

Definition: a predeterminer. This group is limited to a few words which in a nominal slot can precede the determiner without any intervening elements.

Examples: All the new dresses have been sold.

I	1
II	pd d

```
        She  has  lost  both  the  German  books.
I                        _____
                                   4
II                            pd   d
        Many  a  person  must  make  that  decison.
I            _____
                  1
II            pd   d
        Such  a  fine  talent  should  not  be  wasted.
1            _____
                    1
II            pd   d
```

2.3 Notational device: Aj

Definition: an adjective within a slot.

Examples: Have you seen the new car?

```
I                        _____
                               4
II                            d   Aj
        The  little  old  German  family  doctor  is  here.
I            _____
                          1
II            d   Aj  Aj     Aj
        The  tall,  strange-looking  character  is  my  cousin.
I            _____
                        1
II            d   Aj         Aj
        Would  you  do  that  to  little  old  me?
I                            _____
                                  M5
II                            Aj      Aj
        Her  new  dress  was  bright  blue.
I                            _____
                                  5a
II                            Aj
```

2.4 Notational device: H

Definition: the head of a structure of modification. This symbol will always be used in combination with another symbol; e.g., HN, HAj, HAv, HP, HInf, Hing, Hen.

Example: The old coat was a big problem.

```
I            _____         _____
                  1                 5
II            d   Aj  HN      d   Aj   HN
```

Note: other examples will appear as the other symbols are explained.

2.5 Notational device: N
Definition: a noun within a slot.
Examples:

The governor and the senator became very
I   1
II   d   HN   d   HN
unpopular.

Have you seen the white dog?
I   4
II   d   Aj   HN

Take the old blue book.
I   4
II   d Aj Aj   HN

Little Charlie is here.
I   1
II   Aj   HN

A Mr. Walter Smith called while you were out.
I   1
II   d   HN

2.6 Notational device: At
Definition: an attributive noun (or noun adjunct)
within a slot, a noun which functions as an adjective
and is in the attributive position immediately before the
noun modified.
Examples: The dog house needs a coat of paint.
I   1
II   d   At   HN

I missed the school bus.
I   4
II   d   At   HN

The bus driver was upset.
I   1
II   d At   HN

Is that a Nebraska State Highway Patrol car?
I   5
II   d   At   At   At   At   HN

Can I have a chocolate nut fudge ice cream cone?

I			4				
II		d	At	At	At	At	At	HN

2.7 Notational device: N's

Definition: a noun in the possessive case within a slot.
Note: if the possessive noun is the only member of a
slot, it will be identified by the appropriate number on
Level I, and no further identification will be given.

Examples: John's coat is missing.

I		1
II	N's	HN

You forgot the boy's birthday.

I		4
II	d	N's	HN

Bill's attitude is terrible.

I	1
II	N's	HN

Have you seen the doctor's hat?

I		4
II	d	N's	HN

2.8 Notational device: Ap

Definition: an appositive within a slot.

Examples: Tom's dog Rex is missing.

I		1
II	N's	HN	Ap

The new chairman, Dr. Smith, was missing.

I			1
II	d	Aj	HN	Ap

The book, The Hobbit, is very interesting.

I		1
II	d	HN	Ap

2.9 Notational device: Pn

Definition: a pronoun within a slot. In this study it is
distinguished from a noun in that it cannot have an indicator or determiner preceding it.

Examples: He and I are equally responsible.
I   1
II   Pn   Pn

She cheated almost everyone.
I   4
II   HPn

All these are rare.
I   1
II   HPn

I will choose him whom I can trust.
I   4
II   Pn

2.10 Notational device: Pn's

Definition: a possessive pronoun, either personal, quantitative, or reciprocal within a slot. See 2.1.

Examples: My new coat was torn.
I   1
II   Pn's Aj HN

She is everyone's friend.
I   5
II   Pn's   HN

They solve one another's problems.
I
II   Pn's   HN

They have sealed our fate.
I   4
II   Pn's HN

2.11 Notational device: Av

Definition: an adverbial element within a slot.

Examples: He does his work very carefully.
I   M5
II   Av   HAv

We met the very tall stranger.
I   4
II   d   Av   Aj   HN

He did exceptionally well on the test.

```
I              F4
II           Av        HAv
```

Almost everyone was here.

```
I            1
II     Av       HPn
```

2.12 Notational device: P

Definition: a prepositional phrase within a slot. Note: if the prepositional phrase is a complete nominal slot, M, or F on Level I, it will be identified as M, F, etc. Then on Level II the constituents of the phrase will be identified, and this symbol will not appear.

Examples: The boy on the bicycle is my brother.

```
I             1
II        d  HN  P
```

We left just before the buzzer.

```
I             M4
II        Av  HP
```

I must replace the tires on my car.

```
I               4
II           d  HN  P
```

The book is right on top of the television set.

```
I               F4
II          Av   HP
```

2.13 Notational device: (P)

Definition: the word which functions as the preposition itself in an analysis of the whole phrase. Occasionally the preposition consists of more than a single word as in according to.

Examples: Under the tree is shady.

```
I             1
II       (P)     d  HN
```

It is peaceful down the road.

```
I                 M5
II             (P)    d  HN
```

According to Jones this problem can't be solved.

I   M1

II   (P)   HN

We must all suffer because of her decision.

I   M4

II   (P)   Pn's   HN

The chair in the corner should be repaired.

I   1

II   d   HN P

III   (P) d   HN

She put it in the trunk of the car.

I   F5

II   (P) d   HN P

III   (P) d HN

2.14 Notational device: C

Definition: A clause within a slot. Note: the symbol C will not appear when a clause completely fills a nominal slot or is an M or F. It will be identified as M, F, 1, 3, 4, 5, or 6 on Level I and the constituents of the clause will be identified on Level II by the appropriate symbols.

Examples: The boys who broke the windows should be

I   1

II   d HN C

punished.

She had the book that I wanted.

I   4

II   d HN C

On the morning after I got there I lost my money.

I   M1

II (P) d   HN C

2.15 Notational device: ≠

Definition: a subordinating connective, either single-word or phrase, used to introduce clauses, verbal phrases, and occasionally adjectives and adjective phrases.

Examples: <u>If she doesn't come,</u> phone her.

I   M1

II   ≠

Punish her <u>so that she won't do it again.</u>

I   M5

II   <u>≠   </u>

Tell me <u>when she gets here.</u>

I   4

II   ≠

He couldn't win, <u>no matter how he tried.</u>

I   M4

II   <u>≠   </u>

I didn't know <u>how to do it.</u>

I   4

II   ≠

<u>Although defeated,</u> the team was still encouraged.

I   M1

II   ≠

2.16 Notational device: ing

Definition: a present participial phrase used as a constituent of a structure of modification. Note: equivalent forms filling nominal slots are identified as 1's, 4's, etc. If a participial phrase is shifted from its normal appositive position, it will be identified by the proper M on Level I.

Examples: The boys <u>swimming in the river</u> should be

I   1

II   d   HN   <u>ing   </u>

careful.

Do you know the girl <u>washing the car?</u>

I   4

II   d   HN   <u>ing   </u>

<u>After taking my money,</u> he took my car.

I   M1

II   ≠   <u>ing   </u>

The book sitting on the desk is very good.

```
I                 1
II    d   HN  ing
```

2.17 Notational device: (ing)

Definition: the single-word present participle itself.

Examples: Swimming in the river can be dangerous.

```
I                     1
II        H (ing)    P
```

The girls washing the car are doing a good job.

```
I             1
II    d   HN  ing
III              (ing)   4
```

Her job is making pizza.

```
I                5
II             (ing)    4
```

While driving my car, he had an accident.

```
I              M1
II    ≠      ing
III        (ing)    4
```

The swimming team did very well.

```
I             1
II    d   (ing)    HN
```

2.18 Notational device: en

Definition: a past participial phrase used as a modifier in a structure of modification. Note: if the phrase is moved from its normal position following the word modified, it is identified by the proper M on Level I.

Examples: The vase broken by the children cannot be

```
I                      1
II           d  HN  en
```

replaced.

The man wanted by the police was here last week.

```
I                       1
II    d   HN  en
```

The candidate defeated in the primary was our

I   1

II   d   HN   en

choice.

We chose the girl dressed in white.

I   4

II   d   HN   en

2.19 Notational device: (en)

Definition: the single word present participle in a slot.

Examples: The town attacked by the guerrillas could

I   1

II   d   HN   en

III   (en)   1P4

not be defended.

The candidate chosen in the election was not my

I   1

II   d   HN   en

III   (en)   P

choice.

The house painted red is ours.

I   1

II   d   HN   en

III   (en)   5a

We want to buy the car parked in the driveway.

I   4

II   d   HN   en

III   (en)   P

The defeated candidate should have won.

I   1

II   d   (en)   HN

She hit a parked car.

I   4

II   d   (en)   HN

2.20 Notational device: Inf

Definition: an infinitive phrase in a slot. Note: this symbol will not be used if the infinitive phrase constitutes an entire slot since the appropriate symbol for the slot (1, 3, 4, etc.) will be used on Level I, and no further analysis will be needed.

Examples: This is a book to read quickly.

I   5
II   d HN inf

Mr. Jones is the one to see now.

I   5
II   d HN   Inf

2.21 Notational device: (Inf)

Definition: the infinitive itself in a slot, either with or without the function word "to."

Examples: Make her stop that.

I   4
II   1 (Inf)   4

We wanted him to give us the book.

I   4
II   1 (Inf)   3   4

It was his idea to bring her along.

I   1
II   (Inf)   4   F5

For us to be punished was unfair.

I   1
II   1   (Inf)

To do the right thing is not always easy.

I   1
II   (Inf)   4

This is a book to read quickly.

I   5
II   d HN Inf
                (Inf)   Av

2.22 Notational device: x

Definition: The omission of an obligatory filler. This symbol combines with other symbols.

Examples: He saw _____ bird.

I		4
II	x	HN
	d̄	

She ran _____ the block.

I		F4	
II	x	d	HN
	(P̄)		

She gave me a big _____ .

I		4	
II	d	Aj	x
			HN̄

3.0 The analyses of sample sentences having more than a single level of structure.

3.0.1 Example:

Then he told Bob who had been watching all this with

I	M1	1	2				3
II			HN	C			
III				1	2	4	
IV							Pn HPn (P)

a puzzled expression to go to the other end of the

I								
II			(Inf)		F4			
III	F5			(P)	d	Aj	HN	P
IV	d	(en)	HN			(P)	d	

tunnel with the crackers and call Sparky.

I	4					
II		F4		+	(Inf)	4
III		(P)	d	HN		
IV	HN					

3.0.2 Example:

Sparky, knowing food was at the other end of the tunnel

```
I                                             1
II    HN    ing
III          (ing)                    4
IV                        1    2              F4
V                              (P) d    Aj   HN  P
VI                                        (P) d      HN
      raced   through   the   tunnel   with   a   cable   dragging
I       2              F4                          F4
II            (P)     d    HN     (P)  d  HN     (ing)
      behind and received her reward.
I              +     2              4
II        Av               Pn's  HN
```

3.0.3 Example:

Now Jack's father told him that the first thing that he

```
I    M1 (3)    1        2    3              4
II          N's   HN              ≠              1
III                                  d   Aj   HN   C
IV                                          ≠   1
```

should do was to look for the nest that the baby bird

```
I
II                   2b                   5
III    _____        (Inf)  -2-          4
IV                            d   HN   C
V                                 ≠        1
VI                                     d    At    HN
```

fell from.

```
V     2   F4
```

3.0.4. Example: He said, "Henry brush your teeth."

```
I                              1    2    4
II                                  Pn's  HN
```

3.0.5 Example:

And then a little duck said, "I know where the sea is."

```
I    & M1 (2)      1      2   "          4          "
II           d   Aj   HN      I   2      4
III                              ≠     1    2
IV                                  d   HN
```

New Measures of
Grammatical Complexity

John R. Bormuth
University of Chicago

The appraisal of what makes language difficult to read and comprehend has been a continuing concern of educators, writers, publishers, and teachers for many years. Linguistics and linguistics-based studies of children's language suggest previously unconsidered factors of grammatical complexity which may be of great importance. Dr. Bormuth defines some of these factors and reports his research on their significance.

EDITOR

New Measures of Grammatical Complexity

Researchers have been making vigorous efforts to find out why some language is easy to understand while some is difficult. Many have focused their efforts upon the problem of how grammatical structure affects comprehension difficulty. The first purpose of this study was to investigate the sizes of the correlations between comprehension difficulty and three new measures of grammatical complexity. The second purpose was to find out if relationships between comprehension difficulty and measures of grammatical complexity change as a function of the reading ability of the subject.

Finding sentence complexity measures that accurately predict the comprehension difficulty of written language is a matter of considerable theoretical and practical importance. Measures of this sort are of theoretical importance because they suggest hypotheses about the mental processes underlying the act of comprehension. From the standpoint of practice, such measures are of interest because of their utility in improving the accuracy of the predictions of readability formulas, and because they can aid educators in providing children with a systematic sequence of instruction in the skills of comprehending language structures. That is, such measures may serve as criteria for ordering the sequence in which different grammatical structures are introduced in reading instruction.

The second purpose of this study might be rephrased as the question of whether the sizes of the correlations between comprehension difficulty and grammatical complexity variables change as a function of the reading ability of subjects. Gray (6) found some evidence that these correlations increase as subjects increase in reading ability. But, because of his research design, it was impossible to tell whether this effect was due to chance.

If Gray's findings are confirmed, and if the effects are large, the practical result will be to show that different readability formulas are required for predicting readability for subjects at various levels of reading ability.

Until recently the length of a sentence, found by counting the words or syllables in it, furnished the best measure of the complexity of sentences. Flesch (5), for example, found correlations of .66 and .47, respectively, between the comprehension difficulties of passages and the mean numbers of syllables and words in the sentences of the passages. Studies such as the one by Robinson (7) have shown that varying the length of sentences in passages has only trivial effects upon the difficulties of the passages.

Two important educational problems may be traceable to the almost exclusive reliance upon measures of sentence length. First, educators apply readability formulas to instructional materials to determine if students will be able to understand materials. But, as Chall (3) has pointed out, these formulas have validity correlations of only .5 to .7, assuring that many of the materials will not be understood by many of the students. Second, publishers are well aware of the practices of their customers, so they often require their authors to conform to style specifications derived from the readability formulas. Rigid adherence to these specifications must inevitably result in the short, choppy sentences found in reading primers, but not necessarily in materials that are easier to comprehend.

Measures of Grammatical Complexity

Unit of Grammatical Analysis
The independent clause was taken as the unit of grammatical analysis in this study. Until recently the unit of grammatical analysis in studies of this sort has been the sentence unit, which might be defined as the words lying between the initial capital letter and the terminal punctuation mark. In the present study, coordinating conjunctions connecting independent clauses were

treated as if they were terminal punctuation marks rather than as words. Bormuth (2) and Coleman (4) have each found evidence that measures of grammatical complexity have higher correlations with comprehension difficulty when they are based upon the independent clause than when they are based upon the sentence.

Word Depth

Yngve (10) developed the word-depth measure for use in programming computers to produce grammatically correct English sentences. In the word-depth analysis a number is assigned to each word in a grammatical unit. This number represents the number of grammatical facts that a computer producing the sentence would have to be storing at the time it printed out that word. The criterion for deciding if the computer must store a grammatical fact is whether or not the computer must have that fact in order to complete the rest of that sentence and complete it grammatically. In the present study, word depths were averaged for each of the independent clauses and each of the passages studied.

The rationale of this measure states that part of the difficulty people have in comprehending a sentence arises from the grammatical relationships they must keep track of; the greater the number of these relationships per word the more difficult the sentence is to comprehend. Word depth is thought to measure the number of these relationships. Bormuth (1) found that the mean word depths of passages had a correlation of .77 with the passages' comprehension difficulties when sentence length and vocabulary difficulty were held constant.

Pattern Frequency

Strickland (9) devised a method of describing the grammatical patterns of independent clauses. In this method each of the major phrase constituents of an independent clause is assigned a symbol. Each type of constituent is represented by a different symbol. For example, the subject phrase is represented by one symbol, the indirect object of the main verb by another, and various types of adverbial phrases modifying the main verb by still other symbols. The pattern of an independent clause is then defined by which symbols were assigned and the order of these symbols.

Strickland and her students gathered samples of the oral language of elementary school children, analyzed the patterns of the independent clauses used by the children, and then tabulated separately for the children at each grade level the frequency with which each pattern occurred. For the purposes of the present study, the pattern frequencies reported for the samples taken from children in grades 1, 3, and 6 were combined by adding together the frequencies observed for each pattern in the three samples. Each independent clause used in the present study was then analyzed to obtain its pattern and assigned a number corresponding to the number of times that pattern occurred in the samples of children's oral language.

The rationale of this measure of grammatical complexity asserts that people are most likely to be able to comprehend the grammatical patterns they hear frequently and less likely to be able to comprehend patterns they seldom hear. Hence, a measure of the frequencies with which the patterns of a set of independent clauses are used should correlate with a measure of the comprehension difficulties of those independent clauses. Ruddell's (8) findings seemed to show that passages written using only high frequency patterns are easier to comprehend than passages written using only low frequency patterns. However, it is not certain that the difference was significant, since the test of significance did not include an estimate of the item sample error of the test means.

Independent Clause Length

The length of an independent clause is obtained by counting the number of letters in the words within it. In this study, coordinating conjunctions connecting two independent clauses were not counted as a part of either of the independent clauses.

The rationale of this measure of grammatical complexity is

based on the notion that complex grammatical structures are longer than uncomplicated grammatical structures. As mentioned above, measures of the length of grammatical structures based on the independent clause as the unit of grammatical analysis yield higher correlations with comprehension difficulty than measures based on the sentence. Further, Bormuth (2) showed that measures of length based upon the letter as the unit of measurement yield higher correlations with comprehension difficulty than measures based on either words or syllables.

Procedure

Language Sample

The language sample used in this study consisted of twenty passages of about 300 words each. Four passages were drawn from materials in each of the subject matter areas of literature, history, geography, physical science, and biological science. The passages in each subject matter category were about evenly distributed in readability from about the 4.0 to about the 8.0 grade levels as measured by the Dale-Chall formula.

Cloze Tests

Five forms of a cloze test were made over each passage in which each form was made by replacing every fifth word with an underlined blank of a standard length. The five different forms over each passage were made in such a way that every word in the passage appeared once as a deleted item in one of the five cloze test forms. This was done by deleting words 1, 6, 11, etc., to make the first form, words 2, 7, 12, etc., to make the second, and so on until five such forms had been made. No words were deleted from either the first or last sentences of the passage, and these sentences were also excluded from other portions of the analysis.

Test Administration and Scoring

The cloze tests were given to 695 subjects enrolled in grades 4 through 8. The subjects were divided into five subgroups consisting of 139 subjects each. The subgroups were matched for means and distributions of scores on the *Stanford Achievement Test: Reading*. Each form group took a different one of the cloze test forms over each passage. Every subject took one cloze test over each passage. The testing periods were about one hour in length and were distributed over ten consecutive school days. No time limits were imposed on the tests. Responses to an item were scored correct when they matched the word deleted to form that item. Misspellings of the correct response were scored correct as long as they did not make the response ambiguous.

Levels of Analysis

The analyses in this study were carried out first with the variables quantified separately for each independent clause (the independent clause level of analysis) and then repeated with the variables quantified by averaging each variable across the entire passage (the passage level of analysis).

Variables

The dependent variables in this study were the comprehension difficulties of individual independent clauses and the comprehension difficulties of the passages. They were obtained by first finding the difficulty of each word when it appeared as an item in a cloze test. This was done by finding the proportion of subjects responding correctly to each item. Independent clause difficulties were then found by averaging the difficulties of the words within each independent clause. Passage difficulties were found by averaging the difficulties of the words within each passage.

The independent variables were derived separately for each independent clause and for each passage. Mean word depth was found for each independent clause by averaging the depths assigned to the words within it and for each passage by averaging the depths of the words in the passage. Independent clause frequency was found first for each independent clause and then averaged across the independent clauses in each passage to find the mean independent clause frequency for the passage. Inde-

pendent clause length first was found for each passage by counting the number of letters in the passage and dividing by the
number of independent clauses.

Analysis on Results
Correlation with Comprehension Difficulty

In the first portion of this analysis correlations were found
among the grammatical complexity and comprehension difficulty variables derived at the independent clause and passage
levels of analysis. Since it was not certain that these regressions
would be linear, the regression of each grammatical complexity
variable on the appropriate comprehension difficulty variable
was tested for linearity. The test of linearity required the calculation of a correlation ratio, an *eta* correlation, and a Pearson
product moment correlation for the same data. An *F* ratio was
then calculated to see if the *eta* correlation accounted for a significantly greater amount of the variance. In calculating the *eta*
at the independent clause level, the data were classified into ten
categories and at the passage level five categories were used. The
results of these analyses are shown in Table 1.

While the *F* test of linearity showed that the regressions at
both levels of analysis were approximately linear, this result
must be interpreted with caution. This test of linearity loses
much of its power to detect departures from linearity at the distribution extremes where the numbers of replicates are small. An
inspection of the scatter plots showed that this limitation may
have produced misleading results for the regressions involving
independent clause frequency and mean word depth at the
independent clause level of analysis. At the passage level the
scatter plots appeared to be linear.

With the possible exception of the independent clause frequency, all of the grammatical complexity variables appeared
to have significant correlations with comprehension difficulty
at the independent clause level of analysis. The product moment correlation was not significantly greater than zero but the

Table 1

Correlations and Tests of the Linearity of the Regressions at the Independent Clause and Passage Levels of Analysis

Variable	Mean		Product Moment			Linearity Test	
			2	3	4	eta	F^a
Independent Clause Level (N = 405)^b							
1. Frequency	162.82	264.77	09	−06	05	12	.54
2. Mean Word Depth	1.56	.41		28	−20	−26	1.34
3. Length	56.82	41.88			−43	−43	.40
4. Difficulty	32.54	11.98					
Passage Level (N = 20)^c							
1. Frequency	185.74	93.33	−03	06	13	31	.45
2. Mean Word Depth	1.65	.23		51	−55	−50	.32
3. Length	68.20	31.28			−81	−79	.28
4. Difficulty	29.66	9.06					

[a] None of the F ratios in this table has a p = .05.
[b] A correlation of .9 has a p = .05.
[c] A correlation of .43 has a p = .05.

eta correlation was. The results of the *F* test favored accepting the product moment correlation, but evidence derived from an inspection of the scatter plot favored accepting the *eta*. Because there was some possibility that some correlation existed, the variable was retained in the next step of the analysis, which in some respects provided a more powerful test of the hypothesis that a correlation exists.

Only mean word depth and independent clause length had significant correlations with comprehension difficulty at the passage level. But since there were only twenty passages, the correlation between variables would have to be large in order to appear to be significant. Since the pattern of relative sizes of the correlations were about the same at the passage and independent clause levels, and since the power of statistical tests was greatest at the independent clause level of analysis, only the variables derived at the independent clause level were retained in the next portion of the analysis.

Interaction with Reading Achievement

The second portion of this analysis was designed to find out if the sizes of the correlations between the grammatical complexity variables and comprehension difficulty change as a function of the amount of reading achievement of the subject. Because the size of a correlation is a function of the sizes of the variances of the variables correlated and because of the difficulties involved in attempting to match the variances of groups on some measure when the groups differ in ability on that measure, this analysis was carried out using an analysis of variance design. When phrased in terms of an analysis of variance design, the question under study became one of whether varying the levels of reading achievement of subjects and the levels of values on a grammatical complexity variable produce an interaction effect on the comprehension difficulties of independent clauses.

The subjects in each form group were ranked according to the sizes of their scores on the reading achievement test and then split into quintiles. An analysis of variance showed that

there were no significant differences among the mean achievement scores of the groups at each quintile level. The mean
grade placement achievement scores of the subjects at each
of the quintiles were 3.2, 4.2, 5.1, 6.3, and 8.8, and the scores
ranged from about 1.4 to 12.7. Independent clause difficulties
were then calculated separately for the group in each quintile
range. The independent clauses were also ranked with respect
to their values on each of the grammatical complexity variables
and then split into thirds. A two-factor analysis of variance
design was then used.

Table 2 shows the analysis of variance involving the independent clause frequency factor. This analysis answered the
prior question of whether independent clause frequency has
any relationship to comprehension difficulties. The F ratio
for levels of independent clause frequency was significant at
the .01 level. However, when this ratio is compared to the
ratios shown in Tables 3 and 4 which were obtained using
mean word depth and independent clause length, it can be seen
that the frequencies of independent clauses account for only a
trivial proportion of their difficulty variances.

Table 2

*Analysis of the Effects of Independent Clause
Frequency and Levels of Subjects' Reading Achievement
Upon the Comprehension Difficulties of Independent Clauses*

Source	df	Mean Square	F
Achievement Level	4	39,688.89	237.88*
Independent Clause			
Frequency Level	2	2,122.21	12.72*
Interaction	8	938.36	5.62*
Within	2010	166.84	

* $p > .01$.

This analysis also showed that there was a significant effect
produced by the interaction of the achievement levels of the
subjects and the frequency levels of the independent clauses.

In spite of the fact that this interaction was significant statistically, its size was very small when compared with variances associated with the main effects.

Table 3 shows the results of the analysis when the independent clauses were divided into thirds according to the sizes of their word depths. No interaction between reading achievement and mean word depth levels was found. This analysis also yielded some evidence regarding the linearity of the relationship between mean word depth and comprehension difficulty. A plot of the cell and marginal means showed that difficulty increased almost twice as much between the independent clauses of low and medial depth as it did between the clauses of medial and high mean word depth. But this can be taken as being only

Table 3
*Analysis of the Effects of Mean Word Depth and
Levels of Subjects' Reading Achievement Upon
the Comprehension Difficulties of Independent Clauses*

Source	df	Mean Square	F
Achievement Level	4	39,688.89	256.70*
Mean Word-Depth Level	2	17,897.56	115.76*
Interaction	8	67.36	.44
Within	2010	154.61	

* $p > .01$.

suggestive of the shape of the relationship since the levels of mean word depth represented groups containing equal numbers of independent clauses rather than groups differing in mean word depth by equal amounts along the mean word-depth scale.

Table 4 shows the results of the analysis when the independent clauses were divided into thirds according to their length as measured by a count of the number of letters in them. Again both main effects accounted for significant amounts of the variance, and the interaction failed to show a significant effect upon independent clause difficulties.

Table 4

Analysis of the Effects of Levels of Independent Clause Length and Subjects' Reading Achievement Levels Upon the Comprehension Difficulties of Independent Clauses

Source	df	Mean Square	F
Achievement Level	4	39,688.89	286.93*
Independent Clause			
Length Level	2	34,126.62	247.29
Interaction	8	102.51	.74
Within	2010	138.32	

* $p > .01$.

Discussion

The purposes of this study were to see if the new measures of grammatical complexity correlated with comprehension difficulty, and, if so, whether the sizes of these correlations changed as a function of the level of reading achievement of the subjects.

While the frequencies of independent clauses correlate with their comprehension difficulties, the size of this correlation is so small as to make this variable, in its present form, almost useless. That is, the correlation is too small to make this variable of any practical value either for use in predicting readability or for use in sequencing the order in which grammatical patterns are introduced in reading instruction. But this must not be construed as advocacy that this variable be abandoned but rather as a recommendation that the variable be further developed.

Two ways of improving the independent clause frequency variable are evident. First, the analysis of grammatical patterns used for this variable ignores many of the major phrase structures within the independent clause by taking note of only the major structures, such as the subject, verb, object, and adverbial clauses of an independent clause, and ignoring many of the phrases and subordinate clauses and phrases modifying them. For example, the immediately preceding sentence would be classified as having a pattern identical to that of the sentence, "Then, Johnny hit the ball." Strickland devised a more detailed pattern analysis but did not study the frequency with which those patterns occurred. Second, the sample of language upon which frequencies are determined probably should be much larger than that used by Strickland.

Both the mean word depth and the independent clause length variables were found to have significant correlations with comprehension difficulty. These correlations were large enough to make both variables useful for predicting the readability of passages. However, mean word depth, when quantified at the independent clause level of analysis, does not seem to correlate highly enough to recommend its use in predicting the relative difficulties of individual independent clauses.

It appears that measures of mean word depth and independent clause length are as effective in predicting readability for good readers as for poor readers. The independent clause frequency variable did interact with reading achievement to produce an effect upon comprehension difficulty, but when viewed in practical terms the size of this effect was so slight as to be considered trivial.

The fact that the correlations at the passage level of analysis were much larger than those obtained at the independent clause level deserves special attention. This fact might be explained in two ways. It could be said that, since the measures at the passage level were averaged over a large number of independent clauses, they were more reliable. However, this can be partially refuted by the fact that a count of the number of letters or the mean word depth of an independent clause is an exact measure containing little if any error of measurement. Likewise, the cloze test difficulties of independent clauses contain very little error of measurement because of the large number of subjects used in this study. Consequently, it seems reasonable to look for a different explanation. This explanation might be that the difficulty of an independent clause is strongly affected by the difficulty of the context in which it appears. That is, the data suggest that something like intra-sentence syntax may affect the difficulties of independent clauses.

Summary and Conclusions

The purposes of this study were to find out if measures of the frequency, mean word depth, and length (measured in letters) of independent clauses correlated significantly with the comprehension difficulties of independent clauses and, if so, whether the sizes of these correlations changed as subjects increased in reading achievement. Twenty passages, containing a total of 405 independent clauses, were drawn from various subject matter areas. Five forms of a cloze test were made over each passage in such a way that every word in every passage appeared as a cloze item in one of the forms. Each form was then administered to one of five matched groups consisting of 139 subjects each. The subjects were drawn from children enrolled in grades 4 through 8 and varied in reading achievement grade placement scores from about 1.4 to about 12.7.

The difficulty of each word was determined by calculating the proportion of subjects responding correctly when that word appeared as a cloze item. The difficulties of the words within an independent clause were averaged to find the difficulties of those units. These difficulties were then correlated with the measures of grammatical complexity. The subjects were then divided into five groups according to their scores on a reading achievement test and the difficulties of the independent clauses calculated for the subjects at each level. The independent clauses were then divided into thirds with respect to their values on each grammatical complexity measure. An analysis of variance was then performed to determine if the interaction between the reading achievement of the subjects and levels on the grammatical complexity measure was significant.

All three measures of grammatical complexity had a significant correlation with comprehension difficulty; however, the correlation involving the frequency measure was too small to make this variable of value for use in predicting readability or for ordering the sequence in which grammatical structures are introduced in reading instruction.

The sizes of the correlations between the measures of mean word depth and length of an independent clause did not seem to be in any way dependent upon the reading ability of the subject. Consequently, these variables are as effective in ranking the readabilities of written materials for good readers as for poor readers. The relationship between independent clause frequency and comprehension difficulty showed a statistically significant but small change as the reading achievements of subjects increased.

A relatively large difference was observed between the sizes of the correlations obtained at the independent clause and passage levels of analysis. This difference was interpreted as suggesting that the difficulty of an independent clause is strongly influenced by the surrounding text.

The Relation of Regularity of Grapheme-Phoneme Correspondences and of Language Structure to Achievement in First-Grade Reading[*]

Robert B. Ruddell
University of California

Perhaps the first application of concepts from modern linguistics to reading instruction was the attempt to construct materials with regular phoneme-grapheme (sound-letter) correspondence. More recently it has been suggested that the complexity of language structure should be controlled in beginning reading materials. Dr. Ruddell reports a study designed to test the importance of these two variables in actual first-grade reading instruction.

Editor

[*] The research reported herein was performed pursuant to contract SAE2699 with the United States Office of Education, Department of Health, Education and Welfare.

The Relation of Grapheme-Phoneme Correspondences and of Language Structure to Achievement in First-Grade Reading

Introduction

Linguists and psychologists have recently generated numerous hypotheses with direct implications for the teaching of language skills. This is evident from the national meetings of scholars in these related disciplines with language educators during the past two years (5, 13, 14),* related publications which have recently appeared in professional journals (1, 9, 12), the recent publications of textbooks (7, 8), and the development of new classroom materials for reading instruction (3, 4, 10). These hypotheses must be tested in elementary classrooms in experimentally controlled settings over a substantial period of time if progress is to be made in understanding the influence of specific variables on language achievement. The significance of this study in contributing to this goal lies in its provision for increased insight into specific factors in programs of beginning reading instruction and related language variables of children which may contribute to the improvement of primary grade reading achievement.

Hypotheses

The following experimental hypotheses were tested in the study:

1. The first-grade reading programs possessing a high degree of consistency in grapheme-phoneme correspondences in the vocabulary introduced (Program P, Program P +) will result in significantly higher a) word reading, b) word study skills, and c) regular word identification achievement scores than the

* See numbered Bibliography, p. 315.

reading programs making little provision for consistent correspondences (Program B, Program B +).

A related hypothesis stated that the first-grade reading programs making little provision for consistent correspondences (Program B, Program B +) will result in significantly higher irregular word identification achievement scores than the reading programs possessing a high degree of consistency in grapheme-phoneme correspondences in the vocabulary introduced (Program P, Program P+).

2. The first-grade reading programs placing special emphasis on language structure as related to meaning (Program B+, Program P+) will result in significantly higher a) paragraph meaning comprehension and b) sentence meaning comprehension achievement scores than the reading programs placing no special emphasis on language structure as related to meaning (Program B, Program P).

3. Paragraph meaning comprehension, sentence meaning comprehension, and vocabulary achievement of first-grade subjects at the end of grade one are a function of the control which the subjects exhibit over designated aspects of a) their morphological language system and b) their syntactical language system at the beginning of grade one.

Four exploratory questions were developed to study the relationship between the independent background variables of mental age, socio-economic status, sex, and chronological age, and the dependent variables of word recognition and reading comprehension and any changes in these relationships according to the contrastingly different reading programs employed.

Program Description

Two published programs were selected and two supplementary reading programs were developed to encompass the specific characteristics necessary for the experimental testing of the hypotheses.

Program B consisted of a basal reader series (11) encompassing the following characteristics: the grapheme-phoneme regularities were not controlled in the vocabulary presented; the emphasis on phonic training in establishing grapheme-phoneme correspondences was initiated at primer level; the early stages of phonic training dealt with initial consonant correspondences; no specific emphasis on language structure as related to meaning was provided; and the program encompassed a teacher's manual, basal reader, and workbook materials.

Program P consisted of a basal reader series (4), including the following characteristics: the grapheme-phoneme regularities were controlled and programmed in the reading material presented; the emphasis on phonic training in establishing grapheme-phoneme correspondences was initiated in the pre-reading materials; the initial stages of phonic training dealt with the short a, the *schwa,* and four initial consonant sounds; no specific emphasis on language structure as related to meaning was provided; and the program encompassed a teacher's manual and basal reader materials in a programmed format.

Program B+ was developed by the investigator and was designed to stress language structure as related to meaning, supplementing Program B (10). Characteristics of the program include the following: all elements in Program B were common to this program; the vocabulary introduced and developed in Program B was used in the materials and exercises in the supplementary aspect of this program; emphasis in the initial stage of this program was placed on intonation patterns as related to meaning and written punctuation; a variety of basic patterns of language structure (15, p. 29) were developed and the relationship of words and word groups to meaning contrasts in each pattern was stressed. Contrasting meaning changes included:

(1) Word substitution (e.g., *Bill* sees the ball. *Linda* sees the ball. Linda sees the *kitten.*)

(2) Pattern expansion and elaboration (e.g., Ann had a birth-

day. Ann had a birthday *yesterday*. Ann *my friend* had a birthday yesterday.)

(3) Pattern inversion (e.g., *Bill* hit the ball. *The ball* hit Bill.)

(4) Pattern transformation (e.g., *Sam* is in the kitchen. *Is* Sam in the kitchen?)

Detailed teacher plans were developed for each lesson. Words for pattern construction were grouped on the basis of form class and printed on word cards and $1\frac{1}{4}$ inch cubes to provide flexibility in pattern construction and in the development of contrasting meaning changes.

Program P+ was also developed by the investigator and was designed to stress language structure as related to meaning supplementing Program P (10). Characteristics of this program include the following: all elements in Program P were common to this program; the vocabulary introduced in Program P was used in the materials and exercises in the supplementary aspect of this program; the concepts, exercises, and materials were developed, presented, and utilized in identical fashion to the supplementary aspect of Program B+.

Procedure

Twenty-four first-grade classrooms in the Oakland Unified School District, Oakland, California, were selected for the study. These classes represented a wide range of socio-economic levels. Based on the 1960 census report, eight of the classrooms were located in the lowest income areas of the school district, and eight classrooms were located in the highest income areas of the district. The remaining eight classrooms represented the middle income range.

The classrooms on each income level were randomly assigned to each of the four treatment groups (Programs B, P, B+, and P+). A three-day workshop was held at the beginning of the school year for the teachers in each treatment group. At that time the basic instructional rationale, methodology, and instructions for the initial testing program were discussed in detail. Five teacher workshops were held for all treatment groups during the first nine months of the study. Provision for equal time and attention to teachers in each treatment group was carefully controlled throughout the investigation in attempting to generate equivalent interest and enthusiasm in attempting to control for differences which might be produced by the "Hawthorne effect."

The time devoted to the reading instruction period was held constant for each of the four treatment groups. The subjects in Programs B and P devoted 60 minutes in the morning to reading; the second group of subjects in each program devoted 60 minutes in the afternoon to the same activity. Both programs thus used the split-group plan* common to the school district. The first group of subjects in Program B + and Program P + likewise utilized the split-group plan and devoted 45 minutes to basal reading in the morning, while the second group devoted 45 minutes in the afternoon to the basal reading programs common respectively to Program B and Program P. The remaining 15 minutes in the morning and afternoon groups, for subjects in Program B + and Program P +, were utilized for the supplementary program emphasizing language structure as related to meaning.

During the first month of the 1964 school year, the following tests were administered to all subjects: Metropolitan Readiness Test, Form A; Murphy-Durrell Diagnostic Reading Readiness Test; Thurstone Pattern Copying and Identical Forms Test; and the Pintner Cunningham Primary Test of General Ability, Form A. Modified forms of Berko's Test of Morphology (2) and Fraser, Bellugi, and Brown's Test of Syntax (6)

---

* Under the split-group reading plan, the first group of pupils in the reading class arrives at 8:45 A.M. and reading is taught until 9:45 A.M. At 9:45 A.M. the second group of pupils joins the class. At 2:00 P.M. the pupils who came to school at 8:45 A.M. leave the class, and the pupils who entered school at 9:45 A.M. have reading class from 2:00 P.M. until 3:00 P.M.

were administered individually to 160 randomly selected children (40 subjects from each treatment group). The latter two tests were used in measuring the subjects' control over specific aspects of their morphological and syntactical language systems. Chronological age and sex data were collected from the school records. Data on the occupation of parents were collected in order that a socio-economic status level could be determined for each child on the basis of the Minnesota Scale for Paternal Occupations (University of Minnesota, 1950).

In May of 1965 a battery of criterion tests was administered to evaluate reading achievement relative to the hypotheses of the study. These included the following: the Word Reading, Word Study Skills, Paragraph Meaning, and Vocabulary subtests of the Stanford Achievement Test; the Primary Test of Syntax designed by the investigator to measure sentence meaning; the Phonetically Regular Words Oral Reading Test designed by the University of Minnesota Coordinating Research Center to measure children's ability to decode words containing consistent correspondences; and the Gates Word Pronunciation Test administered to measure children's ability to decode words containing inconsistent correspondences. The last two tests were administered individually to a randomly selected group of children drawn from each treatment group. Other criterion measures were also administered; however, the space limitations in this presentation prohibit their discussion.

Findings of the Study

Each experimental hypothesis was stated in terms of its null form for testing. The analysis of covariance was used in testing the hypotheses related to the primary objective of the study. The covariate for each criterion variable consisted of the readiness variable which correlated most highly with the dependent variable under consideration. If significant effects were found on the F test, then individual comparisons of the means were made by using the *t* test. The Pearson product-moment correlation was used in testing the hypothesis exploring the secondary objective of the study. The desired contrasts relative to the four exploratory questions* of the study were examined by using the Scheffé technique of contrasted means.

In relation to the initial part of the first hypothesis, the means for the word-reading, word-study skills, and regular word-identification scores were found to be significantly different, and each comparison favored the program encompassing consistent correspondences, with one exception. This exception was the mean comparison between Program B and Program P on the work study skills test. Although the mean difference was in the predicted direction, the difference was not of sufficient magnitude to reach significance. The experimental hypothesis was thus accepted on the basis of this evidence with the one exception. These findings are presented in Table 1.

The null form of the second part of the first hypothesis could not be rejected on any contrast. It is noted that the mean differences for the irregular word identification scores were in the opposite direction predicted by the experimental hypothesis. Program B+ and Program P+ were found to differ significantly; however, the mean difference between Program B and Program P was not significant. These differences suggest that

---

* In studying the exploratory questions, the independent variables of mental age, socio-economic status, and chronological age were divided into three categories (high, mid, and low) for the analysis of the dependent variables of word-reading, word-study skills, paragraph-meaning, and sentence-meaning comprehension in relation to the four reading programs utilized. The independent variables were divided into two categories (high and low) for the analysis of the dependent variables of regular word identification and irregular word identification in relation to the contrastingly different reading programs employed. The two-category breakdown for the last two variables was necessary due to the small number of subjects in the randomly selected subsample used for this part of the study.

Table 1

Adjusted Means for Word-Reading, Word-Study Skills, Regular Word-Identification, and Irregular Word-Identification Scores for Treatment Groups B, P, B+, and P+

	Group B	Group P	t value	Group B+	Group P+	t value	Covariate
W.R.	17.60 (N = 132)	20.67* (N = 134)	4.86	16.51 (N = 157)	19.70* (N = 124)	5.06	Murphy-Durrell Diagnostic Reading Readiness Test
W.S.S.	32.48 (N = 133)	33.42 (N = 134)	.95	30.93 (N = 155)	34.98* (N = 123)	4.05	Murphy-Durrell Diagnostic Reading Readiness Test
R.W.I.	5.44 (N = 44)	9.09* (N = 41)	3.16	3.08 (N = 42)	10.02* (N = 40)	5.73	Metropolitan Readiness Test
I.W.I.	10.80 (N = 44)	11.83 (N = 41)	.85	9.93 (N = 39)	12.79* (N = 39)	2.25	Metropolitan Readiness Test

* Contrast significant at the .05 level.

the subjects in the treatment groups possessing a high degree of consistency in correspondences introduced were able to deal as effectively, and in one case significantly more effectively, with inconsistent correspondences than the subjects in treatment groups utilizing a high degree of inconsistency in the correspondences. These data are reported in Table 1.

The mean comparisons relative to the second hypothesis revealed the presence of significant differences on paragraph and sentence meaning comprehension scores. The directions of one of the differences favored Program B rather than Program B+. This reversal of predicted mean direction as evidenced in Table 2 indicated that Group B performed significantly better than Group B+ on the paragraph meaning comprehension task. Although the null form of this part of the hypothesis was rejected, the experimental hypothesis could not be accepted because of the former direction predicted.

The mean difference between Program P and Program P+ was significant, favoring the P+ program. The null form of the hypothesis expressing no difference between Group P and Group P+ was rejected and the experimental hypothesis was accepted. These data are reported in Table 2.

The mean differences on the sentence meaning comprehension task was in the direction predicted by the second hypothesis as indicated in Table 2. It is noted, however, that the mean difference between Program B and Program B+ failed to reach significance. Program P+ was found to differ significantly from Program P on the sentence meaning variable. A *post hoc* analysis revealed that Group P+ differed significantly from Group B at the .05 level of significance. These findings suggest a trend favoring the direction of the supplementary programs on the sentence meaning comprehension variable.

The data presented in Table 2 suggest that on both paragraph and sentence meaning comprehension the language structure supplement (+) interacted differently with the P program in the P+ treatment group than with the B program in the B+ treatment group. An interpretation of this interaction may be

Table 2
Adjusted Means for Paragraph Meaning Comprehension and Sentence Meaning Comprehension Scores for Treatment Groups B, B+, P, and P+

	Group B	Group B+	t value	Group P	Group P+	t value	Covariate
P.M.	17.25* (N = 132)	13.78 (N = 156)	3.99	15.66 (N = 134)	17.56* (N = 123)	2.04	Murphy-Durrell Diagnostic Reading Readiness Test
S.M.	22.24 (N = 130)	23.10 (N = 155)	.59	23.96 (N = 132)	29.42* (N = 116)	3.45	Metropolitan Readiness Test

* Contrast significant at the .05 level.

found in the final report to the U.S. Office of Education. Careful observation will be given to these interactions and the suggested trends in the second year of the study.

Relative to the third hypothesis, the correlation coefficients between the morphology test scores and the achievement scores of paragraph meaning, sentence meaning, and vocabulary were found to be .41, .39, and .32 respectively. The coefficients between the syntax test scores and paragraph meaning, sentence meaning, and vocabulary scores were found to be .56, .56, and .53 respectively. (All coefficients were found to be significant at or above the .05 level of significance.) These findings reveal that the child's control over designated aspects of his morphological and syntactical language systems is significantly related to his paragraph meaning, sentence meaning, and vocabulary achievement scores. The third hypothesis was thus accepted. Additional analysis is planned in order to isolate the degree of contribution morphological language development and syntactical language development make in the prediction of reading comprehension achievement when combined with other predictive factors. Additional research is needed in exploring the causal nature of these relationships.

The space limitation in this research summary prohibits the discussion of findings related to the four exploratory questions. The following section on conclusions of the study, however, incorporates four general trend statements derived from the detailed final report relative to the exploratory questions.

Conclusions

Within the limits of the investigation, the following conclusions based upon the findings of the study would seem to be warranted.

1. It was concluded, in regard to part one of the first hypothesis, that the first-grade reading programs possessing a high degree of consistency in grapheme-phoneme correspondences produced significantly higher a) word reading, b) word study skills, and c) regular word identification achievement

than the reading programs making little provision for consistent correspondences, with the exception of one contrast on the word study skills variable.

2. In regard to part two of the first hypothesis, it was concluded that the reading program making little provision for consistent correspondences did not produce significantly higher irregular word identification achievement than the reading program possessing a high degree of consistency in correspondences. However, the reading program which provided for a high degree of consistency and also placed emphasis on language structure as related to meaning produced significantly higher irregular word identification achievement than the reading program which placed no emphasis on consistent correspondences but emphasized language structure as related to meaning.

3. In relation to the second hypothesis, it was concluded that the reading program possessing consistent correspondences and emphasizing language structure as related to meaning produced significantly higher a) paragraph meaning comprehension, and b) sentence meaning comprehension achievement than the program possessing only consistent correspondences. However, the program which did not control consistent correspondences but did emphasize language structure as related to meaning failed to produce significantly higher achievement on either of the comprehension variables than the reading program containing inconsistent correspondences.

4. In relation to the third hypothesis, it was concluded that paragraph meaning comprehension, sentence meaning comprehension, and vocabulary achievement of the first-grade subjects at the end of grade one are a function of the control which the subjects exhibit over designated aspects of a) their morphological language system, and b) their syntactical language system at the beginning of grade one.

The following general statements relative to the four exploratory questions should be considered only suggestive in nature. The smaller number of subjects within the two- or three-category classifications of mental age, socio-economic status, sex, and chronological age greatly reduced the power of the tests of significance on the dependent variable contrasts. As a result, comparatively large differences were required for a mean difference to reach the level of significance. Thus, suggested trends resulting from consistent nonsignificant mean differences have also been included in the statements below. Data collected in the second year of the study should be carefully examined for findings which substantiate or reject these trend statements.

1. The significant mean differences and the consistent nonsignificant mean trends suggest that the reading programs which possessed a high degree of consistency in correspondences benefited the children of both sexes and those classified in the mid and high categories of mental age, socio-economic status, and chronological age on a) word reading, b) word study skills, and c) regular word identification achievement to a greater degree than the reading programs which possessed little control over consistent correspondences.

2. The programs possessing a high degree of consistency in correspondences also produced higher significant and consistent nonsignificant mean values on variables of a) word reading, and b) regular word identification for the children classified in the low category of mental age, socio-economic status, and chronological age than the programs which placed no special emphasis on controlled correspondences. However, the latter program produced higher significant and nonsignificant but consistent mean differences on the variables of word study skills and the irregular word identification, favoring the children in the low mental age, socio-economic status, and chronological age categories.

3. The significant differences and consistent nonsignificant mean trends suggest that the reading program which possessed a high degree of consistency in correspondences, and also placed special emphasis on language structure, was of greater value to children in the male category and those in the mid and high categories of mental age, socio-economic status, and chronological age on the variables of a) paragraph meaning, and b) sentence meaning comprehension achievement, than the read-

ing program which possessed only a high degree of consistency in correspondences. Mean values on both comprehension variables, however, were found to be of greater magnitude for children in the latter program if they were in the female category or classified in the low categories of mental age, socioeconomic status, and chronological age.

4. The reading program which possessed little control over consistent correspondences produced significantly higher and consistently higher (but nonsignificant) mean values on the variables of a) paragraph meaning, and b) sentence meaning comprehension for the children in all mental age, socio-economic, sex, and chronological age categories than the program which possessed little control over consistent correspondences but placed special emphasis on language structure as related to meaning, with one exception. This nonsignificant mean difference favored the direction of the latter program on the mid chronological age category.

Concluding Statement

This investigation represents an attempt to provide increased insight into basic factors in programs of early reading instruction and related language variables of children that may contribute to the improvement of reading achievement. The data to be collected during the second year of the investigation should provide additional information that will allow the investigator to support or reject the experimental hypotheses and suggested trends with greater certainty.

The need for carefully designed longitudinal reading research studies is of great importance if recently developed programs encompassing varied linguistic and psychological rationale are to be adequately evaluated in realistic classroom settings. The recognition of this requisite in research design, which a small minority of reading research studies has achieved, should establish a base that will provide researchers with a more penetrating understanding of factors affecting language skill development.

Linguistics and Materials for Beginning Reading Instruction

Hans C. Olsen, Jr.
Wayne State University

With a somewhat bewildering rapidity materials with linguistic labels for teaching beginning reading are appearing on the market. Variously they claim to be based on linguistics, to use linguistic knowledge, or even to employ "the linguistic method." Dr. Olsen carefully examines the validity and meaning of these claims.

EDITOR

Linguistics and Materials for
Beginning Reading Instruction

As "linguistics" is coming to be a magic word in the world of reading instruction, a rapidly increasing number of reading materials that bear linguistic labels are appearing on the market. These are being introduced by newly-formed as well as long-established publishing houses. Prominent among the authors are well-known professional educators and linguists. Ever increasing numbers of schools and school systems are using these materials.

At least a portion of this growth in the use of reading materials with linguistic labels may be attributed to "the band wagon effect": if it's new (or apparently new) and well-publicized it must be good and "we'd better give it a try." This phenomenon is well known in professional circles. In many sectors of the professional community there is a long story of searching for *the* answer: questing for panaceas. All too often this has resulted in uncritical acceptance of untested, illogical, and/or unsophisticated approaches to instruction that leave practitioners disappointed and disillusioned as it becomes apparent that these approaches will not resolve the problems facing them. While the more professionally sophisticated are well aware that no panaceas are likely to be found, there is always a search for more effective ways than those currently in use. Not all professionals are willing to jump on the band wagon but all are seeking new knowledge that will assist them in providing better instruction.

It is well documented that American education since the 1890's has been characterized by what has been termed the "pendulum" movement. The action of the educational pendulum results from new or different ideas or approaches that challenge the status quo. The "swings" in theory and practice are reactions to established generally accepted patterns. These swings of the pendulum have been evident particularly at the verbal level and much more restrained and restricted at the level of practice. Theorists and educational authorities have been much more fully engaged than have classroom practitioners.

What has been true of education in general has been true of reading instruction in particular. Controversy has swirled as fresh concepts and reworked ideas are introduced, debated, and tested. Frequently the heat has been far more intense than the light, and all too often instructional practice has been affected relatively little. The "either-or," black and white of debate tends to be ameliorated in classroom instruction of boys and girls. Thus the phonics versus sight approach to teaching reading has been, insofar as children are concerned, largely a matter of rhetoric.

Controversy, the swinging pendulum, and the band-wagon effect all play prominent roles in reading instruction because of the importance attached to reading in our culture. Not only do elementary school teachers tend to believe that reading is the most important skill to be learned in the elementary school but school patrons generally concur. Difficulties arise, however, because there is a widespread lack of understanding of the complexity of the reading act, the instructional competence required of teachers, and the number and types of materials needed if children are to learn to read as effectively and extensively as generally hoped or expected. Much of the problem may be traced to the absence of any commonly understood and accepted definition of what reading is or agreement as to when a person has learned to read.

Since World War II in particular it has been popular to inveigh against current school instructional practices, especially those used to teach reading. Reaction to the criticism, no matter how well intentioned, has been one of concern, even bitterness. The criticism has produced a climate of uncertainty as to what constitutes "best" methods and materials. And this climate has led some to an almost desperate search for *the answer*.

Thus, linguistic knowledge and reading materials with linguistic labels are falling on fertile ground. This has come to mean that to a certain extent the new messiahs in the field of reading are linguists. Under these conditions they have a tremendous potential for materially shaping reading instruction for some time to come. Recognized leaders in the field of reading as well as school practitioners are now giving increased attention to this source of knowledge and the relevance of linguistics for reading instruction.

Development of Reading Materials with Linguistic Labels

Bloomfield is generally credited with being the first of the linguists to become seriously interested in utilizing linguistic knowledge in elementary school reading instruction. His interest arose through dissatisfaction with approaches to reading instruction that were prevalent in the early 1930's. He believed that those methods and materials for teaching children to read were unsophisticated and ineffective. From his study of the situation and his knowledge of linguistics he devised a more "scientific" method of reading instruction.

During the late 1930's and most of the 1940's Bloomfield and Barnhart, who had joined in partnership, attempted to have their materials published and tested. However, they were unsuccessful. We are told that commercial publishing houses and university presses refused to publish these materials and that reputable colleges of education were not interested in testing them (1).

In 1942 Bloomfield's two benchmark articles "Linguistics and Reading" (2) were published. These articles outlined the principles he believed should be the basis for reading materials and instruction. They also stressed the need for experimentation to test the approach he was advocating. The articles stirred up interest in reading circles but did not result in getting the Bloomfield-Barnhart materials published.

From the late 1940's others interested in the application of linguistic knowledge began to give attention to the problems of teaching elementary school children to read. Articles authored by linguists began to appear in the literature on reading. However, the major breakthrough probably occurred in 1961, almost two decades after Bloomfield's first article appeared, when *Let's Read: A Linguistic Approach* (1) was published. This book, carrying the names of Bloomfield and Barnhart, presented an introduction to the Bloomfield approach to teaching reading plus the instructional materials they had developed.

Finally, in 1963 a rash of instructional materials with linguistic labels appeared on the market. Among them were the materials that Barnhart himself published. These were the first three books in the series entitled *Let's Read* (3). These materials are essentially those Bloomfield and Barnhart tried unsuccessfully to have published almost a quarter of a century earlier. Also in 1963 the first books in the series entitled *The Linguistic-Science Readers* (11, 12) were published under the authorship of Stratemeyer and Smith. In that same year the Lippincott materials prepared by McCracken and Wolcott were published. These are called *Basic Reading* (4). Two other sets of materials were placed on the market in 1963. One of these was produced by Sullivan Associates and published by McGraw-Hill. These materials are entitled *Programmed Reading* (5). The second set of materials was produced by Scott-Foresman under the name *Linguistic Block Series* (6). Additions to these, as well as other materials with linguistic labels, have recently reached the market or will soon be available.

Within the last three years two interesting phenomena have developed in the textbook publishing field: 1) For the first time within memory publishing houses are rushing basal materials into print as they are completed by the authors rather than printing all books in a series and placing them on the market at one time. This is particularly true of materials with linguistic labels. 2) The term "linguistic" is coming into general use and more or less prominence in publishers' blurbs and materials prepared for use with classroom practitioners. This is almost as true of long-established series as it is of recently published materials. Publishers' representatives often give the impression that conventional basal materials deliberately and consistently follow sound linguistic principles when in reality this is more happenstance than a systematic use of these principles.

Since Bloomfield and Barnhart's *Let's Read: A Linguistic Approach* appeared in 1961, C. C. Fries' landmark book *Linguistics and Reading* (7) became available in 1963 and in 1964 Carl Lefevre's *Linguistics and the Teaching of Reading* (8) was published. Other books on linguistics as related to reading in the elementary school are now available or in process and in some cases sections of books on the teaching of reading now on the market are devoted to a discussion of linguistic knowledge. Thus, within the last five years much linguistic knowledge as it relates to reading, plus many materials with linguistic labels, has become available to those interested in reading instruction in the elementary school.

Description of Representative Reading Materials with Linguistic Labels

Three sets of materials with linguistic labels that are representative of those now found on the market have been selected for review in this paper. As this paper is written they are among the few widely available to schools. Other materials with linguistic labels are in preparation or have been on the market only a short time. These three sets of materials differ markedly one from another. The first of these is *The Linguistic Readers* (11, 12) published by Harper and Row. (Originally entitled *The Linguistic-Science Readers,* the word Science has been dropped.) Of the three it most closely resembles the usual basal reading series. The major authors at the outset were Clara Stratemeyer and Henry Lee Smith. Until recently this series consisted of three pre-primers. However, a primer, first reader, workbook, and teacher's manual have been added. The basic ideas guiding the authors in the construction of these materials are: the presentation of a consistent grapheme-phoneme relationship (although the new teaching manual claims that this is a morphophonic approach rather than a strictly consistent sound-symbol relationship); sentences that are more than one line in length; and the presentation of contractions in the vocabulary, starting with the second pre-primer. The publishers state that the printed material "reflects the child's natural speech" and that the content is an accurate representation of life. An example of the latter is that the animals in these stories do not think or talk. (However, they do dream.) Originally, publishers also stressed that the illustrations were not for the purpose of getting clues to meaning. Rather they were for the purpose of lending attractiveness to the materials. The content was designed to stand on its own merit. The more recently published teacher's manual is silent on this, however. In fact, it shows how the teacher might use the illustrations to help children gain meaning. For example, it recommends that children learn to distinguish Zip from Pud (two frogs) because the latter has spots on his back while the former has stripes (10). The authors have attempted to limit the vocabulary to words that represent a consistent sound symbol relationship. These relationships are initially presented as sight words, and then are repeated systematically. The inevitable inconsistencies in the sound-symbol needed for early reading are introduced in planned patterns. From the start of their experiences with formal reading instruction children are taught to focus on letters rather than words or larger units.

The second set of materials are those prepared by Bloomfield and Barnhart entitled *Let's Read*. These are less like traditional basal materials than are the Harper and Row series. A significant portion of this difference is accounted for by the definition of reading used by the authors. Their contention is that written language is a code and the emphasis in initial reading instruction should be on cracking the code rather than getting meaning. Associating printed symbols with the sounds of vocabulary is the most important task of the child learning to read. No guessing is allowed. Therefore, no illustrations are presented so that children must concentrate on decoding the symbols. The caliber of literature is of no consequence at this point and nonsense syllables are used rather extensively. Indeed, many of the words may be taught as nonsense syllables because they are unknown by children. The authors frankly state that drill on the word lists is of prime importance; the reading lessons are supplementary exercises. The child must learn to "say the word called for by the letters." He learns to spell the word at the time he learns the word for purposes of reading. The authors have selected the regular correspondences of symbol and sound and then present them one at a time. New words are presented by pairing words alike except for one contrasting letter and sound such as cat and rat. But teachers are cautioned not to teach "the sounds of letters." Bloomfield and Barnhart in their materials for teachers claim that their materials consist of letters having only one phonetic value. Emphasis is on the phonetic values of the vowels. No words with silent letters or double letters are included. Neither are the letters x or q and only one duplication of letters having the same phonetic value, c and k. They have also restricted the irregularities to the word "a." The task of the child is to master each step before moving on. Teachers are admonished not to allow children to move ahead until they can say each word with no hesitation; they are told repeatedly of the desirability of having children "overlearn" materials.

The third set of materials called *Programmed Reading* (5) is published by McGraw-Hill and was prepared by Cynthia D. Buchanan for Sullivan Associates. This set of materials is least like the traditional basal reading series. It combines linguistic knowledge with the programmed approach to instruction. It is clearly based on stimulus-response psychology. The materials are designed to maintain a consistent relationship between each sound and the letter that represents it. These regular sound-symbol relationships are systematically developed. Following the principle in all programmed instruction, the intent is to present patterns that gradually increase in complexity. As in the two previously described sets of materials, children must learn to discriminate individual letters in a word. In this series they do it through the use of what are termed minimal pairs. These minimal pairs contain only one contrasting element. This is similar to the Bloomfield-Barnhart approach.

Children are taught to say sounds for letters; for example, the "m" sound. No sound-symbol irregularities are presented in the first portion of the beginning materials. The authors believe that this permits children to *sound out* words precisely and spell them according to regular rules. They further claim that the children learn to spell and to print every word that they can read. However, unlike the Bloomfield-Barnhart approach, meaning is a cornerstone of *Programmed Reading*. A major device in accomplishing this goal is the picture that accompanies each frame. These pictures help tell the story. The publishers also state that the sentences utilized in these materials observe the patterns of modern spoken English and that each new bit of information fits logically with previously presented materials. They further contend that the pictures and sentences that are presented together develop situations in which "children do things from a child's point of view." In accord with the basic tenets of programmed instruction the child is encouraged to move at his own pace. It is recommended that two thirty-minute reading periods be included in the school day. The final claim is that "programmed reading incorporates the findings of structural linguistics, experimental psychology and programming into a skillfully written text which captures the child's imagination and delights him while he learns."

*Analysis of Three Sets of Reading Materials
with Linguistic Labels*

I will confine my presentation of the results of the analysis of these three sets of linguistically labeled materials to four major points, each of which I will describe and document briefly. It must be remembered that in reviewing such diverse types of materials each of the four major points will fit one or two of the materials more closely than others. However, on balance I believe these four points can be substantiated.

First: *There is a concentration on linguistic principles at the expense of knowledge related to reading.*

Interest and motivation are almost totally ignored in the Bloomfield-Barnhart materials. These authors assume that all children want to learn to read and will derive sufficient reward merely from learning to crack the code. Bloomfield-Barnhart ignore and Sullivan Associates restrict the content of the reading materials as a possible source of interest and motivation. The Harper and Row series is by far the most attractive and appealing, based on the pictures, the use of color, and the general layout of the materials. This can be checked out with most six-year-olds. At the same time the stories in this series are rather long, dull, and repetitious.

Certain facts about learning are also overlooked by the authors of these reading materials with linguistic labels. Despite the fact that in each case the authors recommend that children concentrate on individual letters, available evidence indicates that short words can be identified as rapidly and as easily as can individual letters. The Bloomfield-Barnhart and Sullivan Associates materials concentrate on the principle of least differences rather than on the principle of greatest contrast. This despite the known fact that the greater the contrast the more easily children detect differences. The authors of all three series also tend to neglect some of the principles of word recognition long known to reading specialists; that word shape, length, context, pictorial clues and details within the word help children learn the word and that concentration on letters alone may not suffice.

There is a general tendency to neglect the fact that words used frequently by an individual in speaking are usually easier for him to recall when he sees them in print. Bloomfield-Barnhart reject the idea stressed by many reading authorities that pictures are useful in expanding concepts and clearing up misconceptions. And despite the protestations of the authors, the McGraw-Hill materials are subject to the same criticism as Bloomfield-Barnhart for the heavy amounts of practice which can become meaningless and arbitrary to the learner. Perhaps the difference between the two sets of authors is that Bloomfield-Barnhart quite frankly state that meaning is of little importance and that practice is a major focus of their approach. Another fact known to reading teachers and psychologists is that too much emphasis on words destroys the thought carried by the sentence.

Any system of reading instruction based primarily on a standard sound-symbol relationship does not provide for children with auditory and speech problems. It is known that children with both of these difficulties can learn to read. It would be reasonable to assume that if children with such difficulties do learn to read with any one of these three series, such learning takes place in spite of the one-to-one sound-symbol correspondence and that other factors are far more important.

None of the three sets of materials takes into account or makes provision for differences in the direction of reading growth. *Programmed Reading* does make it possible for youngsters to proceed at their own rate but the program is inflexible and must be followed exactly. It should be remembered that the pace at which children move through the program may be quite slow for reasons other than low ability. However, the directional differences such as varying reading interests, the appeal of special words, etc., are not provided for.

Second: There is a concentration on some linguistic principles while other linguistic knowledge is not used.

Goodman has stated that "language has no existence except in association with meaning." (10). Yet the primary emphasis in these three sets of reading materials is on sound-symbol consistency. It must be recognized that the imposition of any controls intended to simplify reading materials for beginning readers inevitably results in artificial language. Thus, we find the now well-known sentence from Bloomfield-Barnhart, "Nan can fan Dan" and in another instance, "Nan can gab. Gab, gab, gab!" Or in the Harper and Row series "Jump Pud. Jump Zip. Jump. Jump." Certainly these illustrate that children's natural speech is altered when controls are imposed to simplify it for initial reading instruction.

Children's natural speech enters in only a limited way. Little emphasis is placed upon intonation, inflectional changes, patterns of word order, and function words. The *Scott-Foresman Linguistic Block Series* (6), perhaps more familiarly known as *Rolling Readers,* or *Rolling Phonics Blocks,* may provide a useful lead. The importance of "the flow of language" in establishing appropriate pronunciation and meaning has not been recognized in the Bloomfield-Barnhart and McGraw-Hill materials. The same could legitimately be said of the Harper and Row materials until the relatively recent availability of the teacher's manual.

Dialect differences also tend to be overlooked. Linguists tell us that all language is equally good; pronunciation, vocabulary, and grammatical structure are important only as they produce effective communication. We recognize that certain dialects are socially more acceptable in our society. However, any reading materials based upon a consistent sound-symbol relationship do not take into account dialect differences of prospective readers. Take for example the Harper, Row series. From the first pre-primer (11) come the following words: pond, log, hop, on, and frog. A dialect difference could account for something less than sound-symbol consistency in that case of the vowel sound. Or from the third pre-primer (12) the phonetic values of "e" in "As the kitten gets to the tree she stops." (Remember the claim advanced in the new teacher's manual that *The Linguistic Readers* present a morphophonic approach rather than a strict sound-symbol relationship.) Or the phonetic values of "a" in this sentence from the third book of *Let's Read:* "A wet rag cannot rot a pot." Perhaps the findings of Loban (13) and Strickland (14) have special significance in helping authors of future materials with linguistic labels avoid these pitfalls. It may be that their influence is already being felt in the revised approach presented in the Harper, Row series.

Third: *There is a considerable amount of inappropriate and/or inaccurate use of linguistic knowledge.*

All those who prepare materials for beginning reading instruction must, before constructing their materials, make basic decisions as to which fundamental principles they will use to guide them. The authors of the three sets of materials considered in this paper originally decided to maintain a consistent sound-symbol relationship. Yet when decisions are made to include some linguistic principles and to exclude others, inaccurate and/or inappropriate uses of linguistic knowledge inevitably result. For example, to present in printed form the spoken language of one sub-culture or social group will undoubtedly mean that the materials do not fit the style or pattern of other children with different dialects, who speak from different experimental backgrounds, and whose vocabularies differ significantly from those whose language is copied. Certainly sound-symbol consistency suffers when dialect differences are encountered. Take for example the words "fog, log, and pond" which are found in the Harper, Row first pre-primer. Pronunciation is not the same across the country. A representative group of Americans, simply by saying those three words, would demolish a claim of sound-symbol consistency. Also, some children do not know what a pond is; they use other words to refer to a body of water that is called a pond in some parts of the United States. This is another dialect problem. All three series present inconsistencies in the sound-symbol relationship early in order to make reading possible. Perhaps the basic question is "How consistent (and arbitrary) should the authors be?"

Fourth: *Professional knowledge made available to practitioners in these materials is limited in quality and in quantity.*

Three supporting points arise from the review of these materials. 1) Inadequate assistance is provided teachers in understanding linguistic principles. In none of the three series are teachers provided with sufficient background in linguistics to understand adequately the meaning of the term "linguistics." Therefore, they tend to get a brief course in what might be seen as advanced phonics and they bring to their teaching little or no understanding of other linguistic principles or, indeed, the real foundation for the linguistic principles they are asked to use. 2) Practitioners are provided little research evidence to support the claims of wide success and great utility of the materials. The authors claim that the materials have been tested successfully and that they may be used effectively in a wide variety of situations. However, they provide little to substantiate these claims. The research cited is very inadequately reported. One is led to believe that the claims boil down to the fact that children can learn to read using these materials. The interesting thing is that many people have reached the conclusion that some children can learn to read with almost any set of materials. Certainly the evidence provided by the publishers and authors of those materials cannot be legitimately interpreted to mean that children can more effectively learn to read with these materials. 3) These materials provide little in the way of new knowledge of method despite the emphasis given to the use of the so-called linguistic approach. As Karlsen (15) has said, the Bloomfield-Barnhart methodology is reminiscent of that in vogue fifty years ago except for the focus on phonetic consistency. The new dimension of the Sullivan Associates materials is the programmed learning approach. And a Harper, Row publicity blurb quite frankly says "The difference between the *Linguistic Science Readers* and any other basic program is not in the method of instruction." Thus, we must conclude with Karlsen that "We probably cannot speak of a 'linguistic approach' to the teaching of reading at the present time, since we are not entirely in agreement as to what this might be."

Conclusions

The following conclusions seem to be warranted on the basis of the preceding analysis and review of reading materials with linguistic labels: 1) There is a need to better integrate linguistic knowledge with other knowledge related to reading. At present, much knowledge about reading is not incorporated in so-called linguistic reading instruction. The purpose in reading instruction is to help children learn to read as efficiently and effectively as possible. To develop a "scientific" system of reading instruction which does no better in this respect than other approaches is not a major contribution. 2) There is a need to better utilize existing linguistic knowledge in reading programs. Attention should be given to the use of child language in reading materials. Greater provision must be made for differences in dialects. Better uses of cue systems such as pattern, inflectional changes, function words, and intonation should be investigated. The importance of the "stream of language" in determining pronunciation and meaning also needs to be recognized. It should be remembered that reading is a part of a communicative process and that meaning is an expectation of all who are involved, including beginning readers. 3) There is a need to test linguistic approaches and materials to determine the extent to which they are effective in producing learning and the extent to which they are more or less appropriate than other approaches and materials. Certainly the cry for more research is not new, yet it is strange that in the field of reading, the most researched area in elementary education, there exists such a paucity of well-documented research substantiating the claims of the authors or publishers of reading materials with linguistic labels. 4) Classroom practitioners need more help in understanding linguistics and the application of linguistic principles in the teaching of reading. When publishers and authors undertake to present allegedly radically new approaches and materials, they assume responsibility for providing teachers with appropriate knowledge for understanding. They cannot be satisfied to assist teachers in "cookbooking" reading instruction. 5) These three sets of materials are pioneers in the field. They are by no means all bad. Each has its strengths and therefore may be appropriately used in some situations. However, they do indicate that future materials with linguistic labels must provide a more rounded approach to the teaching of reading.

A Multidisciplinary Approach
to Language and to Reading:
Some Projections*

Carl A. Lefevre
Temple University

Dr. Lefevre, "a humanist and scholar-teacher" and author of a book-length treatise on reading and linguistics, presents here the case for bringing the knowledge of many disciplines to bear on the study and teaching of reading. He presents his own theoretical view of the reading process and the areas he believes are most in need of researching.

EDITOR

A Multidisciplinary Approach to Language and to Reading: Some Projections*

Our conference title, "The Psycholinguistic Nature of the Reading Process," recognizes that reading involves an overlapping of two disciplines: psychology and linguistics. As a humanist and scholar-teacher of the humanities—an amateur in psychology with English linguistics as one string to my bow —I suggest that a comprehensive study of the arts and skills of reading is truly multidisciplinary. This is true because reading is not a discipline in itself, nor the province of merely two disciplines. To be truly comprehensive, the study of reading must also encompass important elements of anthropology, literature, philosophy, and sociology.

Reading involves a complex of facilitating arts and skills, closely interwoven with speech and writing—none ends in themselves, but communicative means to personal and social maturity, to the ultimate ends of education and of humanity itself, in fact. Reading is not reading unless it gives access to meanings; and it is difficult to refute the proposition that the meanings expressed in speech and writing comprise a large share of communicable human experience. The skills of speech are the essential humanizing skills, because it is language that makes man man. For literate man, reading is the principal further means of acquiring not merely information and concepts, but also attitudes, insights, understandings, and values, required to comprehend the development of human life and human cultures. Reading is a powerful means to maturity and acculturation.

Reading as a Language-Related Process; a Definition of Language

A basic assumption of this paper is that reading is first of all a language-related process. This implies the primacy of speech; that is, language *is* speech, the primary symbol-system. The graphic symbol-systems of handwriting and print—if such systems exist—are based upon and derived from speech; in this sense alone, and in no pejorative sense, the graphic systems are said to be secondary. It follows that study of the skills of literacy, reading in particular for present purposes, should begin with a probing into the complex interplay of the two closely related symbol-systems. This beginning would concern itself especially with basic and primary skills; here *basic* means fundamental , and *primary* means first or introductory. Critical reading, logical thinking, reading in depth, and literary appreciation are neither basic nor primary, but quite advanced reading skills.

A definition of language. Language may be defined as an arbitrary code of audio-lingual symbols by means of which men in a given culture communicate, interact, and cooperate in terms of the culture as a whole; the language of any culture is capable of expressing and communicating as "messages" whatever information, concepts, attitudes, insights, values, and understandings the native speakers may need to express and communicate, including those imported from other cultures. The content of messages is not only mental or intellectual, as the term *code* might suggest, but also emotional (affective) and volitional (intentive); moreover, messages have specific denotative and connotative content, both individual and social. Thus we see that the study of language itself is multidisciplinary.

As a form of human behavior, language is not instinctive but must be learned by every infant and child; he learns it in a creative fashion, generally speaking, by adapting his audio-lingual capabilities so as to develop the systematic habits required by the particular language and dialect he is born to. In this creative learning process, auditory imagery is of primary importance. This definition of language does not overlook significant variations of individual ability to encode and decode messages; on the contrary, individual differences are of considerable interest and importance, ranging from articulation of phonemes to comprehension of extended verbal constructs.

A Multidisciplinary Approach to Language and to Reading

Linguistics, narrowly defined, can describe language as a structural system of interrelated parts, or constituents—language as a code. Psychology, via learning theory, can describe language as a system of habits relating symbols to behavior, and via information theory and communication models, can describe language as a means of transmitting "information." Understanding oral language and comprehending written language also require auditory and visual perception, respectively, both within the domain of psychology. But perception alone is not enough: in both listening and reading, entire meaning-bearing language patterns must be not simply decoded but interpreted and evaluated. Interpretation and evaluation must take into account as part of the "information" in the message, its emotional, volitional, denotative, and connotative content. Moreover, social and cultural dimensions often must be considered—regional, class, and standard dialects, for example, and the many forms of extended discourse, including the forms of literature.

Interpretation and evaluation of meaning-bearing language patterns thus lead us into a consideration of the relationships of language and thought, however we define thought. This, of course, is the traditional realm of philosophy. Every major philosopher beginning with Plato has made the study of language an important part of his work; the philosopher's influence is felt today in some of the attitudes and assumptions we bring to language study.

Reading, Language, Meaning, Thought

If reading is a language-related process of deriving meaning from the printed page, we must turn our attention, even though briefly, to certain relationships among language, meaning, and thought. Our view of language and thought is basic to our definition of meaning. Whatever the precise relationship, and whatever the mechanism or process of the relationship may be, human thought and linguistic patterns appear to be so closely interrelated as to be inextricable, the one from the other. The following discussion is not a survey of this topic, but a quick handling of a few seminal ideas.

Of the specific nature of linguistic symbols, the French psychologist, Joseph Vendryes, in a book published in translation in 1925, had this to say: "Psychologically, the original linguistic act consists in giving to a sign a symbolic value. This psychological process distinguishes the language of man from that of animals" (1). Animals and birds can go no further than to use signs in the immediate presence of the referents of their signs; they cannot use signs symbolically, and especially not at other times or in other places. But signs given symbolic value enable man to communicate with others, both directly and immediately, and at times and in places far removed from the situations or events symbolized in his language structures; linguistic symbols also enable him to think to himself, silently or aloud.

In a famous work first published in 1921, Edward Sapir, arguing that language is primarily a pre-rational function, wrote: "*At best* language can but be the outward facet of thought on the highest, most generalized level of symbolic expression" (emphasis added) (2). He believed "that language is an instrument originally put to uses lower than the conceptual plane and that thought arises as a refined interpretation of its content" (3). Granting that thought and speech may be separate and apart, he noted that speech nevertheless seems to be the only road we know of that leads to thought. It is a road that goes both ways. "We see this complex process of the interaction of language and thought actually taking place under our eyes," he wrote. "The instrument makes possible the product, the product refines the instrument" (4). Language is the instrument, of course, thought the product. Sapir regarded thinking as "An abbreviation of the speech process" (5). He insisted that "Auditory imagery and the correlated motor imagery leading to articulation are, by whatever devious ways we follow the process, the historic fountain-head of all speech and all thinking" (6). In summation, he returned to his original symbolism; "Language, as a structure, is on its inner face the mold of thought" (7).

It is fascinating to note similarities between the insights of Sapir and the Soviet psychologist, Vigotsky, in a monograph published in 1934. "Thought is not expressed in words, but comes into existence through them," wrote Vigotsky (8). "Thought, as it turns into speech, undergoes numerous changes. It does not simply find its expression in words; it finds its reality and form" (9). Regarding the nature of words, he said, "The meaning of a word represents such a close unity of thinking and speech that it is not possible to say whether it is a phenomenon of speech or a phenomenon of thinking. . . . It [meaning] is the word itself looked at from within" (10). Vigotsky was deeply impressed by the dynamic quality of the relationship of language and thought: "The bond between thought and words is a living process: thought is brought forth in words. The word, deprived of thought, is a dead word" (11). His investigations eventually led him to a consideration not only of thought, but of consciousness itself: ". . . thinking and speech are the key for understanding the nature of human consciousness," he concluded. "Words play a central part not only in the development of thought but in consciousness as a whole" (12).

Although much of what Vigotsky had to say about language and thought has deep significance for advanced reading processes, he did not comment on reading specifically in the sense of this discussion. Sapir did, however, and what he said is of special interest to this symposium:

> The most important of all visual speech symbolisms is . . . that of the written or printed word. . . . The written forms are secondary symbols of the spoken ones—symbols of symbols—yet so close is the correspondence that they may, not only in theory, but in the actual practice of certain eye-readers and, possibly, in certain types of thinking, be entirely substituted for the spoken ones. Yet the auditory-motor associations are probably always latent at the least, that is, they are unconsciously brought into play. Even those who read and think without the slightest use of sound imagery are, in the last analysis, dependent on it. They are merely handling the circulating medium, the money, of visual symbols as a convenient substitute for the economic goods and services of the fundamental auditory symbols (13).

This is a fertile suggestion for us.

If the foregoing discussion has suggested some multidisciplinary dimensions of the reading process, it has accomplished its purpose. A synthesis of linguistic approaches to reading cannot be an eclectic agglomeration of elements, nor should it exaggerate out of its due proportion any single element. Such a synthesis should reflect the multidisciplinary dimensions of the reading process itself. The remainder of this paper will explore, first, some of the available territory for such a synthesis, and then project problems and areas to be studied with a view to possible research.

Children's Language and the Skills of Literacy

In considering the child's learning of his first language and dialect—a complete and highly complex system of audio-lingual symbols, let us not forget—we must make a qualitative discrimination between his early random production of vocal noise and his emergent conscious use of vocal symbols. Every baby produces a great deal of vocal noise with no linguistic significance other than giving him practice in articulating sounds that he will later select (and also reject) to form his repertoire of language patterns to be used systematically in speech for communicative purposes; patterns that he selects and rejects include not only phones and phonemes, but the native melodies and rhythms of speech—intonation, in short. This is a qualitative discrimination in that it involves (a) the infant's consciousness, to the point of imitation, of language patterns he hears, as well as (b) an infantile attempt to communicate with others. We must not look for minutely accurate production of patterns or a comprehensive grasp of meaning: all things in due time.

There is ample evidence to establish the primacy of large, overriding general patterns in the early language learning of infants and young children. These patterns are sentences and sentence-like structures, delineated and shaped by basic patterns of native English melodies and rhythms. Even the child's later single-word utterances and patterns of prediction without subjects conform to linguistic descriptions of pitch contours and relative degrees of loudness in English sentences. The same may be said of questions and commands. And while these fundamental structural patterns of intonation may be accompanied by expressive features that are entirely optional, this fact should not obscure the systematic use of the underlying patterns, which are not only of fundamental importance in English language structure, but of prior occurrence in the native language learning process. *Intonation precedes the development of the phonemic repertoire and the formation of vocabulary:* indeed, preschool children often cannot single out so-called words from longer utterances. Publications within the past fifteen years by Lewis (14), Grewel (15), Weir (16), Braine (17), and Huttenlocher (18), to mention five, attest to the truth of these observations. One chapter of my book deals with intonation; the book as a whole focuses attention on the overriding quality of intonation in language structure, and on its importance in reading as a language-related process

(19). It is now time to give greater emphasis to sentence patterns and to intonation in basic and primary reading instruction.

Basic and Primary Reading Theory and Methodolgy

It should be well known now that the language patterns and the vocabulary of children are far more rich and complex than was formerly believed, and that the language used in language arts books is infantile and monotonous, in sharp contrast to the richness and variety of the language spoken by the pupils who use them. Loban and Strickland have independently reached detailed findings in this area (20). Up to the present, the language unit stressed in language arts and reading materials has been the word; whole series of basal readers and language books have been planned to introduce a graded vocabulary, with no rigorous attention to syntax or to sentence patterns. *Intonation as part of English structure,* when it has not been ignored altogether, has been lost in the fog of "reading with expression." Traditional phonics represented an attempt to introduce rigor and discipline into reading instruction by relating sounds to spelling, but all too frequently with no basis in accurate linguistic descriptions of phonemes and graphemes. At its worst, phonics taught "the sounds of the letters," a method derided by Bloomfield as the hiss-and-groan method of teaching reading.

Most of the current so-called linguistic approaches to reading have been based upon, and essentially limited to, spelling or the alphabetical principle (Bloomfield (21), Hall (22), Smith (23), *et al.*); Fries has called his approach a specialized word method (24). Whatever modifications may have had to be introduced later as a result of classroom experience, the basic approach has remained the teaching of phoneme and grapheme relationships or, at most, Fries' morpheme and spelling-pattern method. So far there has been no systematic effort to base reading theory and methodology on anything approaching what we know about sentence patterns, intonation, and other important elements of the structural system of English (25).

To the best of my knowledge, my articles beginning in 1961 (26) and my book, LINGUISTICS AND THE TEACHING OF READING (McGraw-Hill, 1964), represent the only sustained, well-developed theoretical break with phonic and word methods of teaching children to read. *In essence, this theory states that the child should first learn to read and write the language and the dialect he speaks when he comes to school, with no more than minimal attempts to correct or purify it; his idiolect is his most direct bridge to literacy. Conversely, to reject the child's speech, or to attack it, is to reject and attack the child himself; such an attack may place him so deeply on the defensive that he will never effectively learn the basic skills of literacy.* Moreover, it is a great virtue of standard English that persons speaking a variety of English dialects around the world can all read their own speech from the same printed page. *Let the child read his dialect from the page of print; let it talk his language. This is his beginning.* This position is developed extensively in a paper written for the 1964 spring meeting of the International Reading Association and published in ELEMENTARY ENGLISH in February and March, 1966. It is entitled, "Language and Self: Realization or Trauma?"

Speaking generally, reading and all language arts instruction should make maximum use of structural data on intonation, and should link analysis of intonation with the main sentence patterns; with the system of about three hundred structure words; with the system of grammatical inflections; and with the rich and truly remarkable system of English derivational prefixes and suffixes, where vocabulary goes forth and multiplies. The language system, or structure, should be explicitly developed throughout the elementary grades as an integral part of reading and language instruction. In such an approach to the total language structure, moving in from larger structural wholes to smaller and smaller parts, only that amount of attention to spelling that experience proves to be necessary for reading should be given to spelling *as a part of reading instruction.* Spelling would be taken up as a skill largely in relation to writing.

Infants and young children normally learn language in a spirit of play and fun. But if the fun is not taken out of language for them before they come to school, far too often it is soon afterward. Children become fearful of being "wrong," chary after constant "correction." Because we tend to manage spelling as a shibboleth, many children will not use new and interesting words for fear of being caught red-handed in a misspelling. *In some children this fear amounts to trauma.*

The Initial Teaching Alphabet. Proponents of the Initial Teaching Alphabet (i.t.a.) place considerable emphasis upon the children's early writing of original compositions; in addition to studying lessons in the i.t.a. reading program, the children read their own and each other's compositions. Thus writing and reading reinforce each other. In Bethlehem, Pennsylvania, I observed primary classrooms where exceptional work was done in both reading and writing using i.t.a. I also observed that i.t.a., when used narrowly as a synthetic phonics system, was just as deadly as traditional orthography presented synthetically. By design, i.t.a. represents Received Standard British. The best use of i.t.a., simply by permissiveness in transcription of sounds, liberates the child from the tryanny of correct spelling at the point when he is just beginning to build his bridge to literacy. For this reason, and in view of the number of English dialects (and the fact that i.t.a. cannot provide a one-to-one correspondence of printed symbols to speech sounds anyway), teachers using i.t.a. are wise to be permissive. Under the best conditions the result can be: no spelling shibboleth, no trauma; the child is freed to read and write freely in i.t.a. during his first semester of school.

My study of compositions written in i.t.a. showed that neither teachers nor pupils had developed linguistic expertise in transcribing speech sounds, though many of the teachers thought that they had; i.t.a. is in fact not a phonemic alphabet, and should not be treated as such. It is a simplified alphabet designed to prepare children to read materials in t.o. (traditional orthography)—i.t.a. is a transitional alphabet. A subtle visual feature of i.t.a. as a transitional device is that "the coast lines" of i.t.a. and t.o. print are almost identical; (the coast line is the upper half of the line of print). Very few of the children I observed had not completed the transition to t.o. by the end of grade two; many of them had by the end of grade one.

The Role of Spelling. We should reconsider, as dispassionately as possible, the specific role of spelling in the skills of literacy—spelling, writing, and reading. In the basic and primary sense of reading, no active production of letters, words, or sentences is required at all; what is required at this level is the recognition of meaning-bearing language patterns as wholes, sentences predominantly, with their characteristic structural intonation patterns. The reader is not a producer but a relatively passive consumer of graphic counterparts of spoken language patterns; interpretation and evaluation are more active processes, of course, but *not strictly linguistic, or language-related.* Writing, on the other hand, requires the active transliteration of meaning-bearing language patterns into their graphic counterparts as wholes, again sentences predominantly; the sentence, not the word, is the building block of composition. Spelling is an active, productive operation in that it requires the recognition and letter-by-letter writing of single words; but spelling is not a communicative process except indirectly, in *writing.* The relationship of spelling to reading is not well understood. We do know that anyone who literally spells as he reads is not reading; that a good speller is not necessarily a good reader, nor a good reader a good speller. We need to reexamine our assumptions about the function of spelling in basic and primary reading instruction.

*A Capsule Statement of Theory for
Advanced Reading Processes*

Once a reader has mastered the basic and primary skills required to read meaning-bearing language patterns at the sentence level, he then has a foundation for interpretation and evaluation of paragraphs and longer passages of exposition, and for beginning to comprehend and appreciate literature in terms of syntax, language, and form. And while these advanced skills are capable of nearly endless development, they are based upon language-related processes that may be studied by extensions and variations of the analytical methods that have already described linguistic structures up to the level of the sentence: phonemes, morphemes, syntax—*intonation, sentence patterns, and the critically important subsystems of structure words, grammatical inflections, and derivational affixes.* The results of these new extensions and variations should be more than merely quantitative in terms of reading comprehension; they should produce higher and different abilities in successful learners, and consequently reading experiences of greater richness and sophistication.

Zellig Harris was apparently the first American linguist to begin the exploration of "discourse analysis," or structural linguistic analysis of structures at higher levels than the sentence (27). This is rigorously technical, specialized discussion; to the best of my knowledge, no practical applications to teaching have been attempted. On the other hand, Kenneth Pike's theory of tagmemic analysis and some of the experimental investigations reported by his students into extended language patterns and forms seem to promise useful new insights into the larger structures of both expository prose and of literature. Pike explores and seeks to explain composites of form and meaning "beyond the sentence." He uses the linguistic terms *segment, fusion,* and *matrix* as analogues *of particle, wave,* and *field;* his terms *smearing* and *slurring* are applicable to a number of linguistic phenomena. It seems likely that much of this work will be pertinent to reading as well as to writing (28).

This topic, merely touched on here in passing, is explored at greater length in a paper written for the 1964 convention of the National Council of Teachers of English and published in ELEMENTARY ENGLISH in October 1965. It is entitled "A Comprehensive Linguistic Approach to Reading."

Some Projections

Following are suggestions of topics and problems for research listed under selected headings roughly in developmental order of reading skills.

Preschool Reading. Since the O.K. Moore and Doman experiments appear replicable, it might prove interesting to have independent research check on their results. Both experiments seem to me to be too specialized and to involve children who are too young for any widespread application of their methods to be practicable, but perhaps independent research results would have wider implications.

We all know that infants and children naturally learn language playfully. As they emerge from the cradle, they begin to use among themselves verbal riddles, puns, word plays, rhymes, gags of all sorts as part of their normal play. Perhaps a study could be devised to exploit children's verbal play and generally playful spirit in beginning reading instruction. Possibly elements of linguistic play could be combined with the two methods, spelling and oral reading-to-the-child, sketched below.

It should be possible to study both methods under controlled conditions with preschool children, in order to determine whether it would be worthwhile to simulate these conditions in preschool and kindergarten programs. It might be worthwhile to compare the results of experiments using these two procedures, and to investigate further whether elements of either, or of both, might profitably be incorporated into beginning reading programs.

Some children apparently have learned to read by their own spelling method. They learn to identify the names and slogans of products advertised on television and used in the home, such as breakfast cereals, soft drinks and fruit juices, ready-mixes, soaps and detergents, what not; they learn to read traffic signs, street signs, billboard advertising, posted notices, and the like; some of these learnings are reinforced by their perusal of newspaper and magazine advertising, and their exposure to names, titles, and headings in large print; some children study the names and addresses on mail that comes to their home, including advertising matter. They make of this their bridge to reading.

Other children apparently have learned to read as a by-product of listening to children's literature and other materials read aloud to them by interested and affectionate adults, while they follow the text with ears and eyes simultaneously. This method could be simulated in experimental situations by well-trained oral interpreters; it could also be varied and perhaps improved upon by using some of the professional recordings made expressly for children by some of our greatest actors, along with verbatim texts of their readings. For some children, this could be an excellent bridge to literacy.

Basic and Primary Reading; a Comparison of Two Methods. It has been indicated earlier that two different methods have been advanced for reading instruction in the primary grades: (1) a combination of phonics and sight-words; this is the received, or traditional approach, and includes such so-called linguistic materials as those of Bloomfield and Fries; and (2) the intonation and sentence pattern method I have proposed (see pp. 8–11), using word analysis and spelling aids only when the need arises inductively in the course of reading instruction. (One interpretation of my proposal has appeared recently in ELEMENTARY ENGLISH (29); this article is excellent on intonation, but tends to slight the rest of the method.) It would be very helpful to have the results of both methods compared by means of soundly designed research.

It might be possible to use some of the better primary reading materials that are now available as a basis for instruction in such a comparison, but it would be essential to eliminate any portions that are foreign to English intonation. Method 1 would handle the materials traditionally; method 2 would apply the intonation and sentence pattern method mentioned above. The use of identical learning materials, if they were satisfactory with respect to intonation, would in itself constitute one control.

Bi-dialectism in the "Inner City"

There is a strong movement afoot, supported by certain dialect geographers and others, to begin teaching so-called standard dialects—at the phonemic level—in preschools and kindergartens of inner cities across the nation. In theory at least no denigration of the children's dialects will be involved; they will simply be introduced to "another way of saying things." Well enough. Like the poet Hardy, when asked to visit a stable on Christmas Eve to see the oxen kneeling, I shall go along, hoping it may be true.

For my part, I would suggest that another program be drawn up, and that research be designed to compare the results of the two. In my suggested program, the children would at first learn to read their own dialect in print, reduced to standard spellings. There would be no effort to give any special graphic representation to their sounds; on the contrary, the children would learn to associate their own sounds with standard spellings, as a bridge to literacy. So far as practicable, the reading matter at first would be their own in both content and structure; gradually, closely related sentence patterns would be introduced, to prepare the children for their first textbooks. The children would be encouraged to read aloud their own materials, as transcribed in standard spelling by their teacher, and would have the opportunity to hear themselves on tape. At the same time, they would learn manuscript writing, how to copy their own materials visually, and also how to write them down from dictation. Once this basic program became well established, an *optional* program would be offered in "the other way of saying things." Only those children who volunteered for this program would be involved in it, and only so long as they elected to remain involved. If possible, their parents would have the option of participating as volunteers. It is of the utmost importance that no pressures be applied to either parents or children.

The results of such contrasting beginning language programs should prove interesting in terms of fluency of speech, reading, and writing.

Visual Perception. A number of questions concerning the relationship of various units of visual perception might be answered by research. Following are sketches of a few suggestions.

Research might help to settle the vexing question of manuscript versus cursive writing with respect to the child's learning to read. It seems reasonable to suppose that in addition to greater ease of writing for the child, the learning of manuscript writing (or printing), because the letter shapes resemble the print in children's books, would reinforce his efforts to learn to read. To the best of my knowledge, this is an assumption rather than a conclusion based on research. In general, the relationships of handwriting and spelling to beginning reading require more study. It also would be very interesting to compare the correlations with reading skills of manuscript and cursive writing, on the one hand, and the use of the electric typewriter, on the other, with primary school children. If the research design could include other features, auditory and kinesthetic elements might be incorporated into such studies.

Reading lore includes assumptions about the importance of the size of print in beginning reading. Research upon this subject could be enriched and made more significant if the design included not only the size of print, but *size of print in relation to phonological and syntactical constituents.* These are the meaning-bearing patterns, not the letters and words.

Up to now, studies of eye-span and the number of fixations

as the eyes pass along the line of print have ignored phonological and syntactical constituents of language patterns. We do not have an adequate understanding of the relationship between—or of the process that somehow relates—eye-fixations and meaning-bearing language patterns in the brain. Unquestionably, this is a very difficult topic for research design, but until we have research that clears up important questions, we had best avoid making dogma out of untried assumptions. Above all, we should reject assumptions about "meaning units" that do not correspond to meaning-bearing language patterns; they can only be psychological will o' the wisps.

Reading for the Blind and the Deaf. The abnormalities of perception involved in teaching reading to the blind and the deaf create special problems, and our present solutions leave much to be desired. Well-designed research on these problems is sorely needed.

Since the totally deaf can never experience normal intonation patterns as a basis for learning to speak in the first place, they cannot associate intonation directly and simply with handwriting and print. But the partially hearing might be able to receive artificial amplification of intonation, and even the totally deaf could probably associate the language rhythms of loudness and changing rate of utterance with kinesthetic and visual rhythms, if techniques were devised by perceptive teachers who had mastered the principles of intonation. In order to read meaning-bearing patterns of language reduced to print, the deaf, like all other learners, must perceive those patterns as wholes. New visual means of presentation could also be devised to bring out the whole, as well as whole constituent units, of the graphic counterparts of language patterns.

Since the hearing of the blind is usually acute, they should respond very well to instruction in intonation; this instruction might also help to reinforce their learning while listening to recorded readings. It should be interesting to discover whether their interpretation of braille by touch could be improved by association with intonation patterns. Since the braile system in operation depends on the reader's sense of touch, symbol by symbol, it probably has built into it the limitations of spelling as a means of learning to read. Thus it is conceivable that the method could be improved by experiments with new tactile symbols designed to exploit structural features of English that are well above the level of spelling: structure words and affixes, for example, that might be shown by single-letter symbols instead of being spelled out; and units of space with no braille symbols might be used to represent junctures separating phonological groupings, to help the blind reader get the sound of sentences through his sensitive fingertips.

Silent Reading. The very term *silent reading* suggests an intuitive sense of the relationship of print to the sound of speech. Can research instruments be designed to reveal significant aspects of this relationship? If the elements of syntactical intonation patterns were effectively taught (in addition to "reading with expression," which has its own importance), students should learn to read aloud with adequate or minimal control of these patterns. Certainly research could be designed to measure degrees of this learning. But can we measure the auditory-motor associations underlying the reading process that probably account for the fatigue of the larynx, often hoarseness, which frequently follows stimulating or extended "silent" reading? Sapir observed such fatigue after intensive thinking, which he regarded simply as silent speech (30). I myself often develop laryngitis while writing papers such as this. The electromechanical processes in the motor nerves are objective phenomena, susceptible of measurement; could these processes be correlated meaningfully with the similar and presumably simultaneous processes in certain areas of the cerebral cortex during reading?

Experienced readers are familiar with the process of "regressing," or going back to reread silently passages that did not "sound right" on the first reading. It seems very likely that the reader needs to construct, or reconstruct, the language pattern that carries the meaning required by the line of thought stimulated by his reading, including its melody and rhythm. But this is an intuitive explanation. Can research be designed to yield objective evidence that will describe this process?

The direction of this discussion leads toward a consideration of auditory and kinesthetic imagery in silent reading of poetry, with its great dependence on rhythm for its very structure— for example, an entire stanza that is an "incomplete" sentence —and of well-written imaginative prose as well. In dialog, individualization of characters is often shown by the peculiar rhythms of each speaker. A good piece of writing, verse, fiction, drama, has an overall design of sound—a comprehensive intonation pattern of melody and rhythm—that gives the ultimate sense of "form" to a language construct. The creation and evocation of a feeling of completion, of finish, in melody and rhythm, is one of the finest arts of writing; an approach to teaching it can be made through oral readings of students' writing, which in turn can lead to appreciation in reading. John Steinbeck quite deliberately wrote musically in the intercalary chapters of THE GRAPES OF WRATH, and created prose compositions resembling musical forms. And the poet John Ciardi wrote, "The supreme art of poetry is not to *assert* meaning but to *release* it by the juxtaposition of poetic elements. Form, in its interrelations, is the most speaking element" (31). Which reminds us that reading is ultimately a multi-disciplinary process, not all of it susceptible to our present capabilities of research. This topic, literary form, especially as related to music, is developed further in another article (32).

Transformational Grammar

As a final topic, I would like to comment on the current interest in transformational grammar. The term *transformational* refers to the productive, operational grammar as a subjective process within the native speaker (who may be completely unconscious of it).

Despite his scholarly knowledge of the existence of descriptive linguistic data demonstrating the specificity and particularity of many language systems that are quite unlike in their basic structure, Chomsky opened his *Syntactic Structures* with this statement: "The ultimate outcome . . . should be a theory of linguistic structure . . . with no specific reference to particular languages" (33). In this statement, *theory* means *grammar,* and grammar is restricted to the sentence. The proposed universal abstraction embracing all the varied abstract symbol-systems of languages spoken all over the world is more than reminiscent of Plato's Idea as an archetypal form (a general linguistic structure or grammar) in which all particular things participate (structures or grammars of particular languages).

Not long ago a re-statement of this neo-Platonic position appeared in a journal specializing in English composition (34); in 1965, an explication of transformational grammar for English teachers was published (35). More recently, an elementary English series using some of the terminology and apparatus of transformational grammar has appeared (36); the same author has written a programmed textbook of transformational grammar with strong support from Chomsky (37). Today this new-old view of grammar seems quite in vogue.

Transformational grammar impinges on linguistics, logic, mathematics, psychology, language-learning theory, and philosophy, and its influence is being felt in theory and methodology in the English teaching areas of both composition and reading. Psychologists are particularly well equipped to test some of its assumptions, which rest upon an anology that is supposed to explain English sentence structure in terms of the recursive systems of modern mathematics, with an assist from logic (38). The resulting attempt to reduce every detail of English to unexceptionable "rules" is well adapted to computer systems, mechanical translation, and similar applications. But the pretense that English has no dialects (or that only one is "grammatical"); the neglect of phonology, intonation above all; the strong visual bias that tends to regard the English language as *written,* and its "rules" as laws for *writing* and *rewriting;* as well as some of its fundamental assumptions—all raise doubts as to the adaptability of tranformational grammar to the needs of human beings, their speaking, writing, reading.

Transformational grammar replaces study of the objective language system as a code with interpretations of subjective messages carried by the code. This concern with message goes far and deep into psychology. An attempt to give an objective coloration to this subjective concern is made in this assumption: "The native speaker's internalized or 'intuitive' knowledge of language is an empirical fact" (39). This assumption is the basis of a definition of grammar as "an attempt to give an explicit account of this fact" (40). The attempt may be a legitimate one. How is it to be accomplished?

In a recent publication Chomsky puts it this way: "[My work] attempts to formulate precisely the processes of sentence formation and interpretation . . . that underlie the actual uses of language (41)." He further asserts, "The normal sentences of everyday life are formed, characteristically, by a complex series of transformations underlying structures" (42). Despite repeated protestations to the effect that "grammar is autonomous and independent of meaning" (43), the fact is that meaning, supplied by introspection, is the basis for identifying "sentence-like kernels." Which is the kernel, which the transformation? This is a purely subjective decision. The assumption that speakers and auditors, and also presumably writers and readers, actually perform these "certain processes" is also an intuitive assumption. Personally, my intuitions are different.

The arbitrary subjective nature of much of transformational theory is illustrated by the handling of isolated phrases that are said to be ambiguous. A celebrated instance of "ambiguity," much quoted, is supposed to be embedded in the phrase "the shooting of the hunters." This ambiguity can be cleared up by analyzing the phrase into two possible underlying kernel sentences: (1) "the hunters shoot" and (2) "they shoot the hunters." Here is the rationale: "The ambiguity of the grammatical relation . . . is a consequence of the fact that the relation of *shoot* to *hunters* differs in the two underlying kernel sentences." (44) A true believer has repeated and extended discussion of this "ambiguity." (45)

Now, the intuitive knowledge of any native English speaker in a speech community of hunters would not permit him to use the phrase, "the shooting of the hunters," in either of the senses cited—because it is not a part of the language of that speech community. It may be doubted whether it is a part of an English speech community. If a foreigner happened to invent the phrase, it seems quite certain that the context in which it occurred—probably the remainder of the sentence—would make its meaning obvious.

Transformational grammar, for all its claims of "deep insights into human intellectual capacity and mental processes" (46), is meager in concept and scope. It is a theory limited to the structure of sentences. It stipulates, in compensation, that sentences may be infinitely long and complex, at least in theory. (47) What a prospect.

Ramsay MacDonald once warned against "an attempt to clothe unreality in the garb of mathematical reality." This warning might well be applied to transformational theory.

Caveat emptor.

Bibliographies and Notes

Abbreviations

AERJ   —*American Educational Research Journal*
AJP   —*American Journal of Psychology*
AORL —*Annals of Otology, Rhinology, and Laryngology*
CJER   —*California Journal of Educational Research*
CRP   —Cooperative Research Projects
EE   —*Elementary English*
IJAL   —*International Journal of American Linguistics*
JAP   —*Journal of Applied Psychology*
JASA   —*Journal of the Acoustical Society of America*
JASP   —*Journal of Abnormal and Social Psychology*
JEdP   —*Journal of Educational Psychology*
JEP   —*Journal of Experimental Psychology*
JVLVB —*Journal of Verbal Learning and Verbal Behavior*
MSRCD—*Monographs of Social Research and Child Development*
PR   —*Psychological Review*
PS   —Psychonomic Science
QJEP   —*Quarterly Journal of Experimental Psychology*
RER   —*Review of Educational Research*
RT   —*Reading Teacher*

Bibliographies

GOODMAN

pp. 13–26

1. Bloomfield, Leonard and Clarence L. Barnhart, *Let's Read*, Parts 1, 2, 3. New York, 1963.

2. Fries, C. C., *Linguistics and Reading*. New York, 1963.

3. ———— *The Structure of English*. New York, 1952.

4. Goodman, Kenneth S. "Dialect Barriers to Reading Comprehension," *Elementary English* 42:8 (December, 1965), 853–60.

KOLERS

pp. 27–40

Held, R., and Freedman, S. J., "Plasticity in Human Sensorimotor Control," *Science*, 1963, *142*, 455–62.

Kendall, M. G., *Rank Correlation Methods*, London: Griffin, 1948.

Kohler, I., "The Formation and Transformation of the Perceptual World," *Psychological Issues*, 1964, *3*, #4(12).

Kolers, P. A., "Subliminal Stimulation in Problem Solving," *American Journal of Psychology*, 1957, *70*, 437–41.

Kolers, P. A., "Intensity and Contour Effects in Visual Masking," *Vision Research*, 1962, *2*, 277–94.

Kolers, P. A., and Katzman, M. T., "Naming Sequentially Presented Letters and Words," *Language and Speech* 1966, *9*, 84–95.

Kolers, P. A., and Rosner, B. S., "On Visual Masking (Metacontrast): Dichoptic Observation," *American Journal of Psychology*, 1960, *73*, 2–21.

Miller, G. A., *Psychology, the Science of Mental Life*, New York: Harper & Row, 1962.

Neisser, U., "Visual Search," *Scientific American*, 1964, *210*, 94–102.

Smith, K. U., and Smith, W. M., *Perception and Motion*, Philadelphia: Saunders, 1962.

Sperling, G., "A Model for Visual Memory Tasks," *Human Factors,* 1963, *5,* 19–31.

Woodhead, A. G., *A Study of Greek Inscriptions,* Cambridge University Press, 1959.

JONES

pp. 41–57

1. Arnoult, M. D., "Familiarity and Recognition of Nonsense Shapes," *JEP,* 1956, *51,* 269–76.

2. Baldwin, A. L., and Baum, E., "The Interruptability of Words in the Speech of Children." Final Report, Levin, H. *et al.* (Eds.), *A Basic Research Program on Reading,* O.E. CRP, No. 639: Ithaca, 1963.

3. Braine, M. D. S., "On Learning the Grammatical Order of Words," *PR,* 1963, *70,* 323–48.

4. Bruce, D. J., "An Analysis of Word Sounds by Young Children," *British Journal of Educational Psychology,* 1964 (June), *34,* 158–70.

5. Bugelski, B. R., and Cadwallder, T. C., "A Reappraisal of the Transfer and Retroaction Surface," *JEP,* 1956, *52,* 360–70.

6. Carmichael, L., and Dearborn, W. F., *Reading and Visual Fatigue,* Cambridge, Mass., 1947.

7. Carterette, E. C., and Jones, M. H., *Contextual Constraints in the Language of the Child, Final Report,* O. E. CRP, No. 1877, 1965, Los Angeles.

8. Conrad, R., "An Association Between Memory Errors and Errors Due to Acoustic Masking of Speech," *Nature,* 1962, *193,* 1314–15.

9. Dale, H. C. A., "Retroactive Interference in Short-Term Memory," *Nature,* 1964, *203,* 1408.

10. Dirks, D., "Perception of Dichotic and Monaural Verbal Material and Cerebral Dominance for Speech, *Acta-Otolaryngologica,* 1964, *58,* 73–80.

11. Ebeling, C. L., *Linguistic Units,* 's-Gravenhage, 1960.

12. Edfeldt, A. W., *Silent Speech and Silent Reading,* Chicago, 1960, 163.

13. Ervin, S. M., Walker, D. E., and Osgood, C. E., "Psycholinguis-

tic Units," sec. 3.1—"Psychological Bases of Unit Formation." *JASP*, 1954, *49*, (4) No. 2, 50–60.

14. Fodor, J. A., and Bever, T. G., "The Psychological Reality of Linguistic Segments," *JVLVB*, 1965, *4*, 414–20.

15. Fries, C. C., *Linguistics and Reading*, New York, 1963.

16. ———, *The Structure of English*, New York, 1952.

17. Gibson, E. J., Osser, H., and Pick, A. D., "A Study of the Development of Grapheme-Phoneme Correspondences," *JVLVB*, 1963, *2*, 142–46.

18. Glanzer, M., "Grammatical Category: A Rote Learning and Word Association Analysis," *JVLVB*, 1962, *1*, 31–41.

19. Goetzinger, C. P., Dirks, D. D., and Baer, C. J., "Auditory Discrimination and Visual Perception in Good and Poor Readers," *AORL*, 1960, *69*, 121–36.

20. Goldman-Eisler, F., "Hesitation and Information in Speech," in *Information Theory: Fourth London Symposium* (Ed.: Colin Cherry), London, 1964, 162–74.

21. ———, "Speech Production and the Predictability of Words in Context," *QJEP*, 1958, *10*, 96–106.

22. Goodman, K. S., "A Linguistic Investigation of the Reading of Primary Children: An Exploratory Study to Implement a Communicative Theory of Reading." Mimeo., 1963, Wayne State University.

23. Greenberg, J. H., *Essays in Linguistics*, Chicago, 1957, 108.

24. ———, "The Linguistic Approach to Language Behavior," *JASP*, 1954, *49*, 8–19; "The Word as a Linguistic Unit," 66–71.

25. Guilford, J. P., "The Three Faces of Intellect," *American Psychologist*, 1959, *14*, 469–79.

26. Halliday, M. A. K., "The Tones of English," *Archivum Linguisticum*, 1963, *15* (1), 1–28.

27. Hargreaves, W. A., "A Model for Speech Unit Duration," *Language and Speech*, 1960, *3*, 164–73.

28. Harrington, M. J., and Durrell, D., "Mental Maturity Measures versus Perceptual Abilities in Primary Reading, *JEdP*, 1955, *46*, 375–80.

29. Holmes, J. A., and Singer, H., "The Substrata-Factor Theory:

Substrata-Factor Differences Underlying Reading Ability in Known Groups at the High School Level." Final Report covering contracts No. 538, SAE–8176 and No. 538A, SAE–8660, U.S. DHEW, University of California, 1961, 317.

30. Hultzén, L. S., "Information Points in Intonation," *Phonetica,* 1959, *4,* 107–20.

31. Huttenlocher, J., "Children's Language: Word-Phrase Relationship," *Science,* 1964, *143,* 264–65.

32. Katz, P. A., and Deutsch, M., "Relation of Auditory-Visual Shifting to Reading Achievement," *Perceptual Motor Skills,* 1963, *17,* 327–32.

33. Kramers, J. H., "How To Determine the Phonological Word," *Analecta Orientala: Posthumous Writings and Selected Minor Works,* II, 44–54, Leiden, 1956.

34. Ladefoged, P., and Broadbent, D. E., "Perception of Sequence in Auditory Events," *QJEP,* 1960, *12,* 162–70.

35. Lehiste, I., "Acoustic Studies of Boundary Signals, in Sovijärvi, A." (Ed.), *Proceedings of the 4th International Congress of Phonetic Sciences, 1961,* Hague, 1962, 178–87.

36. Lounsbury, F. G., "Transitional Probability, Linguistic Structure, and Systems of Habit-Family Hierarchies," *JASP,* 1954, *49,* No. 4, Pt. 2, 93–101.

37. Lubershane, M., "Can Training in Listening Improve Reading Ability?," *Chicago Schools Journal,* 1962, *43,* 277–81.

38. Maclay, H., and Osgood, C. E., "Hesitation Phenomena in Spontaneous English Speech," *Word,* 1959, *15,* 19–44.

39. Martinet, A., *A Functional View of Language,* Oxford, 1962, 160.

40. McNeil, J. D., and Keislar, E. R., "Value of the Oral Response in Beginning Reading: An Experimental Study Using Programmed Instruction," *British Journal of Educational Psychology,* 1963, *33,* 162–68.

41. Miller, G. A., "Decision Units in the Perception of Speech," IRE Trans. inform. Theory IT–8, 1962, 81–83.

42. ———, "Some Psychological Studies of Grammar," *American Psychologist,* 1962, *17,* 748–62.

43. Miller, G. A., Heise, G. A, and Lichten, W., "The Intelligibility of Speech as a Function of the Content of the Test Materials," *JEP*, 1951, *41*, 329–35.

44. Mosher, H. M., Dreher, J. J., and Adler, S., "Effect of Rate and Phrasing on Intelligibility of Air Messages," AFCRC TN 55–68, May, 1956.

45. Mosher, H. M., Dreher, J. J., Oyer, H. J., and O'Neill, J. J., "Effects of Sequence upon the Reception of Related and Non-Related Message Elements," AFCRC TN 56–55, August, 1956.

46. Nihira, K., Guilford, J. P., Hoepfner, R., and Merrifield, P. R., "A Factor Analysis of the Semantic-Evaluation Abilities," Report, Psychological Laboratory, U.S.C., No., 32, December, 1964, 37.

47. Osgood, C. E., "Hierarchies of Linguistic Units," *JASP*, 1954, *49*, No. 4, part 2, 71–73.

48. ———, "On Understanding and Creating Sentences," *American Psychologist*, 1963, *18*, 735–51.

49. Peterson, L. R., and Peterson, M. J., "Short-Term Retention of Individual Verbal Items," *JEP*, 1959, *58*, 193–98.

50. Pierce, J., "Determinants of Threshold for Form," *Psychological Bulletin*, 1963, *60*, 391–407.

51. Pike, K. L., *The Intonation of American English*, Ann Arbor, 1945.

52. Rubenstein, H., and Aborn, M., "Psycholinguistics," *Ann. Rev. Psych.*, 1960, *11*, 291–322.

53. Siipola, E., Walker, W. N., and Kolb, D., "Task Attitudes in Word Association, Projective and Non-Projective," *Journal of Personality*, 1955, *23*, 441–59.

54. Smith, W. N., "Visual Recognition: Facilitation of Seeing by Saying," PS, 1965, *2*, 57–58.

55. Stene, A., "Hiatus in English," *Anglistica*, 1954, *3*, 102.

56. Suci, G. J., "The Definition of Units in Language," Levin, H. et al. (Eds.), *A Basic Research Program on Reading*, O.E. CRP, No. 639, Final report, Ithaca, 1963.

57. Warren, R. M., and Warren, R. P., "A Comparison of Speech Perception in Childhood, Maturity, and Old Age by Means of the Verbal Transformation Effect," *JVLVB*, 1966, *5*, 142–46.

58. Weissman, S. L., and Crockett, W. H., "Intersensory Transfer of Verbal Material," *AJP*, 1957, *70*, 283–85.

59. Wickelgren, W. A., "Acoustic Similarity and Retroactive Interference in Short-Term Memory," *JVLVB*, 1965, *4*, 53–61.

60. ———, "Size of Rehearsal Group and Short-Term Memory, *JEP*, 1964, *68*, 413–19.

61. Yngve, V. H., Gap Analysis and Syntax, IRE Trans. Information Theory, IT-2, 1956, 106–12.

HANSON AND RODGERS,
pp. 59–102

1. Atkinson, R. C. and Estes, W. K., "Stimulus Sampling Theory." Luce, R., Bush, R. and Galanter, E., Handbook of Mathematical Psychology, Vol. II, Chap. 2. New York, 1963.

2. Bloomfield, L., *Language*. New York, 1932.

3. Bloomfield, L. and Barnhart, C., *Let's Read: A Linguistic Approach*. Detroit, 1961.

4. Bower, G., "Applications of a Model to Paired-Associate Learning," *Psychometrika*, 1961, *26*, 255–80.

5. Brodbeck, M., "Logic and Scientific Method in Research on Teaching. Gage, N. Ed.), *Handbook of Research on Teaching*, 44–94. Chicago, 1963.

6. Brown, R. and McNeil, D., "The 'Tip of the Tongue' Phenomena," *Behavioral Science*, 1965.

7. Chomsky, N., "Formal Properties of Grammars." Luce, R., Bush, R. and Galanter, E., *Handbook of Mathematical Psychology*, Vol. II, 269–322. New York, 1963.

8. ———, "Current Issues in Linguistic Theory." Fodor, J. and Katz, J. (Eds.), *The Structure of Language*, 50–118. Englewood Cliffs, New Jersey, 1964.

9. Carroll, J., "The Analysis of Reading Instruction: Perspectives from Psychology and Linguistics." Hilgard, E. (Ed.), *Theories of Learning and Instruction*, N.S.S.E. 63 Yearbook, 336–53. Chicago, 1964.

10. Fries, C., *The Structure of English*. New York, 1952.

11. ———, *Linguistics and Reading*. New York, 1963.

12. Gates, A., *Interest and Ability in Reading*. New York, 1930.

13. Glanzer, M., "Grammatical Category: A Rote Learning and Word Association Analysis," *JVLVB*, 1962, *1*, 31–41.

14. Greenberg, J. and Jenkins, J., "Studies in the Psychological Correlates of the Sound System of American English," *Word*, 1964, *20*, 157–77.

15. Greenberg, J., "Some Generalizations Concerning Initial and Final Consonant Sequences," *Voprosy Jazyhoznanija*.

16. Halle, M. and Stevens, K., "Speech Recognition: A Model and a Program for Research." Fodor, J., and Katz, J. (Eds.), *The Structure of Language*, 604–12. Englewood Cliffs, New Jersey, 1964.

17. Hilgard, E., "A Perspective on the Relationship Between Learning Theory and Educational Practices," *Theories of Learning and Instruction*, N.S.S.E. 63 Yearbook, 402–15. Chicago, 1964.

18. Harris, C., "Study of the Building Blocks of Speech," *JASA*, 1953, *25*, 962–69.

19. Harris, Z., *Structural Linguistics*. Chicago, 1951.

20. Haugen, E., "The Syllable in Linguistic Description." *For Roman Jakobson*, 213–21. The Hague, 1956.

21. Hockett, C., *A Manual of Phonology*. Baltimore, 1955.

22. Jenkins, J. and Palermo, D., "Mediation Processes and the Acquisition of Linguistic Structure," *MSRCD*, 1964, *29*, 141–68.

23. Lenneberg, E., "The Capacity for Language Acquisition." Fodor, J., and Katz, J. (Eds.), *The Structure of Language*, 579–603. Englewood Cliffs, New Jersey, 1960.

24. Liberman, A., Ingemann, F., Lisker, P., Delattre, P., Cooper, F., "Minimal Rules for Synthesizing Speech, *JASA*, 1959, *31*, 1490–99.

25. Loban, W., *The Language of Elementary School Children*. Champaign, Illinois, 1963.

26. McKee, P., Harrison, M., McCowen, A., and Lehr, E., *Teacher's Guide for Tip*. Boston, 1963.

27. Miller, G., Galanter, E., and Pribram, K., *Plans and the Structure of Behavior*. New York, 1960.

28. Miller, G., "Some Preliminaries to Psycholinguistics," *American Psychologist*, 1965, *20*, 15–20.

29. Morris, R., *Success and Failure in Learning to Read*. London, 1963.

30. O'Connor, J., and Trim, J., "Vowel, Consonant, and Syllable—A Phonological Definition," *Word*, 1953, *9*, 103–22.

31. Osgood, C., and Sebeok, T., (Ed.), *Psycholinguistics: A Survey of Theory and Research Problems*. Baltimore, 1954.

32. Peterson, G., Wang, W., and Sivertsen, E., "Segmentation Techniques in Speech Synthesis," *JASA*, 1958, *30*, 739–42.

33. Pike, K., *Phonemics*. Ann Arbor, 1947.

34. Postman, L., and Rosenzweig, M., "Practice and Transfer in the Visual and Auditory Recognition of Verbal Stimuli," *AJP*, 1956, *69*, 209–26.

35. Rosen, G., "A Dynamic Analogy Speech Synthesizer," *JASA*, 1958, *30*, 201–09.

36. Russell, D., and Ousley, O., *Manual for Teaching the Pre-Primer Program*. New York, 1957.

37. Saporta, S., "Certain Characteristics of Phoneme Sequences." Osgood, C., and Sebeok, T. (Ed.), *Psycholinguistics*, Baltimore, 1954.

38. Stetson, R., *Bases of Phonology*. Oberlin, Ohio, 1945.

39. Suppes, P., and Crothers, E., *Second Language Learning*. New York, 1966.

40. Templin, M., "A Study of Sound Discrimination Ability of Elementary School Pupils, *Journal of Speech Disorders*, 1943, *8*, 127–32.

41. Underwood, B., and Schulz, R., *Meaningfulness and Verbal Learning*. Chicago, 1960.

42. Whorf, B., Linguistics as an Exact Science, *Technological Review*, 1940, *43*, 61–63, 80–83.

43. Zipf, G., *Human Behavior and the Principle of Least Effort*, Cambridge, Mass., 1949.

CARTERETTE AND JONES
pp. 103–166

1. Binder, A. and Wolin, B. R., "Informational Models and Their Uses," *Psychometrika*, 1964, *29*, 29–64.

2. Carroll, J. B., "Transition Probabilities of English Phonemes, Progress Report on Project 52," Cambridge, Mass., 1952. Mimeo.

3. ———, "Linguistics and the Psychology of Language," *RER*, 1964, *34*, 119–26.

4. Carterette, E. C. (Ed.), *Brain Function, Vol. III: Speech, Language and Communication.* UCLA Forum in Medical Sciences No. 4. Berkeley, 1966.

5. Carterette, E. C., and Jones, M. H., "Redundancy in Children's Tests," *Science*, 1963, *140*, 1309–11.

6. ———, "On the Statistics of Spoken American English," *JASA*, 1964, *36*, 1989 (Abstract).

7. ———, "Statistical Comparison of Two Series of Graded Readers," *AERJ*, 1965a, *2*, 13–18.

8. ———, *Contextual Constraints in the Language of the Child.* Final Report to the U.S. Office of Education on CRP No. 1877, Los Angeles, 1965b. [Photo offset, 161 pp.]

9. Chomsky, N., "Three Models for the Description of Language." *IRE Trans. on Inform. Theory*, 1956, IT-2, 113–24.

10. ———, *Syntactic Structures*, The Hague, 1957.

11. Denes, P. B., "On the Statistics of Spoken English," *JASA*, 1963, *35*, 892–904.

12. Dewey, G., *Relativ* (sic) *Frequency of English Speech Sounds*, Cambridge, Mass., 1923.

13. Fowler, M., "Herdan's Statistical Parameter and the Frequency of English Phonemes," in Pulgram, E. (Ed.), *Studies Presented to Joshua Whatmough on his Sixtieth Birthday*, The Hague, 1957, pp. 47–52.

14. French, N. R., Carter, C. W., Jr., and Koenig, W., Jr., "The Words and Sounds of Telephone Conversations," *Bell System Technical Journal*, 1930, *9*, 290–324.

15. Friedman, M. P., and Carterette, E. C., "Detection of Markovian Sequences of Signals," *JASA*, 1964, *36*, 2334–39.

16. Fries, C. C., *The Structure of English.* New York, 1952.

17. Fry, D., "The Frequency of Occurrence of Speech Sounds in Southern English," *Archives Néerlandaises* 1947, *20*, 103–06.

18. Garner, W. R., *Uncertainty and Structure as Psychological Concepts,* New York, 1962.

19. Hayden, R. E., "The Relative Frequency of Phonemes in General American English," *Word,* 1950, *6,* 217–23.

20. Hultzén, L. S., Allen, J. H. D., Jr. and Miron, M. S., *Tables of Transitional Frequencies of English,* Urbana, Ill., 1964.

21. Jakobson, R., Cherry, E. C., and Halle, M., "Toward the Logical Description of Languages in Their Phonemic Aspect," *Language,* 1953, *29,* 34–46; Jakobson, R., *Selected Writings,* I, 's-Gravenhage, 1962, 449–63.

22. Jones, Margaret H., and Carterette, E. C., "Redundancy in Children's Free-Reading Choices," *JVLVB, 2,* 1963, 489–93.

23. Kullback, S., *Information Theory and Statistics,* New York, 1959.

24. Lengyel, P., Speyer, J. F., and Ochoa, S., "Synthetic Polynucleotides and the Amino-Acid Code," I-V. *Proceedings of the National Academy of Science U.S.A.,* 1961, 47, 1936–1942; 1962, 63–68, 282–84, 441–48, 613–16.

25. Miller, G. A., and Chomsky, N. "Finitary Models of Language Users," Luce, R. D., Bush, R. R., and Galanter, E. (Eds.), *Handbook of Mathematical Psychology,* 419–91. New York, 1963.

26. Miller, G. A., and Madow, W. C., "On the Maximum Likelihood Estimate of the Shannon-Wiener Measure of Information," Air Force Cambridge Research Center, AFCRC-TR-54-75, 1954.

27. Newman, E. B., and Waugh, N. C., "The Redundancy of Texts in Three Languages," *Information and Control,* 1960, *3,* 141–53.

28. Newman, E. B., and Gerstman, L. J. "A New Method for Analyzing Printed English," *JEP,* 1952, *44,* 114–25.

29. Nirenberg, M. W., and Matthaei, "The Dependence of Cell-Free Protein Synthesis *E. Coli* upon naturally occurring or synthetic polyribo-nucleotides," *Proceedings of the National Academy of Science U.S.A.,* 1961, *47,* 1588–1602.

30. Reza, R. M., *An Introduction to Information Theory.* New York, 1961.

31. Rinsland, H. D., *A Basic Vocabulary of Elementary School Children,* New York, 1945.

32. Russell, D. H., and Ousley, Odille, *On Cherry Street*. Ginn Basic Readers, Level 1.2. Boston, 1957.

33. Russell, D. H., Wulsing, Gretchen, and Ousley, Odille, *Finding New Neighbors*. Ginn Basic Readers, Level 3.1. Boston, 1957.

34. Russell, D. H., McCullough, Constance, and Gates, Doris, *Trails to Treasure*. Ginn Basic Readers, Level 5. Boston, 1956.

35. Seibel, R., "N-gram (Sequences of Letters N Long) Analysis for English for N from 1 through 12." Paper delivered to Eastern Psychological Association, April 1962.

36. Shannon, C. E., "Prediction and Entropy of Printed English." *Bell System Technical Journal*, 1951, *30*, 50–64.

37. Sheldon, William D., *et al. Our Town*. Sheldon Basic Reading Series, Level 1. Boston, 1957a.

38. Sheldon, William D., *et al. Magic Windows*. Sheldon Basic Reading Series, Level 3.1. Boston, 1957b.

39. Sheldon, William D., *et al. Finding the Way*. Sheldon Basic Reading Series, Level 5. Boston, 1957c.

40. Strickland, Ruth G., *The Language of Elementary School Children: Its Relationship to the Language of Reading Textbooks and the Quality of Reading of Selected Children*. Bulletin of the School of Education, Vol. 38, No. 4. Bloomington, Ind., 1962.

41. Tobias, J. V., "Relative Occurrence of Phonemes in American English." *JASA*, 1959, *31*, 631.

42. Trnka, B., "A Phonological Analysis of Present-Day Standard English," studies in English by members of the English Seminar of the Charles University (Prague), 1935, *5*, 187.

43. Voelker, C. H., "A Comparative Study of Investigation of Phonetic Dispersion in Connected American English," *Archives Néerlandaises*, 1937, *13*, 138–57.

44. Wang, W., and Crawford, J., "Frequency Studies of English Consonants," *Language and Speech*, 1960, *3*, 131–39.

45. West, D. H., and Shor, R. (Eds.) *Children's Catalog*, 10th Ed. New York, 1961.

46. Whitney, W. D., "The Proportional Elements of English Utter-

ance." *Proceedings of the American Philological Association,* 1874, *5,* 14–17.

47. Wilson's *Children's Catalog,* 1961.

ANISFELD

pp. 167–183

1. Berko, Jean, "The Child's Learning of English Morphology." *Word,* 1958, *14,* 150–77.

2. Braine, M. D. S., "The Ontogeny of English Phrase Structure: The First Phase. *Language,* 1963, *39,* 1–13.

3. Brown, R., "Linguistic Determinism and the Part of Speech." *JASP,* 1957, *55,* 1–5.

4. Brown, R., and Berko, Jean, "Word Association and the Acquisition of Grammar." *Child Development,* 1960, *31,* 1–14.

5. Brown, R., and Fraser, C., "The Acquisition of Syntax." C. N. Cofer and Barbara Musgrave, (Eds.), *Verbal Behavior and Learning,* 158–97. New York, 1963.

6. Bruner, J. S., "The Course of Cognitive Growth." *American Psychologist,* 1964, *19,* 1–15.

7. Chomsky, N., *Aspects of the Theory of Syntax.* Cambridge, Mass., 1965.

8. ———, *Syntactic Structures.* The Hague, 1957.

9. ———, "Formal Discussion." Ursula Bellugi and R. Brown, (Eds.), "The Acquisition of Language." *MSRCD,* 1964, *29* –1, 35–42. (Serial #92.)

10. Ervin, Susan M., "Changes with Age in the Verbal Determinants of Word-Association." *AJP,* 1961, *74,* 361–72.

11. ———, "Imitations in the Speech of Two-Year-Olds." Paper read at the meetings of the American Psychological Association, Philadelphia, 1963. (Mimeo.)

12. Francis, W. N., *The Structure of American English.* New York, 1958.

13. Hilgard, E. R., *Theories of Learning.* New York, 1956.

14. Lashley, K. S., "The Problem of Serial Order in Behavior." Hixon Symposium, 1951. Reprinted in S. Saporta (Ed.), *Psycholinguistics: A Book of Readings,* 180–98. New York, 1961.

15. Lees, R. B., "The Grammar of English Nominalizations." *IJAL,* 1960, *26,* No. 3.

16. Luria, A. R., *The Role of Speech in the Regulation of Normal and Abnormal Behavior*. New York, 1961.

17. Menyuk, Paula, "A Preliminary Evaluation of Grammatical Capacity in Children." *JVLVB,* 1963, *2,* 429–39.

18. Miller, W., and Ervin, Susan M., "The Development of Grammar in Child Language." Ursula Bellugi and R. Brown, (Eds.), "The Acquisition of Language." *MSRCD,* 1964, *29* –1, 9–34. (Serial #92.)

19. Piaget, J., *The Child's Conception of Number*. New York, 1965.

20. Postal, P., "Underlying and Superficial Linguistic Structure. *Harvard Educational Review,* 1964, *34,* 246–66.

21. Vigotsky, L. S., *Thought and Language*. New York, 1962.

22. Wallach, M. A., "Research on Children's Thinking." *Child Psychology,* the sixty-second yearbook of the National Society for the Study of Education, 236–76. Chicago, 1963.

23. Watson, J. B., "Psychology as the Behaviorist Views It." *PR,* 1913, *20,* 159–77.

24. Whorf, B. L., *Language, Thought, and Reality*. Selected and edited by J. B. Carroll. Cambridge, Mass., 1956.

Notes

WEIR

pp. 185–199

1. See Richard L. Venezky, "A Computer Program for Deriving Spelling-to-Sound Correlations," M.A. Thesis, Cornell University, 1962. Printed in part in Harry Levin, *et. al., A Basic Research Program on Reading* (Cornell University, 1963).

2. John S. Kenyon and Thomas Knott, *A Pronouncing Dictionary of American English* (Springfield, Mass., 1951). For a summary of English phonology, see Hans Kurath, *A Phonology and Prosody of Modern English* (Ann Arbor: University of Michigan Press, 1964).

3. This model is discussed more fully in Ruth H. Weir, "Formulation of Grapheme-Phoneme Correspondence Rules to Aid in the Teaching of Reading," Final Report, Co-operative Research Project No. S-039 (Stanford, 1964), and Ruth H. Weir and Richard L. Venezky, "Rules to Aid in the Teaching of Reading," Final Report, Co-operative Research Project No. 2584 (Stanford, 1965).

4. This is the approach advocated by, among others, Robert A. Hall, Jr., in *Sound and Spelling in English* (Philadelphia, 1961).

5. See Jean Berko, "The Child's Learning of Morphology," *Word, 14* (1958), 150–77.

EVERTTS

pp. 201–235

1. Inhelder, Barbel, and Piaget, Jean, *The Early Growth of Logic in the Child: Classification and Seriation.* New York, 1964.

2. Strickland, Ruth G., *The Language of Elementary School Children: Its Relationship to the Language of Reading Textbooks and the Quality of Reading of Selected Children,* Bulletin of

the School of Education, Indiana University, Bloomington, Indiana, 1962.

3. Loban, Walter D., *The Language of Elementary School Children*. Champaign, Ill., 1963.

4. ———, Problems in Oral English. Champaign, Ill., 1966.

5. Hunt, Kellogg W., *Grammatical Structures at Three Grade Levels*. Champaign, Ill., 1965. Loban, Walter D. *The Language of Elementary School Children*.

BORMUTH

pp. 237–253

1. Bormuth, J. R., "Mean Word Depth as a Predictor of Comprehension Difficulty." *CJER*, 1964a, *15*, 226–31.

2. ———, *Relationships between Selected Language Variables and Comprehension Ability and Difficulty*. CRP No. 2082, Office of Education, 1964b.

3. Chall, J. S., *Readability: An Appraisal of Research and Application*. Bureau of Educational Research Monographs, Ohio State University, 1958, No. 34.

4. Coleman, E. B., "Improving Comprehensibility by Shortening Sentences." *JAP*, 1962, *46*, 131–34.

5. Flesch, R., "A New Readability Yardstick." *JAP*, 1948, *32*, 221–33.

6. Gray, W. S., and Leary, B. A., *What Makes a Book Readable*. Chicago, 1935.

7. Robinson, F. P., "Comprehension Difficulty and Inspirational Value." *Pedagogical Seminary and Journal of Genetical Psychology*, 1940, *56*, 53–65.

8. Ruddell, R. B., "The Effect of Oral and Written Patterns of Language Structure on Reading Comprehension." *RT*, 1965, *18*, 270–75.

9. Strickland, R. G., *The Language of Elementary School Children: Its Relationship to the Language of Reading Textbooks and Quality of Reading of Selected Children*. Bulletin of the School of Education, Indiana University, 1962, 38, No. 4.

10. Yngve, V. H., "A Model and Hypothesis for Language Structure." *Proceedings of the American Philosophical Society*, 1960, *104*, 444–66.

RUDDELL

pp. 255–270

1. Allen, Robert L., "Better Reading Through the Recognition of Grammatical Relations," *RT, 18* (December, 1964), 194–98.

2. Berko, Jean, "The Child's Learning of English Morphology," *Word, 14* (1958), 150–77.

3. Bloomfield, Leonard, and Clarence L. Barnhart, *Let's Read.* Detroit, 1961.

4. Buchanan, Cynthia Dee, *Programmed Reading.* New York, 1963.

5. Ferguson, C. A., "Seven Statements About the Teaching of Reading," *Linguistic Reporter, 5* (April, 1963), 5–6.

6. Fraser, Colin, Ursula Bellugi, and Roger Brown, "Control of Grammar in Imitation, Comprehension, and Production," *JVLVB, 2* (August, 1963), 121–35.

7. Fries, Charles C., *Linguistics and Reading.* New York, 1963.

8. Lefevre, Carl A., *Linguistics and the Teaching of Reading.* New York, 1964.

9. Ruddell, Robert B., "In a Time of Transition We Seek New and Better Ways to Teach Reading," *California Teachers Association Journal, 61* (October, 1965), 15–16, 56–64.

10. Sheldon, William D., *et al. Sheldon Basic Reading Series.* New York, 1957.

11. Squire, James R., "New Directions in Language Learning," *EE, 39* (October, 1962), 535–44.

12. Steinberg, Erwin R., and William A. Jenkins, "Needed Research in the Teaching of the Elementary School Language Arts," *EE, 39* (December, 1962), 790–93.

13. Strickland, Ruth G., *The Contribution of Structural Linguistics to the Teaching of Reading, Writing, and Grammar in the Elementary School.* Bulletin of the School of Education, Indiana University, Bloomington, Vol. 40 (January, 1964), No. 1.

14. ———, *The Language of Elementary School Children: Its Relationship to the Language of Reading Textbooks and the Quality of Reading of Selected Children.* Bulletin of the School of Education, Indiana University, Bloomington, Vol. 38 (July, 1962), No. 4.

OLSEN

pp. 271–287

1. Bloomfield, Leonard, and Barnhart, Clarence L., *Let's Read: A Linguistic Approach*, Detroit, 1961.

2. Bloomfield, Leonard, "Linguistics and Reading," *The Elementary English Review, 19* (April-May, 1942), 125–30, 183–86.

3. *Let's Read*, Experimental Edition, Bronxville, N.Y., 1963.

4. McCracken, Glen, and Walcott, Charles C., *Basic Reading*, Philadelphia, 1963.

5. Buchanan, Cynthia D., Sullivan Associates, *Programmed Reading*, New York, 1963.

6. Stolpens, B. H., Tyler, Priscilla, and Pounds, E. T., *Scott, Foresman Linguistic Block Series*, Chicago, 1963.

7. Fries, C. C., *Linguistics and Reading*, New York, 1963.

8. Lefevre, Carl A., *Linguistics and the Teaching of Reading*, New York, 1964.

9. Richardson, Jack E., Jr., Smith, Henry Lee, Jr., and Weiss, Bernard J., *Teacher's Plan Book for the Preprimers Frog Fun, Tuggy, Pepper*, Evanston, Ill., 1965.

10. Goodman, Kenneth S., "The Linguistics of Reading," *Elementary School Journal, 64*, No. 7 (April, 1964), 359.

11. Stratemeyer, C. G. and Smith, H. L., Jr., *Frog Fun, The Linguistic-Science Readers*, Evanston, Ill., 1963.

12. ———, *Pepper, The Linguistic-Science Readers*, Evanston, Ill., 1963.

13. Loban, Walter D., *The Language of Elementary School Children*, Research Report No. 1, Champaign, Ill., 1963.

14. Strickland, Ruth G., *The Language of Elementary School Children: Its Relationship to the Language of Reading Textbooks and the Quality of Reading of Selected Children*. Bulletin of the School of Education, Indiana University, 1962.

15. Karlsen, Bjorn, "Children's Reading and the Linguistic Structure of Language," *RT, 18*, No. 3 (December, 1964), 187.

Notes

LEFEVRE

pp. 289–312

1. Joseph Vendryes, *Language: A Linguistic Introduction to History,* translated by Paul Rodin, London, 1925, p. 11.

2. Edward Sapir, *Language: An Introduction to the Study of Speech,* New York, 1921. (See *A Harvest Book,* 1949, p. 15.)

3. *Loc. cit.*

4. *Ibid.,* p. 17.

5. *Ibid.,* p. 18.

6. *Ibid.,* p. 21.

7. *Ibid.,* p. 22.

8. L. S. Vigotsky, *Language and Thought,* Chapter VII, translated in *Psycholinguistics: A Book of Readings,* Sol Saporta, ed., New York, 1961, p. 514.

9. *Ibid.,* p. 515.

10. *Ibid.,* pp. 510–11.

11. *Ibid.,* pp. 534–35.

12. *Loc. cit.*

13. *Op. cit.,* pp. 19–20.

14. M. M. Lewis, *Infant Speech: A Study of the Beginnings of Language,* New York, 1951. (2nd revised edition)

15. F. Grewel, "How Do Children Acquire the Use of Language?," *Phonetica,* Vol. 3, No. 4, 1959, pp. 193–202.

16. Ruth Weir, *Language in the Crib,* The Hague, 1962. (Contains an excellent bibliography.)

17. Martin D. S. Braine, "Grammatical Structure in the Speech of a Two-Year-Old," *Proceedings of the Washington Linguistic Club,* I, No. 1, Fall, 1963, pp. 11–16.

18. Huttenlocher Janellen, "Children's Language: Word-Phrase Relationships," *Science,* January 17, 1964, pp. 264–65. *See also* Julia A. Sableski, "A Selected Annotated Bibliography on Child Language," *The Lin-*

guistic Reporter, April, 1965, pp. 4–6. Note especially items 5, 10, 13, 16, 23, and 27.

19. Carl A. Lefevre, "Intonation: The Melodies of the Printed Page," *Linguistics and the Teaching of Reading,* New York, 1964, pp. 41–75.

20. Walter Loban, *The Language of Elementary School Children:* NCTE Research Report No. 1, Champaign, Ill., 1963. Ruth G. Strickland, *The Language of Elementary School Children . . . , Bulletin,* School of Education, Indiana University, Vol. 38, No. 4, July, 1962.

21. Leonard Bloomfield and Clarence L. Barnhart, *Let's Read: A Linguistic Approach,* Detroit, 1961.

22. Robert A. Hall, Jr., *Sound and Spelling in English,* Philadelphia and New York, 1961.

23. Henry Lee Smith, Jr., *Linguistic Science and the Teaching of English,* The Inglis Lecture, Cambridge, Mass., 1956, 61 pp.
———, *et al., The Linguistic Readers,* Chicago, 1965.

24. Charles C. Fries, *Linguistics and Reading,* New York, 1962, p. 201.

25. Carl A. Lefevre, "A Longer Look at Let's Read," *EE,* March, 1964, pp. 40–45.
———, A review of Fries' book cited in 24 above, in *The Elementary School Journal,* April, 1964, pp. 398–400.

26. ———, "Reading Related to Primary Language Learnings," *Journal of Developmental Reading,* Vol. IV, No. 3, Spring, 1961, pp. 147–58.
———, "Language Patterns and Their Graphic Counterparts: A Linguistic View of Reading," in *Changing Concepts of Reading Instruction, IRA Proceedings,* Scholastic Magazines, New York, 1961, pp. 245–49.
———, "Social Class Influences upon Learning: Linguistic Implications," *EE,* Vol. 38, December, 1961, pp. 553–55, 575.
———, "Reading Our Language Patterns: A Linguistic View: Contributions to a Theory of Reading," *IRA Proceedings,* Scholastic Magazines, New York, 1962, Vol. 7.
———, "Linguistics and the Teaching of Reading," *Reading as an Intellectual Activity, IRA Proceedings,* Scholastic Magazines, New York, 1963, pp. 188–91.
———, "Sound Patterns of English in Relation to Reading Instruction," *The Report of the Saskatchewan Reading Conference,* Saskatchewan Teachers' Federation, Saskatoon, 1964, pp. 29–37.
———, "The Sounds and Tunes We Read By," *New Dimensions in Reading, A Report of the 19th Annual Conference and Course on Reading,* University of Pittsburgh, July, 1963, pp. 61–68.
———, "Linguistics and the Teaching of Reading," *Proceedings of*

the 16th Round Table Meeting on Linguistics and Language Studies, Institute of Languages and Linguistics, Georgetown University, Washington, D.C., 1965. Published in *Monograph Series on Languages and Linguistics,* No. 18, 1965, Georgetown University Press, 139–47.

27. Zellig S. Harris, "Discourse Analysis," *Language,* Vol. 28, 1952, pp. 1–30.
    ————, *Structural Linguistics* (Rev. ed., formerly *Methods in Structural Linguistics,* 1951), University of Chicago Press, Chicago, 1961. See "Preface for the Fourth Impression," 1961.

28. Kenneth L. Pike, "A Linguistic Contribution to Composition: A Hypothesis," *CCC: College Composition and Communication,* May, 1964, pp. 82–88.
    ————, "Beyond the Sentence," *CCC: College Composition and Communication,* October, 1964, pp. 129–135. Both articles provide useful bibliography in the notes. See also two papers by his students:
    Hubert M. English, Jr., "Linguistic Theory as an Aid to Invention," and "A Linguistic Analogy in Literary Criticism," Alan B. Howes, both in *CCC: College Composition and Communication,* October, 1964.

29. Martin Stevens, "Intonation in the Teaching of Reading," *EE,* March, 1965, pp. 231–37.

30. *Op. cit.,* p. 19.

31. John Ciardi, "How to Read Dante," *The Saturday Review,* June 3, 1961, p. 54.

32. Carl A. Lefevre, "A Comprehensive Linguistic Approach to Reading," *EE,* October, 1965, pp. 651–59.

33. Noam Chomsky, *Syntactic Structures,* The Hague, 1957, p. 11.

34. John Viertel, "Generative Grammars," *CCC: College Composition and Communication,* May, 1964, pp. 65–81.

35. Paul Roberts, *The Roberts English Series: A Linguistics Program* (grades 3–9), New York, 1966.

36. Owen Thomas, *Transformational Grammar and the Teacher of English,* New York, 1965.

37. Paul Roberts, *English Syntax: A Programmed Introduction to Transformational Grammar* (Alternate Edition), New York, 1964.

38. *Ibid.,* p. 68.

39. *Ibid.,* p. 69.

40. *Loc. cit.*

41. Noam Chomsky, "Introduction" to *English Syntax* (alternate edition) by Paul Roberts, *ibid.,* ii.

42. *Ibid.*, p. xiii.
43. Chomsky, *Syntactic Structures*, p. 17.
44. *Ibid.*, pp. 88–89.
45. Viertel, *op. cit.*, pp. 79–80.
46. "Introduction," *English Syntax*, p. xiv.
47. Viertel, *op. cit.*, p. 68.

The Participants

Moshe Anisfeld is an assistant professor of psychology at Cornell University. His degrees are from Bar-Ilan University, Israel, and McGill University (Ph.D.). He has taught and done research at Harvard University, Indiana University and McGill. Dr. Anisfeld's articles have appeared in several journals.

John B. Bormuth is an associate professor at the University of Chicago. He is a specialist in reading and language. His Ph.D. is from Indiana University. Dr. Bormuth's major research interest is in problems of predicting and controlling comprehension difficulty of written language. His numerous articles have appeared in educational and psychological journals.

Edward C. Carterette holds degrees from the University of Chicago, Harvard, and Indiana (Ph.D.). He is professor of psychology at the University of California, Los Angeles. Dr. Carterette was a senior post-doctoral fellow at Stanford Institute for Mathematical Studies in the Social Sciences during 1965, and taught at the University of California, Berkeley, during 1966. Author of some forty articles in leading journals, he is editor of a book recently published by the University of California Press.

Eldonna Evertts received her master's and doctoral degrees from Indiana University. She has been an elementary teacher, a college teacher, and a research director. Dr. Evertts served at the University of Nebraska as co-director of the Nebraska Curriculum Development Center. She is now an associate professor at the University of Illinois and is Assistant Executive Secretary of the National Council of Teachers of English. She has written extensively on language arts and elementary education for professional publications.

Kenneth S. Goodman, host for the symposium, is an associate professor of education at Wayne State University. His degrees are from Los Angeles State College and the University of California,

Los Angeles (Ed. D.). Dr. Goodman is author of a number of articles in professional journals of education. He is co-author of a book, *Language in the Educational Process of Dodd Mead,* in press. Dr. Goodman is currently developing language arts materials for elementary schools. He received the Assistant Professor Research Recognition Award from the Wayne State Fund in 1964.

Duncan H. Hansen holds degrees from the University of Chicago and Washington University (St. Louis, Missouri). He received his Ph.D. from Stanford. Dr. Hansen has taught English and mathematics in public schools and at the University of Chicago Laboratory School. He served as reading section leader of the USOE Project on Computer-Based Instruction in Primary School Reading and Mathematics at Stanford Institute for Mathematical Studies in the Social Sciences. He is author or co-author of several articles and books. He is currently on the faculty of Florida State University.

Margaret Hubbard Jones holds degrees from Vassar, Hobart, and University of California, Los Angeles (Ph.D.). She has taught and done research at the University of Alabama, Washington State College, and University of California, Los Angeles in departments of education, engineering, and psychology. She is presently research psychologist, Department of Education, University of California, Los Angeles. Dr. Jones's publications include two books and twenty-four articles. Her current research is on child language development.

Paul A. Kolers is a research associate in the Research Laboratory of Electronics and the Department of Electrical Engineering at Massachusetts Institute of Technology. His degrees are from Queens College and New York University (Ph.D.). Dr. Kolers has taught and done research at Brooklyn College, V.A. Hospital at West Haven, Conn., Wright Patterson Air Force Base, the United States Navy Medical Research Laboratory, Harvard University, and Massachusetts Institute of Technology. He has published extensively.

Carl A. Lefevre is Professor of English Education, Temple University. He has degrees from Western Michigan, University of Michigan, and the University of Minnesota (Ph.D.). Dr. Lefevre has published extensively in professional journals on applied English linguistics.

He is author of *Linguistics and the Teaching of Reading* (McGraw-Hill, 1964), and co-author with Helen E. Lefevre of *Writing by Patterns* (A. A. Knopf, 1965), *English Writing Patterns*, grades 2–12 (Random House-Singer, 1968).

Hans C. Olsen, Jr. is an associate professor of education, Wayne State University. His degrees are from Eastern Illinois University and the University of Illinois (Ed.D.). Dr. Olsen has taught in elementary schools and at Mankato (Minn.) State College and Purdue University. He is co-author of *Choosing Materials To Teach Reading,* Detroit: Wayne State University Press, 1966.

Theodore S. Rodgers holds degrees from Amherst College and Georgetown University. He is a Ph.D. candidate in linguistics at Stanford University. He has taught at the Institute of Modern Language, Georgetown University, and at the University of California, Berkeley. Mr. Rodgers is currently research associate at the Institute for Mathematical Studies in the Social Sciences, Stanford. He has written handbooks, monographs, articles, and language tapes and texts.

Robert B. Ruddell is an associate professor of education, University of California, Berkeley. His degrees are from West Virginia University, George Peabody College, and Indiana University (Ed.D.). His teaching experience ranges from one-room elementary school to university. He has also been a reading supervisor. He received the Annual Research Award of the International Reading Association in 1964.

Richard Venezky is an assistant professor of English and computer sciences at the University of Wisconsin. He holds degrees in electrical engineering (B.E.E.) and linguistics (M.A. from Cornell) and in linguistics (Ph.D.) from Stanford. Dr. Venezky has published in the fields of electronics, technical writing, computing, and reading. His book, *English Orthography: A Synchronic Analysis* will be published soon by Mouton and Co.

Ruth H. Weir, whose untimely death occurred during the year following presentation of this paper, was an associate professor of linguistics at Stanford University. She studied at Charles University in Prague and earned degrees at West Virginia University and the

University of Michigan (Ph.D). She taught linguistics and romance languages in the Foreign Service Institute and at Georgetown University before moving to Stanford. Her books include *Language in the Crib* (Mouton, 1962).

Subject Index

Author Index

The manuscript was prepared for publication by Elvin T. Gidley. The book was designed by Sylvia Winter. The typeface used is Baskerville originally cut about 1750 for John Baskerville.

The book is printed on S. D. Warren's Olde Style Antique white wove and bound in Bancroft's Linen finished cloth over boards. Manufactured in the United States of America.